Dark Horse Records
The Story of George Harrison's Post-Beatles Record Label

Aaron Badgley

sonicbondpublishing.com

Sonicbond Publishing Limited
www.sonicbondpublishing.co.uk
Email: info@sonicbondpublishing.co.uk

First Published in the United Kingdom 2023
First Published in the United States 2023

British Library Cataloguing in Publication Data:
A Catalogue record for this book is available from the British Library

Copyright Aaron Badgley 2023

ISBN 978-1-78952-287-7

Typeset in ITC Garamond Std & AllRoundGothic
Printed and bound in England

Graphic design and typesetting: Full Moon Media

Follow us on social media:
Twitter: https://twitter.com/SonicbondP
Instagram: www.instagram.com/sonicbondpublishing_/
Facebook: www.facebook.com/SonicbondPublishing/

Linktree QR code:

Dark Horse Records
The Story of George Harrison's Post-Beatles Record Label

Aaron Badgley

sonicbondpublishing.com

Dedications

For the fab four women in my life: my mother, Harmony Marion Badgley, my wife, Andrea Badgley and my daughters, Emily Badgley and Linda Badgley.

For George Harrison

Thanks to The Beatles.

Acknowledgments

A lot of people helped me with this book.

Thanks to Stephen Lambe and the staff of Sonicbond Publishing. Thank you for this opportunity and your support. Thank you, Dominic Sanderson for your expert editing and notes.

Tom Brennan, whose website* was beyond helpful. His interviews and detailed information were invaluable. Our discussions helped the direction of the book. He also helped with edits. Thanks, Tom.

Thanks also to Jean Helfer, who allowed me to use his exclusive photos for this book. I cannot thank you enough and I thank you for our wonderful conversations.

Thank you to Hariprasad Chaurasia, Hank Cicalo, Bill Elliottt, Derrek Green, Michael Lanning, Robert Margouleff, Andy Newmark, Tom Scott, Chris Spedding, James Strauss and Alvin Taylor for taking the time to talk with me about their days with Dark Horse.

Thank you to Andrew Brooks, Harry Carter, Margarita Carter, Paul Dean, Evie Elliottt, Stan Harrison, Stephen Lussier, Bruce Spizer, Margot Steinberg, Tony and Cynthia Stuart, Bryan Williston, Kenneth Womack and Allen Goldstein for providing me with information and support for the book.

My family (Kurt and Ruth Badgley, Kerry and Sue Badgley).

Very special thanks to my wife Andrea and daughters Emily and Linda for living with this book for the past few years. Thank you Andrea and Linda for reading and editing several early versions of this book.
Thanks to Emily and Linda for their photographic skills too!
I love you all very much.

*(http://badfinge.ipower.com/Splinter/SplinterLibrary.html)

Dark Horse
The Story of George Harrison's Post-Beatles Record Label

Contents

Introduction

Apple Records was not a failure. It was a label that got tangled up in legal difficulties due to management and the breakup of a band. The label, however, did not fail in itself. In many ways, it was very much ahead of its time. Artist-owned labels were nothing new in 1968 when Apple Records made its debut, but the philosophy behind it was very new, unique and revolutionary. This was the philosophy that George Harrison would take with him when he formed and launched Dark Horse Records. It was Apple's eventual collapse that gave way to the beginning of Harrison's new venture.

Of course, The Beatles were not the first band or musical artist to establish their own label. Frank Sinatra had done this in 1960 with Reprise Records in order to have artistic freedom over his own recordings and because he was dissatisfied with Capitol Records. Because he owned the label, this earned him the nickname 'Chairman of the Board', although he sold the label to Warner Brothers in 1963 while retaining one-third ownership. Another example would be Sam Cooke's label SAR Records, which he formed in 1961. Cook never recorded for the label but used it to help artists he wanted to promote. One of those artists was Billy Preston. Other artist-owned labels included Bobby Darin (Addison), The Everly Brothers (Calliope Records, established in 1961), Bing Crosby (Project Records, 1961), and Nat 'King' Cole (K-C Records, 1961). It is worth pointing out that the first record pressed with the Apple label (Apple 1) was Frank Sinatra singing 'The Lady is a Tramp', changing the word 'Tramp' to 'Champ' as a special birthday gift for Ringo Starr to give to his wife Maureen.

Apple did not start out as a record label but rather as an umbrella organisation protecting The Beatles from taxes and financial issues – a tax shelter, if you will. Apple Corps Limited, as it was called, came into being after the death of Brian Epstein, the original manager of The Beatles, but there is no doubt that the seeds of Apple were planted by Epstein, who was encouraging The Beatles to set up smaller companies for tax purposes. As a result, In April 1967, The Beatles and Co. was formed in addition to Beatles Limited, which continued to exist.

Essentially, the existence of these companies was to allow The Beatles to pay a much lower level of corporation tax. So initially, the idea for Beatles Limited/Apple was that it be made up of various smaller enterprises, such as retail, publishing, electronics and film and Jonathon

Gould, in his book *Can't Buy Me Love: The Beatles, Britain and America*, confirms Epstein's masterplan was to establish a business structure that would assist The Beatles in lessening their tax. Sadly, Epstein died before he could see the end results of his efforts.

But one of the first projects under the Apple Banner was the 1967 film *Magical Mystery Tour,* which was was produced under the Apple Films Division. Although, if one looks carefully at the back of *Sgt. Pepper's Lonely Hearts Club Band,* released in June 1967, Apple is mentioned.

So, in January 1968, Beatles Ltd. became Apple. The Apple trademark (with a logo designed by Gene Mahon) was registered in 47 countries. This included registering the following smaller organisations: Apple Electronics, Apple Films Ltd., Apple Management, Apple Music Publishing, Apple Overseas, Apple Publicity, Apple Records, Apple Retail and Apple Tailoring Civil and Theatrical. The Beatles were ready to launch their own label.

On 19 April 1968, The Beatles ran an advertisement in the UK music press, featuring new general manager Alistair Taylor posing as a one-man band, announcing 'This man has talent'. The poster further added:

One day, he sang his songs to a tape recorder (borrowed from the man next door). In his neatest handwriting, he wrote an explanatory note (giving his name and address) and, remembering to enclose a picture of himself, sent the tape, letter and photograph to Apple music, 94 Baker Street, London, W.1. If you were thinking of doing the same thing yourself – do it now! This man now owns a Bentley!

Apple was officially launched.

On 14 May 1968, John Lennon and Paul McCartney held a press conference at the Americana Hotel at 155 West 47th Street in New York City to launch the Apple Company. Lennon and McCartney tried to field questions about the venture and explain, to the best of their ability, their intentions. Lennon said:

It's a business concerning records, films, electronics, and – as a sideline – manufacturing, or whatever it's called. We just want to set up a system whereby people who just want to make a film about anything don't have to go on their knees in somebody's office – probably yours!

The aim of this company isn't really a stack of gold teeth in the bank. We've done that bit. It's more of a trick to see if we can actually get artistic freedom within a business structure.

Although Lennon and McCartney made a point of saying that the purpose of Apple was to help new artists, of the four Beatles, Harrison embraced this notion the most. The sheer amount of artists he signed and assisted with Apple speaks volumes and with a few exceptions, Harrison signed American artists, which demonstrates the impact American music had had on him. This trend would be repeated with Dark Horse Records. Quite simply, The Beatles were there to help artists receive exposure for their art. Having a number one or a huge seller was not their primary goal. In 1975, Harrison remarked:

Remember, the basic thought behind Apple in those days was that we resented marvellous musicians or singers having to go to the very big, established record companies and go down on their knees. That's what we, The Beatles, had to do with EMI, and so we said the first thing we'd do when we got a bit of money would be to try to beat this part of the system, at least. So many really good musicians had told us they couldn't get a break, make any records, and it made us furious.

On 28 June 1968, Paul McCartney attended the Capitol Records Sales Conference at The Beverly Hills Hilton Hotel. According to Tony Bramwell, McCartney gave a brief speech and then showed a short promo film directed by Bramwell. This was to announce that EMI/ Capitol would be distributing the new Apple label and that all future Beatle recordings would be on the Apple label.

But Harrison was very active with Apple Records from the very beginning. He had the honour of releasing the first album on Apple himself, *Wonderwall Music By George Harrison*, which came out in the UK on 1 November 1968 and one month later in the US and Canada. But by the time it was released in North America, it was the third album to come out in North America, following the release of John Lennon and Yoko Ono's *Unfinished Music No. 1 – Two Virgins* (11 November 1968) and *The Beatles* (25 November 1968).

All of the artists he signed were artists he admired, friends or similarly spiritually inclined, a model he followed when he formed Dark Horse. Indeed, a majority of the musicians were American and rhythm and blues-based. However, Harrison did more than just sign these artists to the label – he took an active interest. He worked diligently on the records, often produced or co-produced. He wrote or co-wrote the songs and even performed on the records as well as doing his best to promote the artists. Promotion was to be one of Dark Horse's problems.

Other evidence of Harrison's enthusiasm for Apple is the fact that Harrison would be responsible for one of the two albums released on the Apple subsidiary Zapple Records, formed in early 1969. The intention of Zapple label was to release experimental, avant-garde music. Many artists and poets were approached and some signed to release albums on this label. Poet Richard Brautigan had planned to release an album *Listening to Richard Brautigan*, which was recorded but was released in 1970 on Harvest Records through Capitol Records rather than Zapple. Then Harrison recorded and produced the album *Electronic Sound*, released on 9 May 1969. But Zapple was shut down after just two albums, the other being John Lennon and Yoko Ono's *Unfinished Music No. 2: Life With the Lions*. Harrison's album peaked at a very low number 191 on the *Billboard* Top 200 album charts. But, like its parent company, huge sales were never Zapple's goal.

Perhaps most telling is the work Harrison did for such artists in the calendar year of 1969. Bear in mind that during this time, he recorded two solo albums, three albums with The Beatles (one being a double album), toured with Delaney and Bonnie, co-wrote what would become Cream's last single, 'Badge' and spent some time with Bob Dylan and The Band.

Harrison's commitment was exemplary. In 1968, Harrison not only signed old Liverpool friend Jackie Lomax, but started work on what would become Lomax's debut solo album and his only album for Apple, *Is This What You Want?* Not only did Harrison produce the album, but he also wrote the song 'Sour Milk Sea' for the project, which became Lomax's debut single. The album itself is a mixture of rock and soul, and with a host of special guests (Leon Russell, Billy Preston, Eric Clapton, Hal Blaine, Ringo Starr and Paul McCartney, to name just a few), with Harrison beginning recording with Jackie at EMI studios in June of 1968, while The Beatles were working on their album *The Beatles*. As a result, Lomax sings on 'Dear Prudence' and 'Hey Jude'.

The single 'Sour Milk Sea' failed to chart in the UK and peaked at number 117 on *Billboard*'s 'Bubbling Under' chart, but it was a moderate hit in Canada, where it peaked at number 29 on Canada's official chart, RPM.

While Harrison was working on that album, he brought two other artists (both American) into the Apple fold: Billy Preston and Doris Troy. Harrison had met Billy Preston while Preston was a member of Little Richard's band. Little Richard was part of a show headlined by The Beatles in Liverpool in 1962, but Harrison became re-acquainted with the keyboardist when Harrison saw Preston performing with Ray Charles in London in early 1969. He later invited Preston to play with The Beatles during the sessions that would result in the *Let It Be* album. As Harrison noted in *The Beatles Anthology*, 'It is interesting to see how nice people behave when you bring a guest in ... Everybody was happier to have somebody else playing and it made what we were doing more enjoyable'. Preston was welcomed with open arms by the band and he eventually wound up playing with them on the Apple rooftop. He holds the distinction of being the only artist to achieve a prominent credit on a Beatle record with 'Get Back', which was credited as The Beatles with Billy Preston. Preston was signed to Apple and from April to July 1969, Harrison worked on Preston's debut album, *That's the Way God Planned It*. Not only did Harrison produce it, but he played guitar and, again, got some friends to help him out: Keith Richards, Eric Clapton, future Apple artist Dois Troy, Ginger Baker and Madeline Bell all took part. Although the album failed to do well in the charts, Preston did have a hit single in the UK and Europe with the title track.

Harrison had seen duo Delaney and Bonnie in the fall of 1968 and their music impressed him. He was very enthused about the band, who were set to release their album *Accept No Substitute* in May of 1968, and brought them to England to sign them to Apple, both parties overlooking the fact that they were already signed to Elektra Records and although a few copies of an album were pressed (exact numbers are not known), the album was scrapped for Apple, although it did appear later on Elektra. In December 1969, Harrison would join their Delaney and Bonnie and Friends tour of Europe and the UK.

While the *Get Back* tapes sat on the shelf, waiting to be turned into *Let It Be*, The Beatles busied themselves with a new album. Beginning in February of 1969 and finishing in September, The Beatles worked on *Abbey Road*. Harrison's role in The Beatles was becoming larger; he would have two songs on the album, one of which became his first A-side ('Something'), the other, a B-side for a non-album single released in 1969, 'Old Brown Shoe', which was the B-side to 'The Ballad of John and Yoko'.

Furthermore, in 1969, Harrison began working with the London chapter of The Radha Krishna Temple. Harrison invited the community to Abbey Road Studios and produced their first single, 'Hare Krishna Mantra', which was released on Apple. The single was a surprise hit in the UK, peaking at number 12 on the national charts. The devotees even got to perform on *Top Of The Pops*, a popular British television show which showcased the popular bands of the day. Harrison produced their 1970 single, 'Govinda', which was another hit in the UK and, once again, landed them on *Top Of The Pops*. By this point, the devotees were sharing stages with the likes of Deep Purple, Joe Cocker and The Moody Blues. Their only Apple album, *The Radha Krishna Temple*, was eventually released in 1971, featuring all of their singles and, once again,was produced by Harrison, but the album failed to chart.

In May of 1969, a single was issued by another American artist, Stephen Friedland, who recorded under the name Brute Force, with 'King of Fuh' and 'Nobody Knows' on the flipside. Friedland had made his name as a member of the band The Tokens (who were credited with producing 'King Of Fuh'), and writing songs for artists such as Peggy March, Del Shannon and The Chiffons. Lennon and Harrison had heard and loved the song. Harrison went to the trouble of having strings (courtesy of the London Philharmonic Orchestra, arranged by John Barham) dubbed onto the song. However, due to the titles' explicit play on words (a song about a 'Fuh King'), EMI refused to distribute it, so Apple pressed 1000 copies and issued it in the UK on mail-order. As a result, this is now one of the rarest Apple releases.

In December 1969, George joined The Plastic Ono Band for a live performance at the Lyceum Ballroom in London as part of UNICEF's Peace For Christmas event. The show was recorded and edited down for release on the 1972 album *Sometime in New York City*. This led to Harrison helping Lennon with 'Instant Karma' in January 1970, where he worked with Phil Spector for the first time. Spector would go on to work with Harrison for *All Things Must Pass*, *The Concert For Bangla Desh* and 'Bangla Desh' single.

By May of 1970, The Beatles had announced their breakup, and Harrison began work on his third solo album, *All Things Must Pass*. But even this did not prevent him from working with other artists. He helped Ringo Starr with the single 'It Don't Come Easy'. Ringo had made attempts to record the single (one with George Martin producing it, when it was known as 'You Gotta Pay Your Dues'), but the song had not been working. Harrison eventually produced the single in March and October of 1970 and contributed to the writing, although he refused any credit. Two members of Badfinger also contributed to the recording. When the single was released in April of 1971 (the same day as Ronnie Spector's 'Try Some, Buy Some'), it went Top Ten around the world.

While Harrison was working with Starr and all the other artists, he was keeping himself busy with Billy Preston's second album *Encouraging Words*, which he co-produced, co-wrote the song 'Sing One For the Lord'. He also gave Preston two songs: 'All Things Must Pass' (listed on the album as 'All Things (Must) Pass') and 'My Sweet Lord'. The album was released on 11 September 1970 (9 November 1970 in North America), meaning that Preston's version of 'My Sweet Lord' was released two months prior to Harrison's version. It was further released as a single in Europe to promote the album and later released in North America as a single after Harrison's version had become a hit, which speaks volumes about Harrison's generous nature. In the 2010 CD reissue of the album, credits were finally added to the liner notes. According to Andy Davis, the musicians on the album include Harrison, Starr, Eric Clapton, Delaney Bramlett and The Edwin Hawkins Singers.

In February 1971, Harrison began working with Phil Spector in producing the 'comeback' single for his wife, Ronnie. The singer had made a name for herself as part of the famous American group The Ronettes. Her single 'Try Some Buy Some', with 'Tandoori Chicken' on the flip side, appeared on Apple on 16 April 1971. The A-side (written by Harrison) would later appear on his 1973 album *Living in the Material World* sung by Harrison. The B-side, 'Tandoori Chicken', was the only time Harrison and Phil Spector co-wrote a song. The follow-up single 'You' was never finished, but Harrison would recycle the song for his *Extra Texture (Read All About It)* album in 1975.

By 1971, *All Things Must Pass* was a worldwide, number one hit album. It spawned the international hit single 'My Sweet Lord' and the North American Top Ten single, 'What is Life'. Harrison helped Lennon with his album *Imagine* in May 1971, and in the same month, Harrison began working with Welsh band Badfinger on their third studio album *Straight Up*. He not only produced four songs for the album but provided some great guitar work. He had planned to produce the entire album but was too busy organising *The Concert For Bangla Desh* (this is the stylisation at the time, so this will be the spelling used throughout this book). Todd Rundgren would complete the production, which was released on 13 December 1971 (North America) and 11 February 1972 (UK). The album produced the worldwide hit 'Day After Day' (produced by Harrison and featuring his trademark guitar work) and the North American hit 'Baby Blue'.

In June of 1971, Harrison worked with Ravi Shankar on a couple of projects. One was the soundtrack for the film *Raga*, in which Harrison appears. Apple Films produced the film, and although the project was completed by July 1971, including the production of the soundtrack album, the film was given a limited release in the US in November 1971. Harrison did his best to promote the film and the album by appearing on the radio, attending a screening at the Carnegie Hall Cinema and even appeared on popular American talk show, The Dick Cavett Show. The soundtrack was released in America only in December 1971.

While Harrison was working on the film and soundtrack, he signed Shankar to Apple. In mid-1971, Harrison produced an EP for Ravi Shankar, released on Apple Records. The A-side was named 'Joi Bangla', which was recorded prior to *The Concert For Bangla Desh*, but released after the concert. It was through the recording of this EP that Harrison, in an attempt to assist Shankar with the project, organised *The Concert For Bangla Desh*. Harrison would also produce *In Concert 1972,* a recording of the 8 October 1972 performance at the Philharmonic Hall in New York City by Ravi Shankar and Ali Akbar Khan. *In Concert 1972* was not released until 22 January 1973 in North America and 13 April 1973 in the UK, and by the time the album was released in Britain, Shankar was working with Harrison on *Shankar Family & Friends* for Dark Horse Records. The album was produced by Harrison, Phil McDonald and Zakir Hussain. It was Shankar's last release on Apple Records, later to be reissued through HarriSongs (2018) and Dark Horse Records (2020). Both reissues were for streaming and download only.

The last artists that Harrison signed to Apple were the American brother team, Lon and Derrek Van Eaton. Both Lennon and Harrison enjoyed their 1971 demo, so they signed with Apple on 15 September 1971, despite interest from other labels. On 19 September, they flew to London to begin work on their album in the newly refurbished Apple Studios, the first band to record in the re-launched Studios at 3 Savile Row.

Harrison loved the duo and even had them stay at Harrison's home, Friar Park. But 1971 and 1972 were particularly busy years for Harrison with *The Concert For Bangla Desh*, Raga, Badfinger's *Straight Up,* Apple, Shankar and writing for his next album. So Harrison was not available to produce the entire album. He did produce one song: their debut single 'Sweet Music' and assembled quite a cast for the song, including Ringo Starr on drums (along with Jim Gordon), Peter Frampton on guitar and Mike Hugg on harmonium. The Van Eatons played all of the other instruments.

Both the album *Brother* and the single 'Sweet Music' received very positive reviews and were held in high regard. But the single failed to make a dent in the charts, which not only confused Harrison but downright angered him. Harrison was so upset that he sent a memo to Apple staff in America: 'What the fuck is the matter out there? 'Sweet Music' is a number-one hit!' This may have been the seeds of Harrison's dissent with Apple and part of the impetus to form his own label. Although they only released one album for Apple, Harrison helped the two move and relocate to Los Angeles and settle with the A&M label, although he never signed them to Dark Horse, who were distributed by A&M. They did record with Harrison on his *Dark Horse* album, as well as playing on Starr's *Ringo* album.

It was also becoming clear that Apple was winding down and that Capitol/EMI was not investing much into the non-Beatle releases from Apple. But Harrison (and Starr, for that matter) wanted to keep helping other artists.

It is clear that Harrison was very generous with his time and his talent when it came to the artists he signed to Apple, and it is the reason Dark Horse Records came into being. At its core, Dark Horse Records was not designed to exploit artists, as other companies had done, but rather, to nurture talent and give artists exposure. It also seemed that Harrison thought that if his name was attached, the music would garner attention; he wanted the label and its artists to be successful.

But even the best of intentions cannot always lead to success. As with Apple, Dark Horse Records had its share of problems. The business model used for Dark Horse Records was, sadly, to be proved a bit out of date by 1974. Not only did Harrison have a great deal to learn about self-promotion, but he also needed to learn how to effectively promote artists on his label.

Dark Horse Begins

By the beginning of 1974, the only artists signed to Apple, other than the four Beatles, were Badfinger and Yoko Ono. In 1973, Badfinger released their final album for Apple, *Ass*, and signed with Warner Brothers. Ono released her final Apple album (*Feeling the Space*) on 2 November 1973, three weeks before *Ass*.

Apple had many successes. James Taylor, Billy Preston, Badfinger, Mary Hopkin, John Tavener and Hot Chocolate, an impressive list of artists, all got their start with Apple. Furthermore, The Beatles (solo and together) released some of the most important music of all time through Apple Records. However, by 1974, it was clear that this chapter of Apple was coming to a close.

But Harrison and Starr wanted to carry on with the Apple philosophy. In 1973, George became aware of Splinter (who had originally been named Half Breed) through Mal Evans, and he was very impressed. Splinter was a duo featuring Bob Purvis (guitar, vocals) and William (Bill) Elliott (vocals, guitar). Harrison liked the duo, in particular, a song titled 'Lonely Man', which he felt would be perfect for a film in which he was involved: *Little Malcolm and His Struggle Against The Eunuchs*. The band appeared in the film singing the song and Harrison felt that it was a hit. Harrison later said on *The Dark Horse Radio Show*: 'I thought this film is not the sort of film that is to sell, and this song is such a hit. I thought if I can make a hit, then maybe the film people would be more interested in the movie'.

The film was directed by Stuart Cooper for Apple Films and released in 1974. Harrison produced a version of the song at Apple Studios, intending to release it as a single for Apple. Backing Splinter (who provided all vocals) were Badfinger's Pete Ham and George himself, both playing guitars, Bill Dickinson and John Taylor (bass), Billy Preston (keyboards) and Jim Keltner (drums). The sessions took place in 1973, and other material was recorded, which became known as *The Apple Demos*. A small portion of the Apple version of the song can be heard in the closing credits of the film. The song 'Lonely Man' would be re-recorded for Splinter's second album, *Harder To Live*, but would never see the light of day as a single.

But in recording the single, Harrison discovered that the duo had a great many songs that could make an album. As he noted, 'I went to do a single with them, but then I heard the rest of the songs and they were so good; I got involved in making the album and the song from *Little Malcolm'*.

With Apple becoming somewhat of a legal mess, Harrison had to figure out the best way to assist new artists and even some of his friends in the music world. According to Alan Clayson, in his 2003 book *George Harrison*, Harrison and Starr made plans to buy Apple in 1973. Harrison discounted the idea, given the numerous legal complications with the label and Allen Klein's involvement. It was simpler to start a whole new enterprise and on 23 May 1974, Harrison officially opened Dark Horse Records. As Harrison discussed in 1974:

> As Newton said, all Apples must fall. Apple was going through such chaos from a business point of view, anyway. At that time, John and Paul didn't really want to know about it and were getting ready to sweep it under the carpet. Ringo and I were planning to try and keep it going, but there were so many problems from old contracts that existed. It seemed simpler to start afresh.

Harrison had learnt a lot from running Apple, especially the loose way in which Apple was originally open to the public. Talking with Ray Coleman in 1976, Harrison was very clear: 'Our 'open door' policy (at Apple) proved impossible to run. We were flooded with every person imaginable who could play or sing a note! We had to clamp down on that because Apple became a lunatic asylum'.

Initially, Harrison did not plan on Dark Horse becoming a huge label with many divisions, but rather a small, boutique operation: 'So Dark Horse will be run pretty tightly, I don't want to be a Kinney (which was a huge music distributor at the time) or an RCA or anything like that. In one way, it's similar to the idea behind Apple, in that most artists we've got at the moment have come into my life without me looking for them'.

Harrison needed distribution for the label and did not have a lot of positive feelings toward EMI/Capitol. In 1975, he noted that McCartney had signed with Capitol Records, which was quickly followed with 'Good luck, Paul!'. He did explore other options and labels, such as Asylum Records, going so far as to meet with Asylum head David Geffen. Harrison even sent a 'demo tape' of Splinter to David Geffen with hopes of securing distribution for the label. He also consulted his good friend Leon Russell (who was the co-founder of Shelter Records) about the running of a label. Eventually, Dark Horse found a home with A&M Records, an independent label known for being artist-friendly.

A&M Records had begun in 1962 and it was owned by Herb Alpert and the late Jerry Moss. The name comes from the initials of their last names, but the label was had originally been called Carnival. By 1962, Alpert had established himself as a musician and composer. He had released a few records on the Dot Record label, but after forming A&M, all future releases would be on A&M Records. Alpert would have immediate success on his label with his single 'The Lonely Bull', which made the Top Ten in 1962. Jerry Moss, on the other hand, got his start in the music business by promoting the single '16 Candles' by The Crests in 1968. By the early 1970s, A&M was the largest independent record label in the world.

According to Derek Green, who was the Senior Vice President of A&M Records Inc and the Managing Director of A&M Records Ltd in the UK, while Dark Horse Records was with A&M, Harrison made the deal directly with Jerry Moss. Green was appointed to help with the label and assessed the situation. Because of Moss's extensive history in the music industry and Alpert being a musician, Harrison felt at home with A&M. Green noted:

George coming from Apple and EMI, A&M was the right place for him. I don't think there was a label of major importance who understood that better. We had worldwide distribution and this was an artistic label – no pressure to sell, you didn't have to be a rocket scientist. He bragged about how artist-sensitive A&M was; it was an artist label and we were very sympathetic to the artist.

Harrison had plans for the label from the start. He was quite clear about his intentions and what the business model would be. Speaking with Ray Coleman in 1975, Harrison said:

There's a certain amount of talent that circulates around, and okay, it's commercial, some of it, I'm not signing anything just through it being commercial. Basically, the people who join Dark Horse are important to me. Maybe, in some ways, a little more than music because I wouldn't like to get involved with somebody who just happened to be a fantastic singer or something, but who I personally didn't like. Some record companies have a bunch of artists whom they don't really like as people – then it creates all this bad feeling, but I must have a decent and friendly relationship with the artist.

Harrison explained his goal for his label on 23 October 1974 during a press conference in Los Angeles. He also took the opportunity to announce his tour of North America with Ravi Shankar, now known as *The Dark Horse Tour*. When asked about the aims of Dark Horse, Harrison said, 'I don't want it to turn into a Kinney. I'd like it to be decently small'. Kinney, at the time, was the corporate owner of Warner Brothers, a company with whom Harrison would eventually sign.

During the same press conference, he joked about the number of demo tapes he had already received: 'To tell you the truth, I've been here just over a week, and if I signed all the people who gave me tapes, I'd be bigger than RCA and Kinney put together, but fortunately, I don't have time to listen to them all'.

By the time Dark Horse Records was ready to launch, Harrison had two artists already signed: Splinter and Ravi Shankar. But now he needed a name and a logo for the label. Harrison had written a song, 'Dark Horse', which would not only be a single (on Apple) but the name of his album, released in 1974. Harrison explained on the promotional album *A Personal Music Dialogue with George Harrison at 33 1/3* the origin of the name Dark Horse:

The song came first. The song, you know, it was funny because it had a slightly different meaning in the States. I didn't realise. Like in England, they'd say, 'Mrs Penguin's knockin' 'round with Mr Johnson. Oh, she's a dark horse'. Something like that, you know? 'Who'd have ever thought?' And so I wrote that song. At that time, I was going through a few different ... trips ... man [laughs]. And I thought of that song, you know: 'I'm a dark horse', and then I thought, 'Running on a dark race course'. I thought, 'That's a bit silly'. And then the next day, I woke up and I thought, 'No, that's not bad, running on a dark race course. That's what it is, you know?' Because it's like the idea is, 'Okay, I'll own up. I'm a dark horse. Who'd have ever thought?' But at the same time, you have to be – because it's a dark race course. Anyway, so I wrote that song and later called the company after that.

On 1 June 1974, an article appeared in *Billboard* magazine on page three announcing that Dark Horse Records had signed with A&M. On

8 June 1974, *Billboard* ran a much longer article, in which Harrison is quoted as saying: 'I feel very happy with the unlimited potential now available through the relationship with Mr A., Mr M. and the entire staff of A&M Records, not only musically and commercially, but also in areas outside of the record industry'. In the same article, Jerry Moss said:

> This is a great moment for A&M Records. The stimulation of working with one of the world's most creative and unique personalities is heightened by our involvement in, and support of his well-known humanitarian activities. I know I speak for Lou Adler when I say that the addition of Dark Horse Records to the A&M/Ode family flatters us immensely and the possibilities for the future are nothing short of dazzling.

The deal with A&M included corporations Clod Holdings (a Netherland Antilles Corporation), Loka Productions and Ganga Distributing. Upon signing with A&M, Dark Horse 'was to get $225,000, an additional $225,000 at the start of the second and third year and $200,000 at the start of the fourth and fifth years' as advances. Dark Horse also received one million dollars in a loan, half of which was to be repaid from the sales of records not recorded by George Harrison directly.

Loka Productions, S.A., owns the Dark Horse Records trademark. According to Encyclopedia Britannica, the word 'Loka' comes from Sanskrit, meaning 'world', and 'in the cosmography of Hinduism, the universe or any particular division of it. The most common division of the universe is the *tri-loka*, or three worlds (heaven, earth, atmosphere; later, heaven, world, netherworld), each of which is divided into seven regions'.

Part of the deal was that Dark Horse Records was to record their artists, whenever possible, outside the United States in an effort to avoid AFM (American Federation of Musicians) payments. However, if there were AFM costs, Dark Horse Records and A&M would share them. Further, according to Sippel, 'A&M and Ganga Distributing agreed to exist on US profits only'. Royalties for non-Harrison albums were very specific. Again, according to Sippel, '12.5% of 90% in the US and 15% outside the US, except in Mexico and Central and South America, where it was 12.5%. Packaging deductions for these acts in the US, Canada and the UK were 10% of the retail selling price for single LPs: 12.5% for double fold and 20% for tape' (Sippel, p. 53). The royalty rate for all singles was 12.5%.

Harrison was also offered shares in A&M, which Jerry Moss noted was the first time an 'outsider' was offered the chance to buy A&M stock. Also, the five-year deal gave A&M a two-year sell-off period of the masters (the master tapes of the music), at which point they would revert back to Dark Horse Records. A&M would absorb all losses during the partnership and would earn 15% of the gross profit for the cost of distribution of up to two million dollars annually.

According to Green, what was unusual was the fact that Harrison already had artists signed to the label before any deal had been made with a distributor. 'With the Dark Horse label, George had already signed Splinter. He had a record ready to go'. Green also pointed out that Harrison's manager, Denis O'Brien, was very involved with the label.

It's possible that Billy Prestson's album *Everybody Likes Some Kind of Music* was to have been released on Dark Horse, perhaps the first album for that label. According to The Daily Beatle website (article 'Life after Apple Records'), test pressings of the album exist on Dark Horse, and given Preston's connection with Harrison, it makes sense that this was considered. It would have been very nice for it to have been the album to launch Dark Horse. The album was released on 21 September 1973 on A&M Records, so the dates do not actually correspond with the creation of Dark Horse, but given Preston's affiliation with Apple, it does make sense. Perhaps Harrison was hoping A&M would allow Preston to release an album on a label that was being distributed by them.

With contracts signed and a distributor – or rather a partner (as the Dark Horse Records labels and sleeves noted: 'Dark Horse Records, A Partnership') – a logo was now needed. Harrison later recounted to Timothy White:

When I got Dark Horse Records, I had a couple of artists come up with logos, and there was one guy who painted one that looked really nice with a nice colour scheme, but it was a Chinese horse. I wanted something kind of different, and I was in India early in 1974 and I just thought I'm bound to find something if I keep my eyes open. One day, I was in this place [in India] called Udaipur and I looked across the street in the market, and I thought I could see some little pictures of enamel. I got across the street and there were tins of paint on this stall. I looked at all the tins, and they all had different labels on them, and one of them had the horse. It was a white horse but it had seven heads, and I thought, there's my logo! I bought the tin can, brought it back and gave it to the artist and got him to make it dark and turn it 'round so it would run the right way around the label. That's the drag now about CDs: you don't get to have any nice logos you can see turning.

George also had the resources at A&M records at his disposal. Derek Green pointed out that the Dark Horse logo came about with help from A&M, 'the imaging of the label, the image of the Dark Horse, George got on very well with my art director. They bonded very quickly, which was very useful. The connection was seamless, it was George's label, but we had all the services'.

In June 1974, one of the first people hired for the label was Jonathon Clyde, who was appointed director of marketing, promotion and A&R in Britain and Europe. He would work out of the London Office. Clyde had worked with Decca Records and Warner Brothers Records, eventually working his way up be the UK label manager for Elektra Records. Later, after heading up Dark Horse Records, he became the UK General Manager for WEA Records. He returned to working with Beatles material on the restored version of *Yellow Submarine*. As of now, he continues to work with Apple Corps.

In the Los Angeles office, which was housed in the A&M lot at 1416 North La Brea Ave in Hollywood, Dino Airali was appointed Managing Director, and in 1975, Louis Newman was named National Promotion Director. In an article for industry magazine *Cashbox*, it was announced that Newman had come from Zappa's Discreet Records (where he had been national promotion and sales director) and Blue Thumb Records (where he had been national promotions director). The Los Angeles office became the headquarters of Dark Horse Records. As Derek Green noted: 'Dark Horse was situated at the A&M office. He (George) didn't have any staff in the UK, but he had staff in LA'. And even though most of the operations were based in Los Angeles, 'George wanted to launch Dark Horse in the UK, and that was my area of responsibility'.

Green went on to note that Harrison's future wife Olivia 'was working for A&M in LA'. Green was spending a great deal of time travelling in order to promote the artists on Dark Horse. 'By that time, I was in California once a month and anywhere in the world where I could spot opportunities for the records we put out'.

The main office was in LA because, from the beginning, Harrison saw the importance of breaking artists in the US. For all intents and purposes, this was an American label. All but three artists signed to the label would be American and from 1975 on, one could argue that the majority of the focus was on the American market.

According to Green, one part of the contract that was not completely made public was that when Dark Horse signed with A&M, Harrison signed a deal with the label as well. Bearing in mind that he was still signed to EMI/Capitol until 1975, it was part of the contract that Harrison was part of the deal and he would be recording for Dark Horse/A&M when he was contractually able to do so. Green related, 'He was building relationships and the signing with A&M was kept contractually quiet. It was not to be announced'. This was very important: 'George, as a recording artist, was involved in that contract. When we signed Dark Horse, we signed George from EMI. During that time period, he was signed to us. I was working with both the head of the label and the superstar recording artist'. This would cause more than a few problems in the future.

It was clear that part of the appeal of taking on Dark Horse was having an ex-Beatle signed to the label. Remember, at this time, The Beatles had only ended four years before, and all four solo Beatles were having a great deal of success. Harrison, in particular, had a very high profile and had a remarkable track record for sales. Apple in the 1970s may not have been selling a lot of records by non-Beatle artists, but the solo Beatles made up for any losses.

In 1975, when asked if he would be recording for Dark Horse, Harrison confirmed: 'Yeah, there's a good chance that I would do that', he told radio host Dave Herman, 'Because there's no point in forming a label and then going on RCA'.

A&M was a successful and well-respected independent label. It would be a major feather in their cap to have signed a solo Beatle. Beyond that, there was plenty of reason to believe the artists signing to Dark Horse would find success on their own accord. Splinter were courted by several labels and must have been considered commercial, as can the bands that were signed in 1974/1975.

It is safe to say that there were great hopes for it. Harrison had his own goals and plans for the label and his career. In 1974, he told *Melody Maker*:

There isn't really a concept or goal; the goal in life is to manifest our divinity. Because each one is potentially divine. All we can do is try and do that, and hope that influences our work.

The label was set up, announced and ready to launch.

Dark Horse in 1974

Splinter were the first band signed to Dark Horse. The duo had a warm, English folk sound, which Harrison captured on their first album, technically the first to be released on Dark Horse. It was released alongside *Shankar, Family and Friends* on 20 September 1974 (in the UK). As mentioned, Harrison originally intended to release 'Lonely Man', featured in a film Harrison financed, *Little Malcolm and His Struggles Against the Eunuchs* (1974). That film would be the first in which Harrison acted as an Executive Producer, but it was not his last; three years later, he formed Handmade Films. Harrison financed the film, having been a fan of the original play. Once again, Harrison was getting involved in projects that he not only believed in but of which he was also a fan.

Splinter consisted of two members: Bob Purvis and Bill Elliott. Based in Tyneside, the two formed a duo in 1970 and later formed a band with other members. That band, Stone Blind, evolved into Half Breed. They recorded some demos and their manager at the time sent the tapes to various record companies searching for a label. One of the tapes reached the ears of Mal Evans. Former employee and friend of The Beatles, Evans had become somewhat of an A&R man for Apple Records in the early 1970s, as well as producing and co-producing a few singles, with 'No Matter What' by Badfinger being his biggest success and he produced *No Dice* with Geoff Emerick.

Starting in 1961, Mal Evans became a regular at The Cavern Club, watching The Beatles. He eventually struck up a friendship with George Harrison, who put a good word in with Cavern's owner Ray McFall. McFall hired Evans as a doorman; given his size (six feet, six inches), he was the perfect doorman and bouncer. After befriending The Beatles in The Cavern, he became their roadie, confident and bodyguard, eventually working for Apple Records as a personal assistant.

Evans decided to find out more about the band, and he travelled to Newcastle to hear more of their music and produce more demos with the band. Evans took the tape back to Apple to play for Lennon and, eventually, Harrison to see if Apple would sign them. However, at the same time this was going on, there was some turmoil in Half Breed. Bob Purvis, the main songwriter, had left the band. Apple were impressed with his writing and the singing but not with the band.

Although Apple did not sign the band, Bill Elliott was asked to sing lead on a new single that Lennon and Ono had written in support of the magazine *Oz*. In May 1970, *Oz* magazine published an issue that was edited and written by secondary school students. The issue, known as *Schoolkids Oz,* was deemed obscene in the UK. Lennon was asked by friend Stan Demidjuk, who was a member of 'Friends of Oz', to assist in raising money for the legal costs. Lennon agreed and went to work on a single intended to raise awareness and money for the magazine. He wrote the songs 'Do the Oz' and 'God Save Oz', later changed to 'God Save Us'. Lennon later said the change from 'God Save Oz' to 'God Save Us' was to promote sales, especially in the US. Although Lennon takes the lead vocals on side 'Do the Oz', he never intended to sing 'God Save Us'. As Lennon explained to *Sounds*:

We got one singer in, and he was all right, but he'd never had much experience recording or singing actually, because he needed some experience singing and holding vaguely around the note. I can't hold a note – all my songs are sung out of tune, but I can get fairly near it sometimes. This guy was way off, but it didn't work, so then I sang it just to show him how to sing it, how it should go, and we got this guy that Mal had found in a group called Half-breed or something, and he sounded like Paul. So I thought, 'That's a commercial sound'. It would have been nice to have Paul's voice singing 'God Save Oz', but the guy imitated more of my demo, so he sounds like himself because he doesn't sound like me, really, but he doesn't sound like Paul either.

The single, credited to Bill Elliott and The Elastic Oz Band, was released on Apple, with Mal Evans receiving a co-production credit, in July of 1971. Although it is a catchy tune and features excellent vocals, the record got little airplay and did not chart on either side of the pond. But Lennon must have had some affection for the record as he discussed it in 1974 when he was a guest disc jockey on WNEW on 28 September 1974. He played 'Gravy Train' from Splinter's debut album as well.

Meanwhile, Purvis and Elliott decided to get back together and, in 1972, formed the band Truth. By this point, Mal Evans was Purvis's manager, and when that band disbanded, he assisted Purvis in recording some demos with Mike Gibbons, drummer of Badfinger. By the end of 1973, Purvis and Elliott figured out that they worked best as a duo and formed the band Splinter, who received interest from a number of people and labels. Tony Visconti (who was making a name for himself producing David Bowie) offered them a deal, as did Threshold Records, owned by The Moody Blues. But they held out for a contract with Apple Records. Little did they know that Apple was crumbling from within. George Harrison explained in a *Melody Maker* interview:

> The Splinter thing happened when I was making a movie. I was raising the money for a movie to be made, *Little Malcolm and His Struggles Against the Eunuchs*, and there was a scene where they needed a couple of singers in a nightclub. A friend of mine Mal Evans brought these guys down. I liked their material and we did an album.

The album was recorded at Harrison's home studio, F.P.S.H.O.T. (Friar Park Studios, Henley on the Thames) and according to Purvis in an interview with *The Newcastle Evening Chronicle* in 2001, they spent 17 months recording it. Harrison produced the album and brought in some of his friends, including Billy Preston (electric guitar, organ, keyboards), Alvin Lee (guitar), Klaus Voormann (bass), Gary Wright (piano, keyboards), Jim Keltner (drums), Willie Weeks (bass), Mel Collins (horn arrangements), Graham Maitland (accordion) and Mike Kelly (drums). Other instruments were handled by Harrison under such pseudonyms as P. Roducer, Hari Georgeson and Jai Raj Harisein. Harrison was not fooling anyone. Introducing the song on WNEW, Lennon remarked: 'I heard them on your radio station the other day ... it sounded like George'.

Purvis said in 2001, 'Harrison was brilliant. He made us feel at home and it was awesome working with a legend'. Bill Elliott was equally thrilled to work with Harrison and be on Dark Horse. He told Tom Brennan in 2014:

> The first album was a miracle as George put huge amounts of his time into it. I think George was going through a bad time personally, so there were a few strange moments, but at the time, being young and naïve, I guess most of it went unnoticed. Nobody can imagine how it felt to be a 24-year-old singer harmonising with a Beatle in his own home, 40 years later, I still feel proud and very privileged to have been there.

Simon Leng, in his book *While My Guitar Gently Weeps: The Music of George Harrison*, notes that Harrison continually pushed Purvis and Elliott in order for them to play and perform their best. He would stay in the control room with engineer Kumar Shankar. At the end of the sessions, he would escort the two out and Harrison would be left alone to overdub guitar and other parts. When Splinter returned, Harrison would play what he had recorded and ask for their feedback. In total, Harrison would end up contributing acoustic guitar, electric guitar, bass, dobro, harmonium, 12-string guitar, synthesiser and backing vocals.

Purvis recalls working with Harrison: 'George has an amazing amount of energy, so he'll work for 24 hours straight and not realise that the people he is working with don't have that much energy. He'd still be going strong when everyone else was exhausted'.

Bill Elliottt, in an interview at the time in *Record Mirror*, commented: 'With George, there's still the thing where he is a Beatle; it's like working with an idol. So when we recorded the album (*The Place I Love*), he was producing it, so we let him get on with it. We just accepted the fact that he knew far more about it than us'.

Gary Wright had very good memories of recording the album with Splinter. According to Wright, he got along so well with the duo, that they wrote a song together, 'Kyle', which appeared on a later Spooky Tooth album entitled *The Mirror*.

Quite wisely, one week before the album was released, 'Costafine Town' was selected as the first single. Promotional copies of the single were sent out to radio stations around the world. In the UK, Dark Horse followed the industry standard by sending the regular single to the radio stations with a notation on the label that it is a promotional copy. In North America, however, all Dark Horse singles released through A&M would have a mono version on one side and the stereo mix on the other. This would continue until the label was distributed by Warner Brothers.

Bill Elliottt recalled that the song was the obvious choice as a single. In a 2020 interview with this author, he recounted how the song came about. 'When we brought the first album out, *The Place I Love*, and the song 'Costafine Town', originally, it just lacked the little certain something'. According to Elliott, they added something that made the song stand out: 'There is this accordion player (Graham Maitland) in a Scottish band, Glencoe; we brought him down and he triple-tracked the accordion, and as soon as he did that, we thought: right, great, that's a single'. He further added, 'you get that little bit of fairy dust, you know. Once you've dusted it with fairy dust, there is no going back'.

'Costafine Town' became the first Dark Horse single to make the charts. It proved to be a decent hit in the UK, where it made it to number 17 on the national charts. It also reached number 16 in

Australia. Sadly, the single did not fare as well in the US, where it peaked at number 77 on the *Billboard* charts. The album was a minor chart success in North America, however, reaching number 89 in Canada on their national RPM charts and number 81 in the US *Billboard* Top 200 Album charts. This was a very encouraging start for Harrison, Splinter, A&M and Dark Horse. Elliott stated at the time to Rosalind Russell for a 1975 *Record Mirror and Disc* article: 'We were surprised, as any new band would be, that it got into the charts and we were literally flabbergasted when it (the single) got into the Top 20',

The Place I Love was released by Dark Horse in September 1974. It got the attention of critics. Although not a rave, Chris Irwin, writing in the UK's *Melody Maker,* gave it a good review, stating: 'In terms of a debut album, it is outstanding', and Harrison's production is 'clean and unmuddled'. Further, he referred to the songs as 'melodic, instantly listenable, not too bad lyrically'. *Cashbox* gave it a neutral and factual review in their 5 October issue, but they did compare their music to The Beatles, which is quite a compliment. Ken Barnes, in writing for *Rolling Stone*, noted that Splinter is Dark Horse's 'first rock act', and they received the 'royal treatment' with the packaging, guests and 'a perfectly immaculate recording'. He gave the album a positive review, highlighting the songs 'China Light', 'Haven't Got Time', 'Situation Vacant' and 'Drink All Day (Got to Find Your Own Way Home)' as 'catchy' and 'striking'. Overall, he referred to the album as 'impressive'.

Billboard magazine, in their 'Top Album Picks' gave the album a rave review, stating that FM and AM airplay should be a sure thing. They referred to the album as a 'very pleasant surprise' and noted the famous musicians playing on it. But even with the star power, they were very clear, 'the set, nevertheless, remains theirs (the band's)'. They did note the Harrison influence and picked the future single 'China Light' as one of the best cuts.

All the stops were pulled out to promote this album. To their credit, A&M did a fine job with print ads, posters (in which Harrison appeared with hopes it would help sales) and in getting the band to tour the UK and the US. Harrison helped out by releasing an interview album to all radio stations titled *Dark Horse Radio Special* promoting Splinter and the Dark Horse label. Everything seemed to be coming together. A&M appeared very committed to Dark Horse, as did Harrison. Harrison had to be pleased with how A&M was working with the label and the artists; there seemed to be a great deal of excitement as the label was launched.

Splinter completed their first-ever BBC Radio session for the show *In Concert* for Radio 1. This was aired on 2 November 1974. Following in the footsteps of The Beatles, the band performed only three songs from the album they were promoting: the title track ('The Place I Love'), their then-current single ('Costafine Town') and the future single from the album ('China Light'). Other songs included future album tracks (both 'Lonely Man' and 'What is it (If You Never Ever Tried)' would appear on the 1975 album *Harder to Live,* while 'Silver' would be on their third Dark Horse album *Two Man Band*), a future B-side released only in Japan ('White Shoe Weather') and a song they never released on any album ('Split Crow Road') were also included in the set.

And yet something went wrong, despite the fact they had a Top 20 single, had made several television appearances (including *The Old Grey Whistle Test*) and the good promotion the album received. *The Place I Love* did not sell as well as hoped. Although Splinter spent 1974 promoting the single 'Costafine Town' and the album, they could not generate a great deal of interest. They even performed on the all-important *Top Of The Pops* on 24 October 1974. Splinter appeared on Granada Television (the television show *45*, performing 'Costafine Town') and Dutch television (the show *Top Pop*, where they performed 'Costafine Town'). They also opened for the up-and-coming band Supertramp at Kings Road Theatre, Chelsea, London. Of course, Supertramp were label mates in a sense, as they were signed to A&M. A promotional film was made for the single, which was not the most common method of promotion at the time. They also made the cover of *Melody Maker* on 31 August 1974, where they are pictured alongside Harrison with the subtitle 'Harrison's Splinter Group'. The issue featured an interview with the duo.

So, what went wrong? Why the album did not sell is anyone's guess. It did not chart in the UK and all future singles failed to chart on either side of the Atlantic. Their second single, chosen for release in the UK and Europe, was the very folky 'Drink All Day (Got to Find Your Own Way Home)'. It seemed like the perfect follow-up to 'Costafine Town'; it had most of the same ingredients, excellent playing and wonderful harmonies.

The members of Splinter were not always in favour of decisions made in terms of singles. Green reported to this author that Harrison had the final say as to which singles were released from albums. Derek Green, who was assigned to promote Dark Horse, assisted Harrison in determining the best course of action for promoting the records and artists. According to Green, 'the singles were chosen under discussion with George. He trusted me better than others. We discussed singles, what we might do – a very healthy working relationship'. But in the end, even with a Beatle's involvement, Green admits, it was 'impossible to get it played'.

Elliott, very diplomatically, offered his opinion of the second single during an interview he gave for *Record Mirror*. "Drink All Day' was a majority decision. We don't think it's the best track on the album, but everyone seemed to think it should be released as a single, including George's Dad. We hope it'll do better than 'Costafine Town".

However, it turned out that the single had some controversial lyrics. 'Drink All Day (Got to Find Your Own Way Home)' was banned by the BBC due to the use of the word 'bloody'. Derek Green even tried to use his relationship with the BBC in order to get the ban lifted: '... they were going to refuse to play the record, it being a swear word at the time. Luckily, I had a relationship with Doreen Davis, programmer on Radio 1, and got Dori to recognise that it was not that offensive'. However, the ban was not lifted, which did not help in promoting the single. Elliott, in speaking with Tom Brennan in 2014, has a different understanding: 'Unfortunately, Doreen Davis didn't like the fact that it might influence the youth at the time to consume alcohol, so the song didn't make the playlist, which is a pity because, in my opinion, it was a more happy-go-lucky song and I think it would have charted given the chance'.

'China Light' was remixed and edited for its single release, their third UK single and their second for the North American market. In her review of it, *Record Mirror* and *Popswop* critic Sue Byrom makes mention of the confusion: 'This was originally the B-side, but due to certain persons objecting to the A-side, the record has been repackaged with the sides switched. It's a soft, gentle sound, much in the 'Costafine Town' vein, but possibly having it as the original B-side was right. It lacks a little something'. She never identified that 'certain person'.

Harrison had to have been disappointed that the follow-up singles did not match the success of the debut. However, the album and the singles did have airplay in pockets throughout North America and the band were developing a following. Opening slots on tours and even radio broadcasts helped the band gain a foothold in North America. The album is now regarded as a lost classic. Self-effacingly, Bill Elliott said to Rosalind Russell in 1975: 'We make no bones about the fact that people probably bought the album because Billy Preston or someone was on it'. Elliott is not giving the record enough credit. Most who heard the album loved it.

Perhaps there was a backlash against the group given Harrison's involvement, being on his label and his appearance on the album with some very famous friends. 'People are bound to say that, because of George Harrison, we have a head start', Elliott stated in 1974, 'But we've been trying for five years. We've been through it, as well as having the rewards, maybe'. But given the popular albums and artists of late 1974, Elton John, Neil Diamond and Ringo Starr were all in the US *Billboard* Top Ten album chart, the mellow folk sounds of Splinter might easily have found a large audience.

Harrison assembled a top-notch studio band and demonstrated, very clearly, that he could produce. Phil McDonald, the engineer who had worked with The Beatles, was brought in to record the whole affair, and as *Rolling Stone* noted, it was recorded perfectly. The album was beautifully packaged with a gatefold sleeve in North America with lyrics and a fold-out sleeve in the UK. The cover photograph was taken by Terry O'Neill, with the cover design by Jack Katz, Fabio Nicoli and Nick Marshall. Nicoli and Marshall, both employees of A&M Records, did a fantastic job with the entire design.

Although many saw the album as an extension of Harrison's solo career, it was clearly not. 'It's a Splinter album and he's done it as a Splinter album', Elliott said at the time. 'I don't think it sounds at all like a George Harrison album'.

Splinter's *The Place I Love* was a strong debut for a new record label. The album, along with *Shankar Family & Friends* gave a clear indication that Dark Horse Records was a diverse and unique label. A British folk album and an Indian Ballet were released on the same day by the same label. Harrison must have been pleased to see his vision, if not his dream, come true. However, was North America ready for such diversity and alternative styles of music that did not conform to the standard tropes of pop music? Harrison was also very aware of the existing pigeonholes in the music industry, having seen it play out with Apple.

While Harrison was working with Splinter, he was also quite busy with Ravi Shankar. It should have come as no surprise that one of the first artists Harrison signed to Dark Horse was his old friend and mentor whom Harrison first met in 1966. Shankar, born in India in 1920, began his career as a dancer at the age of ten. By 18, he gave up his career in dancing and began seriously studying music under famed Indian musician Allauddin Khan. Khan's sons Ali Akbar and Annapurna Devi studied alongside Shanker and would later perform with him in concert and on record. Shankar began his recording career for HMV India in 1949 and came to international attention in 1955 when he composed music for Satyajit Ray's *Apu Trilogy*. His first album *Three Ragas*, on World Pacific Records in 1955, earnt him worldwide attention. Harrison met Shankar through The Byrds and the founder of World Pacific Records Richard Bock, in 1965.

Harrison's first meeting with Shankar had been at a dinner at the home of Patricia and Ayana Deva Anghadi, who ran the Asian Music Circle in London. Harrison recalled in his book *I Me Mine* that Shankar '... Came to Esher and gave me a quick sitar lesson ... John and Ringo came to watch'. He further added that 'the first sitar lesson was interesting in that it was so nice to find somebody who was such a master at being able to start from scratch with a beginner'.

In the same book, Harrison pointed out that he was not doing everything correctly when it came to how he held the instrument and that there were other aspects of the sitar he was simply not aware of. He gave a very good and somewhat amusing example: 'The telephone rang and I put the sitar down, stood up and went to step across the sitar to go to the phone and Ravi whacked me on the leg and said: 'the first thing you must realise is that you must have more respect for the instrument".

When Harrison first heard Indian music, he took an instant liking to it, and this developed into a profound love of the music. Harrison wrote in *I Me Mine*:

> When I first consciously heard Indian music, it was as if I already knew it. When I was a child, we had a crystal radio with long and short-wave bands and so it's possible I might have already heard some Indian classical music. There was something about it that was very familiar, but at the same time, intellectually, I didn't know what was happening at all.

Harrison studied with Shakar from 1966 until 1968, an example of a lesson during this time was filmed and used in the film *Raga,* filmed in Big Sur, California and finally released in 1971.

He had developed an interest in the sitar before he met Shankar, most likely while filming *Help!*, which is where he noted that he first 'messed around with one'. The first time Harrison played the sitar on a Beatle record was *Rubber Soul*'s 'Norwegian Wood (This Bird Has Flown)', released in 1965. He experimented even further on The Beatles' *Revolver* (1966) with the song 'Love You To', which was his first successful attempt at total Indian music immersion. His love of the music continued with *Sgt. Pepper's Lonely Hearts Club Band* (1967) and the stunning 'Within You, Without You'. He also scored his first official Beatle B-side, 'The Inner Light', which was released in 1968 on the 'Lady Madonna' single and featured Indian music. The song itself was recorded while Harrison worked on the soundtrack for Joe Massot's film *Wonderwall*, the first album released on The Beatles' Apple label in 1968. It was a precursor to what he had hoped *Shankar Family and Friends* would be: East meets West. It was an attempt to introduce and expand what Harrison had already done with The Beatles, with Harrison believing that given the chance, music fans would enjoy Indian music as much as he did.

Once Apple Records was up and running, Harrison signed Ravi Shankar and produced two albums: *Raga* and *In Concert 1972* – the latter was credited to Ravi Shankar and Ali Akbar Khan. He also produced the Ravi Shankar EP *Joi Bangla*. The songs on the EP were recorded to raise awareness and money for refugees of The Bangladesh Liberation War with Harrison producing the single during the sessions for his charity record 'Bangla Desh'. Shankar's pleas for his people of Bangladesh, formerly known as East Pakistan, touched Harrison and he wanted to help as the press of the time reported a population of people who were facing war and the effects of a cyclone in early 1971. Harrison, on hearing the proposal that Shankar was planning a benefit concert, offered to help.

Harrison had another idea to help his mentor and friend: a benefit concert featuring himself and his other rock friends. Keep in mind that, at this time, Harrison had just scored his first worldwide number-one album with *All Things Must Pass*, had a worldwide number-one single ('My Sweet Lord') and, in North America, another Top Ten ('What Is Life') – Harrison had emerged from The Beatles split as the most popular Beatle at that point.

'When I asked George for his thoughts about raising money for the refugees of Bangla Desh, he quickly organised what became the now historic concert at New York's Madison Square Garden', Shankar said in the liner notes of the CD box set *In Celebration*.

Harrison was very matter of fact when asked why he was doing the concert: 'Because I was asked by a friend to help', said Harrison during a press conference on 27 July 1971 to discuss the upcoming *Concert For Bangla Desh*. In his usual understated manner, Harrison was discussing a concert that he had organised in a very short time that was to occur at Madison Square Garden on 1 August 1971. There were to be two concerts, an afternoon show and an evening show: both shows were instant sellouts.

The album, released later in the year, won Album of the Year at the 1973 Grammy Awards, topped the charts in the UK and made number two in Canada and the US. The film, released through 20th Century Fox in 1972, did extremely well in its own right. According to Simon Leng, despite the film's success, Harrison was never happy with it.

Although the concert, film and album raised awareness and money for Bangladesh, there were numerous legal and tax problems. But Harrison pioneered what we now know as the 'Benefit Concert' with *The Concert For Bangla Desh*. Yes, there had been benefit concerts before, but none featuring such a large number of artists. Live Aid organiser Bob Geldof noted in his memoir that when he organised his concert, he found an ally in George, who met with him and gave him some advice about administering the money earned from the concert.

Harrison signed Shankar to Dark Horse as soon as he could. The pair were very close, with Shankar viewing Harrison as part of his own family. But while Splinter's *The Place I Love* was recorded at Harrison's home studio, *Shankar Family and Friends* was recorded at A&M studios in Los Angeles in April of 1973, just after Harrison finished his album *Living in the Material World*. Harrison was also in LA to assist Ringo Starr with his classic *Ringo* album so many of the artists working with Starr also contributed to the *Shankar Family and Friends* album. This included Billy Preston, Klaus Voormannn, Nicky Hopkins and Starr himself. It was also at this time that he met saxophonist Tom Scott, who would soon become a friend and collaborator.

Scott, in conversation with this author, paints an exciting picture of A&M and Studio A, noting that many of the rock/pop elite could be seen there, such as Joni Mitchell, The Carpenters, Billy Preston, Carole King and Cheech & Chong. But meeting Harrison was on another level. Scott recalls that Harrison put him at ease and wanted to talk about their mutual love of Indian music. 'He said, 'do you enjoy listening to Indian music?' And I said 'sure'. He said 'come with me' and, at that moment, I became George's sidekick off and on for the next three or four years'. According to Scott, 'that is how I got to know him. I spent a great deal of time at Friar Park, obviously working on his records'.

Scott's connection to Shankar is very interesting. While he was a high school student, Scott had the opportunity to attend summer courses. He studied at UCLA, where he took two summer courses with jazz musician, writer and arranger Don Ellis. Ellis offered a course on jazz arranging and composing and jazz improvisation. According to Scott, 'I found out that Don was very much into East Indian rhythms. And he formed a group called the Hindustani Jazz Sextet. One of the members of this Sextet was Harihar Rao, who was also a teacher at UCLA. He had also studied under Ravi Shankar'.

At this time, Scott was also starting to get some work in Los Angeles as a session musician. Scott had many opportunities to work within many genres. However, the fact that he was familiar with Indian music afforded him an opportunity to work on the soundtrack for the film *Charly*, which Shankar had scored.

Shankar was equally impressed that Scott had studied with Harihar Rao at UCLA. Scott said that when he met Shankar, 'he looked at me and he said, that makes you my grandson. He reached out and gave me a big hug. I thought at that moment, I am the happiest fucking guy on the planet. Getting a hug from Ravi Shankar, how cool is that?'

According to Leng, in his book *While My Guitar Gently Weeps: The Music of George Harrison*, sessions for the album started on 1 April 1973 at A&M Studios and continued into May of that year. Other 'western' musicians participated in the recording at Harrison's invitation. This included Tom Scott (saxophones and flutes), Emil Richards (marimbas), Ringo Starr (drums), Robert Margouleff (Moog synthesiser), Billy Preston (organ), Paul Beaver (Moog synthesiser), Malcolm Cecil (Moog synthesiser), Nicky Hopkins (piano), Klaus Voormann (bass), Dennis Budimer (guitar), Jim Keltner (drums) and David Bromberg (guitar). Harrison had worked with Bromberg on his album *David Bromberg* and co-wrote the song 'The Holdup', while Emil Richards would feature on Harrison's *Dark Horse* album, as would Scott. Harrison knew Keltner from working with Harry Nilsson in the early 1970s. Harrison also played on the album as well as producing the entire project.

Scott also recalls seeing Harrison in London prior to the tour when the saxophonist was performing with Joni Mitchell:

I came through London with Joni Mitchell, opening for her and accompanying her on the *Court and Spark* tour of 1974. We did a concert at Odeon Hammersmith, and George came to that concert and drove a bunch of us back to his home, his castle – his home is his castle, by the way. Literally. He kind of sussed us out, he was considering having us as his band for his tour. He was planning the tour in the back of his head. I wasn't aware at the time, exactly. We went there and Joni Mitchell went as well. He decided the people he liked the best were me and Robben Ford.

Much like on Harrison's *Wonderwall Music*, Harrison and Shankar wanted to blend Indian music with current, modern 'Western' music. This was not a new concept to Shankar either. In 1967, he collaborated with Yehudi Menuhin on the now-classic *West Meets East album*. That album was a huge success, both critically and commercially, winning a Grammy in 1968 for Best Chamber Music Performance. Shankar became the first Asian musician to win that esteemed award.

The impact of *West Meets East* cannot be overstated. This album, along with The Beatles' use of sitar and Harrison's excursions into Indian music, especially on *Revolver*, influenced a whole generation of musicians and had a tremendous impact on the British folk scene. Bands such as The Incredible String Band and Renaissance can partially trace their origins to that album. By the late 1960s, the British folk scene was exciting, vibrant and new, due in part to Shankar.

According to Scott, recording *Shankar Family and Friends* was a great experience. He remembers:

We did the sessions over a week or two and it was very interesting. 'Ravi didn't compose in a conventional Western kind of way. He had some themes written out, but most of the time, he would walk around and assign parts of them to various instruments. You can hear the Indian influence, obviously. It was just wonderful.

Flautist Hariprasad Chaurasia, who was part of the Indian Orchestra, has similar memories. During a conversation with this author, he stated:

I remember the record that was recorded in Hollywood Boulevard. This was a World Music project composed and arranged by Pt. Ravi Shankar and George Harrison, released later by Shankar, Family & Friends. This was the best musical experience for everyone who was a part of this project. It was my good fortune that I was a participant.

Harrison worked very hard on the album and he had every right to be proud of it, especially as he was releasing it on his own label. Harrison must have thought he had a surefire hit on his hands. As with Splinter, he certainly pulled out all the stops to promote the album upon its release.

The packaging for the album was very elaborate, complete with a beautifully designed insert describing the album and how it was made. Similarly to Splinter's debut, the album art was put together by Jack Katz, Nick Marshall and Fabio Nicoli. Nicoli was A&M's art director and had a great deal of influence on the album sleeves, while Dark Horse was with A&M.

According to Derek Green, promoting the album was not an easy task. He recalls that it was 'Impossible to get it played. We could get press on Ravi and George', but radio play did not happen. Green continues, 'I remember going to George's wonderful home in Henley, and I went up to the studio. Kumar Shankar, who was his engineer at the studio, was there. That is where they played me the Shankar tracks'.

But 'It was a difficult meeting', says Green. The expectation was for Green to promote the album and the single, but, as Green remembered, 'how do you promote it? Well, with great difficulty, that is how'.

And to a certain extent, Harrison shared this view. In November 1974, Dark Horse released the first album by George Harrison on the label, although it was a promotional interview album distributed to radio stations. The album *The Dark Horse Radio Special* features Harrison talking about the label, Splinter and Shankar. The idea was to send the album to radio stations and the station would have an hour of free radio programming, simply by playing the album.

In the interview, Harrison admits, 'People in the West will realise there is more to Indian music. It is so complex that Indian classical music is light years ahead of anything in the West, and the nearest anybody's come to it, I suppose, is certain jazz musicians. They are usually the ones who acknowledge that Indian music is far out. Even John Coltrane; he studied with Ravi'.

Nevertheless, Dark Horse did promote *Shankar Family & Friends*. Full-page ads were taken out in *Billboard* stating, 'Only one artist was at the three most significant music events of all time: *Monterey Pop*,

Woodstock and *The Concert For Bangla Desh*. Dark Horse is proud to present his new music'.

Shankar Family & Friends was met with very positive reviews. *Cashbox* went so far as to write: 'the album is a must for listening as the new sounds of Shankar and Harrison may be the new sounds of today'. In the *Billboard* review, it is mentioned that if feels like two different records. They note there is one side of 'short commercial cuts' and the other side is a ballet. They go on to call Shankar a 'master at his craft' and that not all music 'need be of Western origins', a line that Harrison must have loved.

But it did not sell as well as hoped. In the UK, the album failed to chart, while in the US it charted on the *Billboard* Top 200 for three weeks, peaking at number 176. A single from the album was released in September 1974, 'I Am Missing You', which featured Ravi Shankar's then sister-in-law Lakshmi Shankar on vocals. Harrison noted in an interview with Andy McConnel of *Sounds* magazine, 'it should be top of the pops because it's lovely'.

Shankar comments in the liner notes for *In Celebration*, 'We actually recorded two versions of this song, one of the few that I wrote in English. George and I wanted to include this 'pop' version, which George arranged and we performed each night for the finale of our concert tour together'. The other version of the song on the album is more of a traditional folk song, owing more to the Incredible String Band than Classical Indian music. Tom Scott noted that 'Hariprasad Chaurasia's playing of the bansuri is fantastic'.

Harrison put a great deal of work into the album, and when he released the interview album to radio stations in November of 1974, he was very vocal about the reception *Shankar Family & Friends* received. 'It is not strictly classical. 'I Am Missing You' is a composition by Ravi Shankar, and it is the first song he has written in English', Harrison noted. 'The first time he sang it to me, it just blew my mind'.

To Harrison's credit, he felt that he had a hit on his hands. 'I heard it from my pop background. I said, 'that is a hit, it's so lovely. It's a lovely song. You should write more of these Ravi', and he said, 'I have been trying not to write these for years".

In fact, Harrison became very protective of the song and the album.

People always put people into pigeonholes. He is one of the world's greatest classical musicians, but if he wants to write a song in English, it doesn't take away or distract from his talent as a classical musician. People want to lock everything up. Like in *Melody Maker* this week. Some guy did an interview on Ravi, whoever you are, you know it really is just a bitchy article. Just saying, is he going heavy! He is going light. This is what *Melody Maker* thinks is heavy, and in actual fact, it is light compared to Ravi just playing on his sitar. It is very, very light.

In the end, *Shankar Family & Friends* (for the record, the '&' is actually the Sanskrit OM sign) is an album Harrison held close to his heart. In an interview in 1979 with *Rolling Stone*, Harrison referenced the album as one of his favourites released by Dark Horse. He was also not so quick to give up on the album being a success. According to *Rolling Stone*, Harrison and Shankar had met up in India in February 1974 to plan a North American Tour. This was to be a double bill, Ravi Shankar and George Harrison, not Shankar merely opening the show, but a joint headliner. Harrison began assembling his band while Shankar put together his orchestra. The tour, which has now come to be known as the *Dark Horse Tour* – because Harrison was promoting both his then-latest album *Dark Horse* and as well as the launch of the label – was named *George Harrison/Ravi Shankar 1974*, as indicated by the actual tour programme.

Harrison's backup band was quite incredible: old friend Billy Preston (keyboards and a couple of solo numbers), Andy Newmark (drums), Willie Weeks (bass), Emil Richards (percussion), Robben Ford (guitar) and Tom Scott (of the famed LA Express). Scott brought along two players, Chuck Findley and Jim Horn, to round out the horn section. Harrison had met Newmark and Weeks when he was helping Ronnie Wood of The Rolling Stones with his first solo album *I've Got My Own Album To Do in* 1974.

The tour would encompass 26 dates with a total of 45 shows, with some dates featuring two shows. A&M were in full support. Derek Green joined the tour. The concert was set up so that Ravi Shankar and his Orchestra opened the show, followed by an intermission, before Harrison and his band would come on. For the last few numbers, Shankar and Orchestra would join Harrison for 'Anurag', 'I Am Missing You' and 'Dispute and Violence', all three songs from *Shankar Family & Friends,* with Harrison ending the show with 'My Sweet Lord'.

When Harrison began assembling a setlist for the show, Scott noticed that there were only four songs from The Beatles' catalogue, even though he was encouraged by tour promoter Bill Graham to include more. Rehearsals began in October 1974 in the A&M soundstages. Shankar even noted that Harrison wanted to 'perform all his new songs and was insisting on not singing his old favourites which people were clamouring to hear'.

According to author Nicholas Schaffner in his book *The Beatles Forever*, as people filed in to find their seats to see Harrison, and during intermission, the music of Splinter's debut album was played through the speakers. It was an excellent idea; although they were on their own tour, Harrison still felt that they should get some exposure at his shows.

Drummer Andy Newmark remembers the tour. 'The tour was …the whole thing was… in hindsight, difficult for him. He lost his voice early on and the record wasn't doing particularly well. This is what I have read from other writers. I observed – I knew his voice was gone'. Furthermore, according to Newmark, 'The press was not particularly kind to him on the tour; a lot of people didn't care for the Ravi Shankar and Orchestra opening act'.

The audience's response to Ravi Shankar and Orchestra is confirmed, at least for the Toronto evening show, by musician Blair Packham, who was in attendance:

It was embarrassing, even at my age at the time, which I think was 15. I was embarrassed at how uninterested the audience was. They weren't as welcoming and as open as I hoped they would be and I think, as well, there were a lot of people there who wanted to see 'George The Beatle', not George the semi-mystic, spiritual God he became.

From the very beginning, Harrison was under a great deal of stress. Keep in mind that Harrison had just launched his own label, had a new album out and was riding high in the public affection at this time. His first two studio solo albums had both hit number one, and both featured number-one singles. People still had very positive memories of *The Concert For Bangladesh*, and The Beatles were still riding high in the charts with the two compilations released in 1973 (*The Beatles 1962-1966* and *The Beatles 1967-1970*). Expectations were high, there was a lot riding on the tour and he was having some personal and professional problems.

Newmark recalls:

He was under a lot of stress. His marriage was breaking up as the tour began; he and his wife broke up. I think it was a difficult time for him.

As far as the audience was concerned, people came to the show and probably must have enjoyed it, thought it was ok. And then his throat went and he couldn't sing and the critics were really pounding him.

Although the record company was very supportive, it was clear from their perspective that there was a great deal riding on this tour. But for George, issues kept arising. On 30 November 1974, Ravi Shankar was taken to hospital with a suspected heart attack. Luckily for all concerned, it turned out to be indigestion, but it did mean that he missed the next few concerts. Harrison recalled the meeting in Ravi Shankar's autobiography, *Raga Mala – An Autobiography*:

Unfortunately, I had the first alert from my heart while we were in Chicago. I was hospitalised in intensive care for five days. Luckily, it was not that serious, but I was cautioned to take care of my heart in the future. The cause of the trouble seemed to have been the thunderous noise I'd had to endure from the stage monitors for those few weeks on tour. I managed to finish the tour.

And there were clear highlights, such as Harrison being invited to The White House by then-President Gerold Ford, whose son Jack was a fan of Harrison's. Shankar recalled the meeting in his autobiography:

They organised our visit in two tours. Billy Preston, Tommy Scott, Ravi, myself and my dad were all taken in early to meet the President. We were taken up into the private apartments, had lunch up there, came down and went into the Oval Office, and as we came out, we bumped into all the others from the Indian band, who had arrived later ... I couldn't believe the place felt as comfortable as it did, after going through that Nixon period.

For Newmark, an experienced, albeit young musician at the time, the treatment of Harrison by the fans did not seem to make sense. After all, this was the first tour undertaken by an ex-Beatle and the first tour of America by a member of the band since 1966.

When I was in it, it was a different matter. He was really struggling, having to go to all those cities in front of all those people and not have his voice. At the time, I probably would not have had that much compassion or sympathy or understanding because I was young. But I was thinking, this is George Harrison. How could anything be difficult in the life of a Beatle? If you are a Beatle, you have everything, you have tons of money, success. At that age, it was hard to imagine him not being in a good headspace. On the surface of it, he made everything look like it was ok. He was on an indestructible high after *Bangla Desh* and *All Things Must Pass*, and then I don't know what happened. He fell from grace. It was going incredibly well, and it seemed like he could do no wrong. I can only see that in hindsight. It didn't feel like that at the time.

Scott agrees that the tour was hard on Harrison:

He took a terrible beating on that tour. I love George, we supported him fully throughout the whole thing and we were happy to help him out, any way we could. The issue was his voice. He wasn't prepared. He'd never headlined as a solo singer, and physically, it was just too much for him. Bill Graham, a concert promoter I adored; he was passionate, ballsy, outspoken, opinionated and I loved him. But he assumed that George would be capable of handling the strain of a tour of that length. It was relentless. He lost his voice early on, and never quite got it back; he was kind of hoarse the whole time – dark horse, literally. That made it tough.

For many of the Indian musicians, it was their first trip to America and their first tour, albeit with a rock band. Indian flautist Hariprasad Chaurasia, who toured with Harrison and Shankar, said, 'I do remember the American tour. More than 50 concerts, I think ... but what superb organisers! The arrangements were very good, the musicians were great. It was, overall, a super amazing tour. I enjoyed every moment of it'.

And as well intended as Harrison was to have the show an equal split with him and the Indian musicians, years later, Shankar acknowledged that it was somewhat of a problem:

There were troubles with the half-and-half combination of Indian and pop music. I suppose only a tenth of the audience came for me, and the rest of them were there mainly for George. Neither camp was fully satisfied! Reviews were lukewarm, but financially, it was not a failure, and in spite of the difficulties, we all immensely enjoyed the performing and especially the touring together.

Scott had good memories of the tour as well:

George treated us well; we stayed at all the best hotels. He had a 747 jet or whatever it was that it was outfitted with ... the first class section, the seats had been removed and replaced with two rows of bean bag chairs with seat belts. We flew on that from place to place, which was George and the rock band and Ravi and his entourage. We all flew on this jet; we ate very well. The Indians had their own cook. Sometimes I would go over there because George had made me a fan of Indian food. I loved the tour and I felt bad for George. He took a terrible beating from the critics.

Sadly, for Scott, criticism was not limited to Harrison. In fact, Scott has one memory of a review written in a Toronto paper. Scott remembered that the *Toronto Star* reviewer 'was not very complimentary of George's performance', but Scott further recalled that the critic went on to say something like, 'somewhere in the middle of the concert, saxophonist Tom Scott took over and did a tune of his. He's a perfect example of someone who should never stand out in front of a band'. 'I remember this very well, and I even made a button out of it'.

By the end of the tour in New York City on 20 December 1974, on what should have been a celebratory day, Harrison was dealing with The Beatles' business issues. In fact, this concert would serve as a meeting place for all of The Beatles to discuss the end the band. Ringo, who was unable to come, had signed the documents in Europe, but John Lennon and Paul McCartney were planning on coming to the show in order to sign the papers. McCartney attended the show while wearing a very obvious disguise (a wig and fake moustache).

Lennon, however, disappointed Harrison. On NBC's *The Today Show*, on 16 December 1974, Lennon was talking about his relationship with the other Beatles and stated, 'and I may be working with him this Friday, folks. He's in town performing and we're still friends, you see. We might have a laugh. It's the last night of his tour; see you Friday!' Lennon never showed up, perhaps because he did not want to deal with the legal paperwork. Lennon had attended Harrison's show at Nassau Coliseum in Uniondale, New York, the previous week, and spoke highly of the performance.

Instead of attending the show, Lennon sent a balloon: 'Listen to this balloon'. Harrison was not impressed. He immediately called Lennon but got his employee May Pang on the phone. By all accounts, Harrison is said to have asserted to Pang: 'tell him that I started this tour on my own and I'll end it on my own'. Lennon later told Ray Coleman that he did not attend the show that night because 'I was a bit nervous' and he didn't sign the forms as his 'astrologer told me it wasn't the right day'. Lennon did observe, however, that he had seen the show on a previous night and although it was great, he noticed that 'George's voice was shot'.

By the next day, the storm had blown over and Harrison, through a very young Julian Lennon, got a message to Lennon to come to the end of the tour party at New York's Hippopotamus Club. Lennon did attend; as fate would have it, it was the last time Harrison and Lennon would see each other in person.

However, the tour was very successful in many ways. First of all, it was a predecessor to such concerts as WOMAD and other world music festivals. The *Dark Horse* album, while not making number one, did extremely well in terms of sales and the tour, for the most part, did good business, with sold-out concerts throughout. Bob Dylan attended a show in Los Angeles and reported that he enjoyed it very much and although some critics were unnecessarily harsh, several local newspapers at the time gave the show a favourable review.

Sadly, few ran to their local record store to pick up *Shankar Family & Friends* after the concert. Harrison's *Dark Horse* album did extremely well in the US, peaking at number four on 25 January 1975 after the tour was completed while the number one album that week was *Elton John's Greatest Hits*. On that same date, Shankar's album sat at number 188 on the same *Billboard* chart. The album failed to find an audience; very sad, given the quality of the musicianship and excellence of the album.

But Harrison loved it, as did those who took the time to listen. It, along with the entire A&M Dark Horse catalogue, was eventually taken out of circulation, but it continues to have a life. It was one of two Dark Horse albums to be reissued in its complete form when the box set *Collaborations* was released by Dark Horse in 2010. Harrison also chose tracks for the album included in the 1996 box set *In Celebration* to commemorate Shankar's 75th birthday. George not only compiled the album but co-produced it as well.

Los Angeles, 1975

After a busy 1974, Harrison was not to have any respite in 1975, as it would prove to be another busy year. Not only did he write, record, produce and release his last studio album of original material for Apple, *Extra Texture (Read All About It)*, but he also threw himself into Dark Horse. It was slowly dawning on him that running a record label on your own was a lot of time and hard work.

While he was in Los Angeles, George took the opportunity to check out bands for consideration for Dark Horse and by the end of 1975, Harrison signed four more bands to the label, all but one being American. One was Jiva, who were the first American band signed to the label.

Harrison went to Los Angeles to record his album, *Extra Texture (Read All About It)*, but using studio time, he booked to record Splinter's second album at the A&M studio from the end of April until the end of June. The plan was to have Tom Scott produce their album. The saxophonist was also invited to play on Harrison's album. Harrison trusted him, no doubt also thinking that Scott could bring an American sound and more commercial appeal for the band.

Record Mirror, in their 19 April 1975 issue, stated:

Splinter have left for the States with George Harrison to start a new album at A&M Studios in Los Angeles. It will be produced by George Harrison, and feature Jim Keltner, Willy Weeks, and Billy Preston. Release of the album is hoped for late summer before Splinter's proposed tour of the US, with no plans to play in the UK.

Note that Harrison was noted as producer, yet Scott was ready to take the helm.

However, those plans changed; Splinter never made it over to Los Angeles to record what would become *Harder to Live*. In an interview with Dave Herman in Los Angeles, Harrison noted that 'in fact, they should have been here in the States to do that last week, but they couldn't get here with work visas'. But according to Bob Purvis, there was a different reason the duo did not make it to Los Angeles to record, later recounting that 'The pollen count is really high in Los Angeles. It would have been no fun for me out there'. Indeed, one article titled 'Hopefuls Splinter Have Been Out on the Road, Sneaking in the Back Door' in *Record and Popswap Mirror*, points out that Bob Purvis wanted the album done by May because, according to Bill Elliott, 'after the hayfever deadline, he can't sing a note'.

Harrison did not want to lose the studio time, so he used the studio in LA instead. It also gave him a chance to check out some bands and musicians. As he said to Paul Gambaccini at the time, 'When I get the time, I go out on genuine talent-spotting exercises'. While recording the album in Los Angeles, Harrison began to explore the music scene, and since Dark Horse had an office in Los Angeles, he began spending more time in the city, playing with other musicians, jamming and establishing roots.

In 1975, Los Angeles was a major music hub. One look at the US *Billboard* and *Cashbox* charts at the time demonstrates that Los Angeles had developed a healthy and extremely successful music scene. As Jiva's bassist James Strauss remarked to this author, 'When Jiva came out, the bands in LA would, end to end, reach all the way down the 405 to San Diego'.

While in Los Angeles, George also developed his relationship with Olivia Trinidad Arias.

Arias was a native of Los Angeles, but her grandparents had migrated there from Guanajuato, Mexico. In 1972, she started working for A&M Records, and by 1974, she had worked her way up to being part of the marketing department. In this role, she had several trans-Atlantic conversations with Harrison dealing with Dark Horse artists. Harrison was impressed with her work on his behalf, and once the Dark Horse offices were set up at the A&M studios, he requested that she work exclusively for his label.

Michael Lanning of Jiva recalled in 2013:

> Linda and her sister Olivia Arias, who later became Mrs George Harrison, were friends of ours and they turned our record onto George. George loved the record and he came to a place called the Topanga Corral to hear us perform. He said he loved our songs and loved our energy, and he pretty much signed us on the spot.

So, in 1974, Olivia was working with Splinter and Ravi Shankar in order to break them in North America, and, given the chart placings for Splinter, she did an excellent job. It also meant that she was assisting with Harrison and Shaknar's 1974 tour. Author Robert Rodriguez noted in his book *Fab Four FAQ 2.0: The Solo Years, 1970 – 1980*, that she was 'a capable and even-tempered administrator, ably handling the routine chaos involved with setting up a record label and dealing with all manner of personalities'. Harrison and Arias also became romantically involved. Her face (well, half of her face) adorned the record labels for the Dark Horse album and the singles 'Ding Dong; Ding Dong' and 'Dark Horse'.

Chris O'Dell, whom Harrison brought into The Beatles' inner circle, documents Harrison's attraction to Olivia in her book *Miss O'Dell*. She recalls Harrison talking to her about Olivia and saying:

'Well, I've been talking to [Olivia] on the phone a lot', [George] said a little sheepishly. 'You know, we really have a connection. Sometimes we talk for hours. I just want to know if she's as beautiful as she sounds'.

O'Dell states that it was 'love at first sight'.

Like Harrison, Arias already practised meditation and, like Harrison, very much embraced her spirituality. This included a vegetarian diet. Part of her spiritual journey and exploration led her to Prem Pal Singh Rawat (also known as Prem Rawat, Maharajji, Guru Maharaj Ji, and Balyogeshwar). Followers or devotees were known as 'Premies'. Members of Jiva were 'Premies', indeed, the name Jiva (pronounced Gee-vaa) comes from the Sanskrit root 'jiv', which means 'to breathe'. Jiva is 'that which breathes' and is commonly used to signify the soul.

'This is one band I'm proud to have found', Harrison noted in the Dark Horse Press Release for the Jiva album. 'They are positive musicians and have a lot of influences from the 1960s as well'. The Beatles were clearly an influence on the band, as Strauss noted during his conversation with this author, 'Everybody who had two guitar players, a bass player and a drummer wanted to be The Beatles'. By the time Harrison became interested in the band, they had already released one album, *Music For Hans Jayanti Festival,* on the independent label Box Canyon Records in 1974.

When Harrison first saw Jiva perform in a club, they were a four-piece comprised of Michael Scott Lanning (guitar, lead vocals, vocals), James Strauss (he is known as 'Jim' at the time) (bass, lead vocals, vocals), Thomas Walter Hilton (guitar, lead vocals, vocals) and Michael Randolph Reed aka Reedo (drums, percussion). Like most bands at the time, Jiva had been paying their dues. According to bassist James Strauss, the band had been around for quite some time, with various members and different band names. At one time, members of Jiva were in the band Titan.

Strauss recalled, 'we were sort of funk-oriented and Michael (Lanning) and I had a band that was a Tower of Power (the American funk band) kind of thing with a horn section'. The road to a record contract was not easy for Strauss: 'Actually, they fired me out of Titan'. Strauss, looking back, understands the conflict: 'I sort of pushed very hard, I had been in Vegas showbands, and I pushed really hard getting this thing visible and nailed down, not just in a garage, goofing off, getting high'.

Jack Reed was involved with the band from the very start and became their manager. He explained how he became involved:

> The guys that were in Jiva were a bunch of guys from San Bernardino, California, that I was managing as a High School band. When my wife and I moved into L.A., when they graduated High School, we brought them in there and got them an apartment. At one point, we were an eight-piece group with horns and were called Titan. Two trumpets and a sax player. Of the eight players, five were named Michael, so only Michael Lanning, as the lead singer, got to keep his own name ... all the others had to adopt nicknames. We did a lot of covers and that sort of thing. We finally settled down as a four-man group and we were looking for something to happen. I personally nurtured them through several 'salad years' before we met George (Harrison) and also served as a recording engineer and mixer on the road.

Dark Horse was not the only label interested in the band. They were on the radar of a lot of companies. Strauss says that the thought of working with and for George Harrison was too much of an attraction, and the band went with Dark Horse:

> A&M was courting us. At the time, the President Gil Friesen told me in his office... 'you guys are in the luxurious position of being a band that everyone in town wants'. A&M literally offered me the fucking moon, but wow, to get to record with a Beatle. Think about it, when you are 22 or 23 years old and The Beatles were The Beatles. It's a total no-brainer and it is also the stupidest business advice anyone on the planet of Earth had ever taken ...

For Harrison, they were simply Jiva, a four-piece band. In 1975, during an interview with New York Disc Jockey Dave Herman, while he promoted *Extra Texture (Read All About It)*, he commented on how positive Jiva were. He saw them as a 'little rhythm and blues band' who could be 'pretty funky too'.

However, an important couple came to the aid of Jiva and introduced the band to George. According to James Strauss, 'Patricia Pelham – Lady Tricia. She was the one who introduced us to Alan Pariser, who became our manager. She was key to the Jiva history'. Lady Tricia was The Lady Patricia Pelham-Clinton-Hope. She is the daughter of Henry Edward Hugh Pelham-Clinton-Hope, 16th Earl of Lincoln and 9th Duke of Newcastle-under-Lyne. In 1975, she was married to Alan Pariser. Pariser had made a name for himself in rock music as a photographer and entrepreneur and he was also the manager of Delaney and Bonnie (with whom Harrison toured in 1969) and Dave Mason. He contributed to Jackie Lomax's Apple album, *Is This What You Want?*, 1969, produced by George Harrison, and he was a good friend of George Harrison.

Harrison trusted Pariser and Lady Tricia. Pariser became Jiva's business manager and earnt a credit on the back of the album sleeve (Direction: Alan Pariser). Lady Tricia would get a 'special thanks' on the back of the same sleeve.

According to Jack Reed, 'She went to George and said there is this group who is really good and have a nice sound, you should go hear them. And so George came to hear us at one of the clubs and was impressed and it went forward from there'. Jiva were also being touted by Arias. She was a fan of their music.

Reed maintains that it was not a quick signing. 'It didn't happen instantly, but the way things go in this business, it went pretty fast'. He remembers that there were a couple of months of back and forth, but in the end, 'the deal with George was very straightforward and generous'. Reed recalled that the band received $150,000 as an advance and Harrison financed the album.

Strauss remembers Dark Horse headquarters in Los Angeles as pretty spectacular. 'Dark Horse, it was insane. A beautiful facility'. Strauss also recalls Harrison having something of a kindred spirit with the band. 'When he saw us in Topanga, this little club we were playing in, he said 'it reminds me of the Cavern club''. He also noted that the band, due to their association with Prem Pal Singh Rawat, were a bit more serious and were not typical rock 'n' roll party animals. He notes, 'It was one of the key things that George liked about us. That we were not anywhere near interested in throwing TVs out windows or being coked-up idiots'.

Harrison did not produce the album, but he did want to leave the band in what he considered to be good hands. At the time, Harrison noted, 'I think this will be the first album they're making with a guy, a producer, called Stewart Levine, who has just done Minnie Riperton's second album. And he's the producer of The Crusaders'.

Levine came to the band through Pariser. By 1975, he was an established music producer. Along with producing Riperton and The Crusaders, Levine also produced Hugh Masekela, with whom Levine attended Manhattan School of Music, where the two were roommates, Van Morrison, Randy Crawford and Lamont Dozier. He also (along with Masekela) had formed his own record label, Chisa Records. He would go on to produce artists such as Simply Red, The Allman Brothers, Lionel Ritchie and B.B. King.

Strauss recalls the production of the album was a collaborative effort, 'Alan, George, Stewart Levine and Jiva all had input on the songs of the album, the order, et cetera'. Michael Lanning, during a Facebook performance in 2020, remembers the creation of the songs being a group effort as well:

> There was a time when one person, either Tommy Hilton or Jim Strauss, would bring a song, it would be unfinished and someone would bring an idea and we would throw in a verse. There were a couple of songs on that Dark Horse record that each of us contributed a verse too, and a few we all wrote together. But most of the time, the song would come almost fully formed into the fold and we would create an arrangement around it, so we basically said, let us put Michael Lanning, James Strauss and Thomas Walter Hilton and take an equal cut because we are all in this together.

Drummer Michael Reed was not listed as a co-writer.

Both Jack Reed and Strauss remember Harrison having a 'hands-off approach', while still being quite supportive. Strauss recalled Harrison coming into the studio for a couple of sessions, but he left them alone. But Strauss remembered that Harrison provided $125,000 for recording and 'little per diem'. Strauss said, 'we were pretty conscious of the studio time and how much we were paying'.

Reed recalled that Harrison was very active during the recording: 'He was in our sessions all the time. Offering tips. We were recording at the Record Plant that no longer exists'. Michael Lanning goes even further: 'George (Harrison) was deeply involved in not only signing us but the making of our record as well. He served as executive producer and was there quite a lot of the recording time. He even helped in the demo sessions, picking out what tunes would be on the record and even playing piano on one of the demo tracks'.

Although Harrison did not play on the finished album, he was able to bring in a well-known, talented musician, Gary Wright. According to Strauss, 'George got him in, they were fast pals. He is a sweet guy'.

Gary Wright was born the same year as George Harrison (1943) but across the pond in New Jersey. Harrison would play a very big role in Wright's life and career, and Wright contributed a great deal to Harrison, so they became very good friends. Wright came to Harrison's attention through Klaus Voormannn, who had been friends with Harrison since The Beatles' Hamburg days. Voormannn had played on Wright's debut solo album and it was through Voormannn that Wright wound up on Harrison's album *All Things Must Pass*.

In 2009, in a conversation with *Popdose*'s Mojo Flucke, Wright recalled: 'Well, I was living in London at the time, and I had just finished my first solo album *Extraction*. One of the people that played on my album was Klaus Voormannn. He called me when I was in the studio producing an artist and asked me if I would be into playing on a track on George's album, and I said, 'Absolutely''.

Wright worked with Harrison on several records, including Ringo Starr's singles 'It Don't Come Easy' in 1971 and 'Back Off Boogaloo' in 1972, which Harrison produced. He also contributed to Ronnie Spector's 'Try Some, Buy Some' single, which Harrison wrote and co-produced for Apple. As Strauss noted, Harrison and Wright became very good friends based both on music and Indian religion.

Wright worked with Harrison on Splinter's debut album, providing keyboards and, according to author Simon Leng, acting as 'a sounding board and musical amanuensis' for the album. Strauss recalled, 'Gary loved working with George, he paid triple scale, and he went all night long. He would fly Gary over to Henley, and they would record eight or ten hours a night/day'. By 1975, Wright had relocated to Los Angeles, left A&M Records and signed with Warner Brothers. It was with Warner Brothers that Wright would have his biggest success with the album *The Dream Weaver*. Interestingly, half of the band Attitudes – David Foster and Jim Keltner – appear on *The Dream Weaver*. The Attitudes would soon sign to Dark Horse as well.

Gary Wright, who passed away in August 2023, in his autobiography *Dream Weaver: A Memoir; Music, Meditation, and My Friendship with George Harrison*, wrote about his friendship with Harrison:

> George and I immediately hit it off and became really good friends ... we shared a mutual interest in Eastern philosophy, and our relationship really blossomed into something really special. A unique relationship like I've had with no other person. We went to India together, and did a lot of travelling together, and wrote songs together, and he produced some tracks on my album. I consider him as one of the most important people in my life.

Harrison was instrumental in having Wright perform keyboards on Jiva's album. But there was one other connection as well. Jay Lewis, who engineered and recorded *The Dream Weaver,* was related to one of the members of Jiva. Lewis was the brother of James Strauss's then-wife. Lewis also engineered and recorded the *Jiva* album.

Jiva's self-titled sophomore effort was released in October 1975. The album was well received by critics in the US and Canada, with *Cashbox* giving it a very good review, noting that Jiva 'managed to take the best of Latin, rhythm and blues, and a spacey sort of pop' to make an album that is a 'highly acceptable listen'.

The UK press was not so kind. Ray Fox-Cumming in *Record Mirror* gave it a rating of 'C' in the 1 November 1975 edition, summing up the record by comparing them to The Average White Band, and stating that '... everything about this record sounds second hand and old hat and it's very boring'. Other than some print ads, the album was not well-publicised in the UK. In James Strauss's words, the album received 'zero' promotion in the UK and Europe. Strauss was clear that, in his opinion, there was 'no exposure in the UK'. In fact, there was no single released off the album in the UK, although 'Something's Goin' on Inside LA' was released as a single in North America and Australia a full two months after the album was released. For collectors, the US single is a bit of a holy grail, as stock copies (copies one would have bought in a store) seem non-existent. Promo copies pop up for sale, but stock copies are very rare.

This must have been surprising and disappointing to the band. At this stage, it seems that Harrison and Dark Horse were focusing on the US market and little money and time was spent on Europe and the UK.

Although there were a few print ads, including for the *Jiva* album, it is doubtful many in Europe would have known of its existence. Jiva would have benefited from Harrison introducing them to the UK and arousing attention from the likes of John Peel or even the very popular television show *The Old Grey Whistle Test*.

On 11 February 1976, Jiva's only Dark Horse single 'Something's Goin' on Inside L.A.' was released in North America. Strauss was not in agreement with the choice of single from the album. "L.A.' seemed the obvious choice for a single; in retrospect, 'Don't be Sad' would have been better, in my opinion'.

Given that the Top Ten singles on *Billboard* the week it was released featured Paul Simon (number one with '50 Ways to Leave Your Lover'), Donna Summer ('Love to Love You'), former Apple band Hot Chocolate ('You Sexy Thing'), Neil Sedaka ('Breaking Up is Hard to Do') and Electric Light Orchestra ('Evil Woman'), it is somewhat a mystery as to why 'Something's Going on Inside L.A.' did not receive airtime and become a hit record. It is also worth noting that when the single was released, Jiva were touring with Fleetwood Mac, which should have guaranteed them more interest.

The song was not without a bit of controversy, at least for the band. According to Lanning, during a Facebook performance of Jiva highlights, he told an interesting story about the record.

> When we submitted the lyrics for publication, they came back without the comma for 'Something's Going on Inside, L.A.', which changes the meaning of the song completely, at least the title of the song. It is supposed to mean something's going on inside L.A. It is like the difference of 'Let's eat, grandma, and let's eat grandma'. Commas are important, grammar's important.

Lanning further noted in the same Facebook performance, 'We recorded it when I was 22, and my take on the vocal on the original recording is just horrible. I hate it. It's bratty, smug, arrogant and blech…'

Lanning is being far too hard on himself. The vocals are perfect for the song, and by all rights, it should have been a hit. It certainly should have been the first of several singles from the album, as a number of songs were crying out to be singles. As for the rest of the album, *Jiva* had everything right. It is a well-recorded, extremely well-played, strong album full of very melodic and catchy songs. Given that it was released in 1975, it should have found an audience – a very large audience. The lyrics are based around love, relationships and love for your fellow passengers on this journey. Given the popular music of the day, it is a mystery as to why the album did not get much attention, as it could have easily fit onto many radio station playlists.

Strauss has the likely answer. 'Because Stevie Wonder released *Songs in the Key of Life*, Steely Dan blew up, The Eagles were kicking it, Jackson Browne was rocking it, so many other bands were really going on'. In other words, competition was stiff and a Beatle's involvement was not enough to guarantee success.

The single was released while Jiva was on tour as the support act for Fleetwood Mac. On 11 July 1975, Fleetwood Mac released their album *Fleetwood Mac*, the first to feature Lindsey Buckingham and Stevie Nicks. The album was a number one success.

Reed had met Nicks before Jiva worked with the band:

I had met Stevie before. I hardly knew anything about Fleetwood Mac. I was working in a restaurant, Great American Food and Beverage in Hollywood. I was a sandwich cook and an omelette cook and sometimes a waiter. A waiter came in and said, 'hey Jack, there is a girl out there who wants something from this omelette and something from this omelette. Can you do that, can you mix up the ingredients?' I said, of course, the ingredients bins are just there. I don't care what I put in the omelette. So I made her a special omelette. It was a slow day, so I went out to her table and asked her if she approved. She said she loved it. She explained that she and her boyfriend had just joined Fleetwood Mac and they were rehearsing on a soundstage a couple of blocks away.

It would be a while before he saw her again.

Harrison and Mick Fleetwood were friends as Harrison knew him in London in the late 1960s and was a fan of Fleetwood Mac's music from the start. But there was another connection. Mick Fleetwood was married to Jenny Boyd, who happened to be the sister of Harrison's first wife, Pattie Boyd. Harrison and Fleetwood remained friends after his split from Pattie, and there was a great deal of mutual admiration between the two. It was through this connection that Jiva was offered the opening spot on the tour.

Once the album had been recorded and released, Jiva were eager to tour to promote their record. According to Reed, 'When the album was done, we wanted to get out on the road. So we looked at George and said, 'Dude, you know everybody in this business, help us get out on the road'. They were very well received by the audiences. 'Our music was basically straight-up rock 'n' roll with influences from the Beach Boys, with harmonies'.

Harrison got them the slot on the tour. 'So he called up the Fleetwood Mac organisation and, just by the luck of the draw, they were out on their breakout tour with Stevie and Lindsey'. Jiva joined them in Atlanta, Georgia, on 7 March 1976.

James Strauss remembers Harrison getting the band involved, with typical Harrison humour: 'Mick was going out, and George said to Mick, 'why don't you take Jiva with you?' And Mick is going, 'we don't use opening acts', and George said, 'ok, you don't have to, but don't talk to me again'. I am pretty sure it was very light-hearted'.

By all accounts, Jiva did extremely well on the tour and Fleetwood Mac were very generous to Jiva. According to Strauss, Jiva was given 'half the PA sound and a third of the lights'. Reed agreed in his conversation with Tom Brennan: '(John) McVie was always an incredibly gracious person and never treated us as 'just the opening act', nor did any of the rest of the Mac. We remained friends with them for years after our tour'.

Reed got a chance to meet up with Nicks again: 'I said, 'Hey Stevie, had any good omelettes lately', and she whipped her head around and said, 'Jack, what are you doing here?'. I said, 'well, I am managing your opening act".

Both Strauss and Reed agree that Jiva was welcomed by Fleetwood Mac fans. Reed recalls, 'When we were touring with Fleetwood Mac, we got fantastic audience responses. On more than one occasion, I can recall John McVie telling us that he thought we had a better rapport with the audience on a given night than the Mac did'. Strauss agrees, 'We were totally hot, and (had a) very strong stage presence. John McVie told me that, at one show, Fleetwood Mac were afraid to go on after us'.

But just before the tour ended, things went wrong for Jiva. Strauss:

We were out on the road, everything was going good. I think it was Houston. Terry Doran is our road manager, and we are all there in Houston playing with Fleetwood Mac. I come downstairs, and I say to Terry, 'what are we doing?' I was expecting we were going to the radio station; you know how you used to do that back then, all the promo stuff. I was excited to talk my damn fool head off, and Terry goes, 'nothing. Go talk to Alan'. Alan says A&M just cut us off. That was the end of the tour with Fleetwood Mac.

Reed agrees, 'George (Harrison) admitted that some poor choices were made in the management team of Dark Horse Records'. What Jiva was unaware of at the time was that the Harrison and A&M partnership had broken down. Lawsuits were being threatened, and it looked like A&M was no longer interested in distributing Dark Horse. It is a shame that Jiva got caught in the crossfire. As far as Reed is concerned, the album should have done better than it did, even before the plug was pulled on the tour.

Jiva were to be caught in the crossfire of the Dark Horse break with A&M, but that was still to come, and for Reed, beyond the legal issues, the main problem was the lack of promotion.

It got air time in the South, it got air time in a lot of places. What we think happened was, while George loved the idea of having a label, they weren't doing a lot of promotion. They weren't spending a lot of money, and what happens in that business – and I know this well because I was working a side job with another guy doing promotions – even if you are getting a good response and the station manager notices you are not doing a lot of promotional things, giving up prizes, or billboards, if they get a feeling that the label is not fully behind the artist, then they start moving other people into the rotation. So, we got airplay, but we didn't get good backing from Dark Horse. There were a lot of good songs on that album, but the label was not being proactive. And I don't really blame George; he turned it over to other people to run, and he had his life to lead, and he was a very busy man. He admitted that to us later on.

There was no second album for Jiva on Dark Horse Records. Once Dark Horse moved to Warner Brothers, not every artist made the leap with Harrison. Jiva toured with Donovan and then Strauss left the band. Lanning regrouped and Jiva signed a deal with Polydor Records, where they released the album *Still Life* in 1978.

In Reed's opinion, 'After the album was out, he didn't do much. He (Harrison) had his own things going on, which is why I think he downplayed Dark Horse. Dark Horse was not prepared to do a second album and get behind it. George was just winding down Dark Horse'.

Since 1978, each of the members have carried on with their lives. Michael Lanning has been the most prominent in the music world. He has continued singing, both as a session musician (he performed with Trans Siberian Orchestra) and as a solo artist in his own right, writing, acting and appearing in musical theatre. His strong, distinctive rock vocals can be heard on many albums and he has written songs covered by Dave Edmunds, The Stray Cats and Sylvie Vartan.

While Harrison was working with Jiva, Splinter were getting ready for their sophomore album. *The Place I Love* was a breakthrough album, and with the hit 'Costafine Town', Splinter were beginning to make inroads in the music world, especially in the UK. The year 1975 started on a very positive note. In the 25 January 1975 issue of *Record and Popswop World* magazine, Splinter rated quite high on two reader polls. They came in at number ten for Best Newcomers (Sparks were number one) and they came in at number four in 'tip for '75'. They were beaten by Pilot, Hello and Queen. This was good company and an honour as it was only their first album. It seemed that 1975 was not only going to build on their successes of 1974 but catapult them into the bigger arenas.

In the same article, Elliott is quite clear on the hopes for the album and the continued success of the band: 'But all the tracks are written and ready, more than they need or know what to do with really. They're hoping that this album will take up where the other one left off'. Further, Purvis stated that they are happy with the success of *The Place I Love*, which was getting some attention in the US: 'We're really pleased to see it selling so well in America ... And George is really pleased with it. And when he's pleased, we believe it because he knows what he is talking about'.

Work on what would become *Harder to Live* started in July 1975 at Harrison's home studio F.P.S.H.O.T. According to Purvis, Tom Scott recruited the musicians who performed on the album, including the musicians who recorded the overdubs in Los Angeles. Scott himself performed horns, synthesisers and made his debut on steel drums (on the last song of the album, 'What is it (If You Never Ever Tried It Yourself)'.

It has often been said that a musician has their entire life to record their debut album and less than a year for the second. Second albums are often seen as more difficult to formulate. After all, the band are often gifted with a wealth of time to write, produce and record for a debut; the second album is sometimes a rushed affair and the quality can sometimes suffer for that reason. This is, obviously, not always the rule, but certainly, it must have been weighing heavily on Splinter's mind. They had had international success with their debut; now, the second album was due. In the press kit that accompanied the record to radio stations, however, Purvis, who was the primary writer for the band, made it clear that there were plenty more songs where the first album came from: 'We have enough to make good albums for six years. It's good for us that we didn't make our first album until we had a hundred good songs ... and we write new ones whenever they come to us. I got in last night and wrote one at 2 am'.

Once he finished his duties with Harrison's *Extra Texture (Read All About It),* Scott left for England to go to Henley-on-Thames. According to the promotion package, the album was recorded over nine days in July, while Scott remembers this as three or four days, with a few days of overdubs in Los Angeles.

Scott had previously worked with Harrison at Friar Park Studios and was familiar with the studio. Scott enjoyed recording there: F.P.S.H.O.T. 'was state-of-the-art at that time. It had a warmth to it that I just can't describe'. He reports that the studio had a wonderful vibe and was full of guitars. 'I walked in there and I said, 'I've never seen so many guitars in one place in my life', and George said, 'you know, when I was just starting out poor, I couldn't even afford a guitar. Now, every time I turn around, somebody hands me one".

Scott remembered that Harrison simply asked him if he would like to produce Splinter. 'I don't know if he did it in person, I don't know if I was with him, or whether he called me. He was doing something that prevented him from recording the Splinter album, or maybe he didn't want to, I don't remember the reasoning, but he said, 'Tom, do you want to produce them?' I said, 'sure', why wouldn't I?'

Unlike with their debut album, Harrison only appeared on one song, a re-recording of 'Lonely Man'. It was the song that attracted Harrison in the first place. Scott assembled a very tight, strong and brilliant backup band for the album. Although not household names, the musicians on the album were all very established and very important in the history of rock 'n' roll, especially drummer Earl Palmer.

Noted journalist and author Paul Du Noyer identified Palmer as one of the inventors of rock 'n' roll. Indeed, he was inducted into the Rock & Roll Hall of Fame. He drummed for Little Richard, Fats Domino, The Strollers, Sam Cooke, Lloyd Price, Richie Valens and Eddie Cochran, to name just a few. His style influenced drummers for generations. But if

Earl Palmer was a living legend, the rest of the backing band for the album was also impressive. Indeed, for Scott, assembling the backup band was quite easy: 'Earl Palmer was already in London with (American vocalist) Maria Muldaur; he was there long enough to do two or three days of sessions with us, which was awesome. Pianist John Taylor – fantastic, great talent – played with me at Ronnie Scott's. Bill Dickinson was with Maria Muldaur as well'.

Along with Palmer, bassist Bill Dickinson was also in London performing as part of Maria Muldaur's backing band at Ronnie Scott's Jazz Club. Although a relative newcomer, he had established himself playing live in Los Angeles, but he would go on to work with Lee Ritenour, Sergio Mendes and record with Maria Muldar. Famed British jazz pianist John Taylor, supplied piano. He was well known at Ronnie Scott's Jazz Club, backing up many performers there (including British jazz singer Cleo Laine) and was part of Maria Muldaur's band. He was also a member of Ronnie Scott's Quintet. So even though the album was recorded, for the most part, in England, the backup band and producer were American. Although Harrison was not successful in bringing Splinter to L.A., he did get L.A. musicians to Henley.

Rounding out the band in the UK sessions was renowned British guitarist Chris Spedding. According to Scott, 'Spedding's name came to me; he was a session guy in London with a rocking flare, very good, very good'. Spedding had made a name for himself, both as a session player and for his own records ('Motor Bikin' was a Top 20 hit in the UK in 1975). He has played with Jack Bruce, Elton John, Harry Nilsson, and Cass Elliott. He would go on to play with Paul McCartney, Bryan Ferry and Roxy Music. He was also part of the band The Wombles, based on the popular UK children's show. Spedding recalls getting a telephone call from Scott: 'You get a phone call, people call you up. The telephone, the usual thing. I was called in because one of the tracks needed a Chuck Berry-style guitar; I don't know which track that was'. It was 'Green Line Bus'. 'The sessions were taking place in the afternoon. The band had been brought over to England to back-up Maria Muldar at Ronnie Scott's, and they were working every night'.

Spedding recounted a rather amusing situation when he was initially called in to perform. 'So I came in at night to do this song ...' Spedding explained that there are two types of beats: swing (or more jazz) and even, which are standard rock beats. So Chuck Berry-style guitar would, logically, go on an even beat. He remembers that Scott wanted ...

... me to do the Chuck Berry beat over the swing beat, so you had a conflict. So I told them, 'if you guys are coming in every afternoon, why don't you come in and do this song again, tomorrow afternoon with the even beat, and I will come in tomorrow in the evening and put my part in with the beat that matches it. I thought I was being smart, you know. So I came in the following night, and the message from Tom Scott was, the guys were kind of scoffing at my suggestion. And the drummer said, 'why don't you go back and listen to the old records?'

He was suggesting that Spedding listen to the old rock 'n' roll records. Spedding continues:

I then found out who the drummer was;the drummer was Earl Palmer. He played on the Little Richard hits, Fats Domino hits, and Eddie Cochran when he moved to Los Angeles. He's the original rock 'n' roll drummer. And if you do listen to those 1950s things, when the people hadn't quite got it together, a lot of the drummers are jazz-influenced and playing the jazz beat, while the piano players and guitar players are playing that even beat. So I just had to swallow my pride and go ahead and do it. It was like a 1950s-style record, with the two different grooves going on.

The recording worked out, and Spedding can be heard on all but one track. For Spedding, the sessions were quite pleasant. 'I enjoyed the sessions, I got along with two guys from Splinter. They liked me, and I got on well with Tom Scott, the producer. I never met Earl; they were working in the evenings at Ronnie Scott's, the rhythm section recorded in the afternoon. I was brought in to do overdubs. I never met those guys. I never met Earl. That would have been an interesting encounter, I would have had to eat some humble pie and apologise'.

Although Splinter did enjoy recording at F.P.S.H.O.T. studios at Harrison's home, sometimes, the vegetarian diet became a bit much for the duo. Elliott related to Tom Brennan: 'It was wonderful working in the studio at George's place. If we wanted a meal, we'd just walk down the street into Henley. We don't eat meat in George's house out of respect for his beliefs'.

Purvis was clear that, for the most part, the songs for *Harder to Live* were all new compositions. The two exceptions were 'Lonely Man' and 'Half-Way There', which he states in the press package for the album, he wrote in 1967.

Although Harrison was not there to produce, he still had a lot to contribute. Scott remembers the duo coming into the studio with songs that Harrison had basically given his approval too.

> I think George had already approved the songs. We made the songs that they presented. I am sure that George exercised some overseeing in that regard. So my job was to write the arrangements for the studio players so that they didn't have to learn the songs from memory and steer a little bit here and there: Suggest a few things, just by instinct and try to make the best take on every tune we do. I believe the songs were fairly complete, I don't think I added to them. I may have extended a fade or something, but not in terms of the actual composition of the songs. My job was to help them realise their music to the best of my ability.

Scott, who was well known for his arrangements for artists such as Bonnie Raitt and Joni Mitchell (his arrangements can be heard on Mitchell's album *Court and Spark*), found the process of producing and arranging *Harder to Live* very professional and, overall, the sessions were smooth.

> The good news is, when you have musicians of that quality, things move fast. Because Earl Palmer and, I think, Bill Dickinson, both had to get back to London to play with Maria Muldaur at Ronnie Scott's, so we had to do it in the morning and afternoon to get them out. Two or three days of six-hour sessions, something like that, and we cranked it out.

After the basic recording was completed at Friar Park, Scott took the tapes to Los Angeles for overdubs, recorded at A&M studios in August of 1975. This included guitar overdubs from Robert 'Waddy' Wachtel. Wachtel, at this point in his career, was well known as a session player in Los Angeles and up to 1975, had worked on albums by The Everly Brothers (and toured with them), Buckingham Nicks, Guthrie Thomas and John Stewart, to name just a few. Percussionist Ralph MacDonald (misspelt on the sleeve as McDonald) was also involved in the overdub sessions in Los Angeles. MacDonald was part of Tom Scott's New York Connection band in 1976 and was a well-known and well-respected session player, having worked with Grover Washington Jr., Ron Carter, Bob James and Arif Mardin, to name just a few. Finally, Bill Nuttycombe added string arrangements to the album.

There were significant changes made to the album. According to *Record Mirror*, in the 16 August 1975 issue: 'Splinter have completed recording their second album, *White Shoe Weather,* for late September release'. The song 'White Shoe Weather' does not appear on the album, and most fans did not know of its existence. Some songs were dropped and others were added.

In popular music, it's a regular occurrence that songs are recorded during recording sessions do not find a place on the album for which they have been recorded. Often, these songs turn up as non-album B-sides. For *Harder to Live,* three other songs were recorded during the sessions that were not released until 1976: 'Love is Not Enough', 'White Shoe Weather' and 'Lonely Man (Japanese Version)'. These tracks, in these forms, were only released as singles in Japan. Scott remembers all of those songs being recorded during the sessions for the album. 'Lonely Man (Japanese Version)' was recorded with the intention of having a hit in Japan. It was released following the success of the 'Love is Not Enough' single.

With the album recorded, it was ready for release. *Harder to Live* was released in October 1975. To promote the album, 'Which Way Will I Get Home' was released as a single. In the press release accompanying the album, Purvis is quoted as saying, 'we recorded this album trying to make every song a possible single'. He further added that having recorded the album and living with the songs, 'I've lost perspective on what could be a single'. He highlights 'Which Way Will I Go Home', singling out Tom Scott's string arrangement on the song. Leng noted that Harrison agreed with Purvis and not only reportedly loved the song but thought that it would be a hit. The single was listed in *Billboard*'s 'Top Singles Picks' in the 14 February 1976 issue of *Billboard* magazine in the 'Recommended' section.

Although it is a beautiful song, as it is extremely well produced and arranged, it may not have been the best choice as an introductory single for the album. The week the single was released, half of the Top Ten on the *Billboard* Top 100 charts were in the disco genre. Sadly, the song did not seem to get much airplay in North America; it was simply out of step with the current hits. In the UK, it failed to chart, even though, as journalist Russell Rosalind noted, it did receive '..heavy airplay'. Why it failed to be a hit in the UK remains a mystery.

The second single in the UK was 'Half Way There', released on 21 May 1976, with hopes of resurrecting interest in the album. It didn't do that or succeed as a single. In North America, Dark Horse gave the nod to 'After Five Years' as the second single. Again, it failed to gain any significant airplay and did not chart.

The Japan-only single 'Lonely Man' was also re-recorded in Japanese. The band had help from Masatoshi Nakamura, who was then an up-and-coming actor and singer, going on to great success in Japan. 'Lonely Man (Japanese)' (as it was titled) was released in October 1976 on Dark Horse (CM-2006), making it the first of three Japan-only releases by Splinter on Dark Horse.

Perhaps due to the lack of a hit single, the album did not fare well with the record-buying public of 1975, failing to chart on both sides of the Atlantic. There were attempts to promote the album in their native UK and in America, Splinter received some assistance from A&M Records promotions in the form of PR guy Richard Pachter. He helped arrange a tour in the Eastern area of the US in late October and November, which included at least four radio appearances. The most significant was for WCMF-FM radio in Rochester. In December, they toured the West Coast, accompanied by Harrison associate Terry Doran.

They continued promoting the album in early 1976. They even had the opportunity to open for The Kinks in England (27 February through to 10 March 1976) and did the same for them for their European tour (26 March to 31 March 1976). They even returned to the television programme *The Geordie Scene* and performed six songs from *Harder to Live*, as well as the song that had yet to be released, 'White Shoe Weather'. Later, Splinter would complete a ten-week tour of the US in the summer of 1976, following two dates with The Ozark Mountain Daredevils in Europe in April.

The duo also made themselves available for interviews and were very candid. In an interview with *Record Mirror and Disc*, Elliott was expressed the importance of breaking into the American market: 'Once you're in, you're IN. It's hard breaking it, but America is going to be very important to us'. He was equally honest about working with George Harrison: 'We thought it would work out 50-50. We had a few snags in the past year, but it has all been smoothed out. George was going to produce our new album, but he was in the States and we couldn't come over because we were busy, so he suggested Tom Scott, which was tremendous'.

A hit in the US effectively means a hit worldwide; the same is true today. The album received very positive reviews, such as in *Cashbox*, who categorised it in the 'Easy Listening' genre (while noting 'strains of jazz and funk'). The reviewer noted that the album 'allows subtle access to different layers of the meditative musical mind'. The review highlights the title track ('Harder to Live') and the more rocking 'Green Line Bus'.

Furthermore, while the 8 November 1975 issue of *Record Mirror and Disc* gave the album an overall positive review, the reviewer noted that the band was getting nearer to their full potential. Writer Jan Iles notes that the album is 'musically flawless' and that some of Purvis's writing is 'poignant', but the album does not have anything 'extraordinary happening'. The best review they received was from David McGee in *Rolling Stone* magazine. He compares them, favourably, to the likes of Robin Gibb and ABBA while, at the same time, highlighting Purvis's writing ability. He also highlights Spedding's guitar and Scott's production.

However, there were negative reviews, such as the scathing write up in the 29 November 1975 issue of the UK's *Melody Maker*. The reviewer calls the songs weak and boring. Obviously, this review is extremely harsh, but it was also the style of reviews for *Melody Maker* at the time, there were few genres that would, especially in England, get the wrath of critics more than 'easy listening'.

Once again, Fabio Nicoli designed the sleeve with photography by Gered Mankowitz, a British rock photographer famous for his photos with The Rolling Stones and Jimi Hendrix. Although the packaging of the album was not as elaborate as *The Place I Love*, it did contain a lyric sheet and the overall presentation was good.

The fact that the album did not do well must have been a mystery to all involved. Harrison picked great songs and Scott did everything right. He assembled the perfect backing band and ended up with a strong album. Scott remains very pragmatic about the whole thing:

> I don't invest myself in the outcome, in the sales. Once I have done the thing that I do, everything that happens to it after that is totally out of my hands. I hope people appreciate it. There are records I have made that I thought were hits that weren't, and there are records I made that I didn't think were hits and were huge.

Three other songs recorded during this time, produced by Tom Scott with the same musicians who worked on *Harder to Live*, were released in 1976. These were the aforementioned Japan-only releases. 'Love is

Not Enough', written by Bob Purvis, was entered into the World Popular Song Festival, a music competition in the same vein as The Eurovision Song Contest. The song was placed in the ninth position. Because of its success at the festival, Dark Horse released a single with the song 'White Show Weather' on the B-side. 'Love is Not Enough' would be re-recorded for Splinter's third album, *Two Man Band,* in 1977. 'White Show Weather' is only available on this single and was released only in Japan. Splinter collectors have a very difficult time finding this, as well as the Japanese 'Lonely Man' single.

In reflection, however, Purvis was not happy with the single. 'Love is Not Enough' dates back to the famous Apple demos album, and Purvis thought that was the best version. Purvis, in speaking with Tom Brennan, was very critical of some of the production on Splinter songs.

(The) 'Love is Not Enough' Apple version was the best. I hated the song contest version we did in Japan. The *Two Man Band* version – rubbish. Me and Billy did a good live one. We would finish a gig with it. The song was written around the time I wrote 'Elly-May'. I didn't like what happened to that song either; it was nothing like the song I wrote.

Later, Purvis also noted he was not happy with the production on *Harder to Live,* or their next album, *Two Man Band*: 'No one really captured the music'. After all is said and done, it is an album that is remembered by few people, but it did and does deserve a much bigger audience.

Splinter had one other album released in 1975, but this was limited to a very small number. The album, simply titled *Splinter* (DH 2), was released in 1975 and consisted of an acoustic recording Splinter made at Harrison's F.P.S.H.O.T. in 1973. It is just the two members and an acoustic guitar. There is no producer noted and there is also no mention of A&M records on the label or the packaging. The album was given out to friends, some media outlets and to some very lucky fans. Of the 13 songs found on this album, only one resurfaced on a Splinter album, which is packaged in a white sleeve with very little information noted on the front. The album is nearly impossible to find, which is unfortunate as it gives a glimpse into the more folky side of the band. It also gives an insight into their early years. Bob Purvis was not entirely happy with the recording and in an interview with Tom Brennan, Purvis stated: 'The acoustic album was made when we were messing about in

George's studio; we didn't know it was being made. I hated it, but now, after all these years, I don't mind it. George did it with good intentions'. Harrison's intention is not completely understood. It was not sent to enough radio stations to be considered a proper 'promotional' record, and it is doubtful the album brought much attention to the band. But in hindsight, it may have been the best album to represent Splinter's sound and it may also have helped them find an audience in the folk/acoustic music world.

Harrison would be much more involved in the third Splinter album. Until then, he had some more artists to sign in Los Angeles as he continued to spend a great deal of time at his Dark Horse office there.

More Adventures in L.A.

While in Los Angeles, working with Jiva, Attitudes, and The Stairsteps (about whom more later), Harrison managed to hear an unreleased album by an artist he knew very well, Henry McCullough. McCullough had finished recording an album, which was produced independently.

McCullough, born in Portstewart in Northern Ireland, had always had an interest in music and by his late teens, he was playing professionally. The musician recalled during an interview with Carl Wiser:

I had an apprenticeship in Irish show bands and I went on the road when I was seventeen. I got offered this gig with a dance band that sat down with little music stools and stuff. They didn't know anything about rock 'n' roll or Chuck Berry or Elvis or Hank or Jerry Lee – it was all old-fashioned dance band stuff. But it made me want to learn more, and I learned chords so that I could keep up with this horn section. The dances would start at nine and finish at one. So, for me as a young fella, it was truly exciting to see what was going on over the top of the horizon.

Through playing with these dance bands, McCullough gained a great deal of experience, even forming his own band. This eventually led to him joining the band Sweeney's Men – when he replaced Andy Irvine – who were part of the Irish Folk Music revival, which included bands such as The Dubliners and The Clancy Brothers. He joined and left the band in 1968. Upon returning to London in 1969, he was invited to join Joe Cocker's Grease Band, at which point he was catapulted into the world of rock stardom.

McCullough, reflecting on his career later in his life, gave a lot of credit to his early days with the Irish show bands. He told Wiser:

With the dance band, I was able to play all the top pop and dance tunes and what have you. So, anything that I did after that, like working with Joe (Cocker) and then doing Jesus Christ Superstar, I was able to figure out quickly because of the apprenticeship in show bands. And with the Grease Band, that's what we did. We were very experienced players in all figures of music and we were able to take care of everything from whatever Joe was looking for at a particular time or sessions with Donovan, Marianne Faithfull, Eric Gordon and everything else.

As a member of The Grease Band, McCullough toured North America with Joe Cocker, actually performing at Woodstock in 1969. In his book *Wingspan*, McCartney remembers McCullough coming to his attention through mutual work acquaintances:

> Our roadies happened to know Henry McCullough, who had been in Joe Cocker's Grease Band. They said he was really good, so we invited him along to a rehearsal and we all got along well. He became Wings' lead guitarist, and so now we had a complete five-piece band ready to rock.

McCullough joined Wings in 1972, which consisted of Paul McCartney, Linda McCartney (keyboards), Denny Laine (guitar) and Denny Seiwell (drums), staying with the band until 1973. He left following the recording of the 'Live and Let Die' single. He was part of the band when they recorded their first US number one album *Red Rose Speedway,* and his guitar solo is the highlight of the 'My Love' single (which also made number one in North America). 'My Love' proved to be a very interesting recording.

McCartney wrote the song 'My Love' about his wife, Linda. He had a specific sound in his head and wanted to record the song as artists had done in the past, live with an orchestra. With help from arranger Richard Hewson, McCartney set about recording the song at Abbey Road Studios in October 1972. McCartney had the song arranged, but McCullough had another idea in mind, as he recalled in 2011 on *Hitchannel*:

> I was in the studio. Paul used to write everything and he wanted a solo. I didn't want to be told by the management or by anyone what to play. I know what to play; I'm the guitar player. I had very little time to think of a solo to play, so I played what came out of the top of my head. I don't like the solos to be different from the other part of the song; it's all one. I was alone in the studio with one other person, there was no management there, no one to tell me what to play, and I played that.

McCartney agrees:

> I'd sort of written the solo, as I often did write our solos. And he walked up to me right before the take and said, 'Hey, would it be alright if I try something else?' And I said, 'Er ... yeah'. It was like, 'Do I believe in this guy?' And he played the solo on 'My Love', which came

right out of the blue. And I just thought, fucking great. And so there were plenty of moments like that where somebody's skill or feeling would overtake my wishes.

The solo worked out for all concerned. It, no doubt, helped propel the single to the number one spot.

But being in Wings was not all plain sailing. Although they had had successful UK and European tours, Top Ten singles in North America, three Top Ten singles in the UK and a number one album, Wings were starting to fall apart. McCullough decided it was the right time to leave the band, and did so on the eve of the departure to Lagos, Nigeria, to record what would become *Band On The Run*. He acknowledged that he left at the very wrong time and the manner in which he did was possibly the most unprofessional thing he had done in his career.

McCartney has maintained that McCullough and Denny Seiwell, who had also decided to leave, left due to the band's plans to record in Nigeria. But, according to McCullough, that was just the tip of the iceberg, and McCartney's official reasons weren't completely true:

Less than a week later, Denny Seiwell left. It wasn't for the same reason as me, but we were friends in the band and he didn't want to be there if I wasn't going to be there. You know, there was a huge bond within the band before we went out to play one note of music. It was Paul's first time out with Wings, and we were all very protective of him and wanted to do our very best with him. But he very quickly became Paul McCartney again. After Denny and I left, I saw a little bit of Paul on TV, where he said, 'Well, the guys just didn't want to go to Africa'. That sort of says it all. They had no more story. But he's a great musician and a great man. I have nothing but the utmost respect for him. What happened between us was too many years ago to bother about.

In addition, Denny Seiwell also wanted some form of legal agreement for the band members. Something that had not happened. However, McCartney did not want another legal mess as The Beatles were still in court and McCartney wanted to avoid another situation like that at all costs. In 2018, Denny Seiwell commented to Nick Deriso:

I was really pushing for an agreement; we were all working on a handshake. We had no contracts or anything like that in those days.

I don't think we could have even had one that was legal, because of the Apple receivership and the court case that was going on at the moment. So, I was there at the best and the worst time, if you will.

McCullough said that this was also part of his decision to leave. The lack of signing an agreement left him feeling like a session player, not a member of a band that were doing extremely well and becoming very big. McCullough felt the success was not being shared with the band. Much later in his life, in interviews, he acknowledged that Wings worked very hard, but management did not pay what McCullough felt was a fair amount. He does not blame McCartney but rather the band's management. Years after he left Wings, McCullough still harboured very strong opinions about his days with the band that represented for him a missed opportunity to form a tight, rocking band. He spoke to Max Bell in 2016:

We were still on this feckin' retainer and we'd been told that as things progressed, we could contribute material, become part of a 'band' as such, but it never came to that. I can remember it well – we had a row one afternoon. I wanted to contribute, you know, 'Give me a chance – if it doesn't work out, we'll do it your way'. I felt it was time he allowed the musicians to have some of their own ideas used as part of this 'group' vibe. But all that was slowly being lost; the idea from the university tour, the van, the craic and all that started to go out the window.

Paul McCartney, Linda McCartney and Denny Laine would continue on with their plan of going to Nigeria to record what would become one of the biggest albums of all time in *Band on the Run*. As for McCullough, he did not harbour any negative thoughts about McCartney and Wings. As he told Wiser, 'I had a good relationship with Paul and Linda and Denny Laine. Everyone had. I think Paul is fantastic'. He was able to meet up with McCartney many years later:

I saw Paul's show last year in Dublin and he played a lot of Beatles songs. After the show, I went backstage and we met. We hadn't met for 35 years. We still had a great respect for each other's work and art. We had a lot of respect for what we did together many years ago. I can say that Paul McCartney is now a lot happier than he was in the past. After Linda passed away, he didn't stop and continued to make music and there aren't many men who can do this.

He's been ever so generous over the years with his talk about how this Irish guy was in the studio telling him the solo he wrote wasn't good enough.

After leaving Wings, McCullough decided to strike out on his own. He did some session work with a number of musicians and most importantly, he also started writing his own songs, which led to recording his first solo album.

I don't really class myself as a songwriter. I've written a few songs, but I'm a bit of everything. Songwriting was something that came accidentally to me, as did singing.

He said to Wiser in 2011:

A real songwriter does it day in, day out. I do it whenever the notion's there, and if it doesn't happen, I'm lazy and I won't go back to it. But I know there's a huge bubble of stuff there that if somebody said, Look, Henry, write some songs for this album, I can do that sort of thing. I can wait around and not push myself to pretend that I am a songwriter. But I like what I came up with, like 'Failed Christian', 'Belfast to Boston', some good stuff in there. But it's not a huge catalogue or anything. I come up with bits and pieces and that's what they are. I don't have the discipline unless there's something attractive enough at the end of it to get involved in it.

Although he may not have considered himself a writer, he did write a number of songs, and while on tour in the UK, he found the time to record some of them:

I was on the road and I had recorded the *Mind Your Own Business* album, my first solo album which came out in 1975. I didn't have access to people who knew how to distribute the stuff. George got to hear one of the songs and he gave me a call. I went down to the studio and he said he'd like to put my album out and I said okay. He took it to a distributor and all of the rest of it.

In 1975, he joined Frankie Miller's band. McCullough appears on Miller's 1975 album *The Rock* (credited to The Frankie Miller Band), which had been recorded in San Francisco in 1975. Some of the musicians in that band appear on McCullough's *Mind Your Own Business* album. As he told Jason Saulner: 'After I went to America with a singer named Frank Miller, and I had this album in the can', recalled McCullough. He had the chance to play the album he had recorded to Harrison:

> It just so happened that he liked it. We had dinner, talked about it, and that was it. It was fantastic, great large billboards on Sunset Strip and everything else. I was delighted as well for him to give me a ring and ask me if I would be interested and he heard the stuff anyway. There was one track he really liked and spoke about it. Not every day you get George Harrison on the phone.

In Michael Heatley's liner notes for the *Henry McCullough Band Live at Rockpalast* CD, Harrison also stated in an interview that he had found 'a kindred spirit in Henry' because he claimed McCullough, 'like himself years before, had lost confidence after playing in a band with McCartney'.

Mind Your Own Business was recorded in 1975 at Ramport Studios in London, which was owned by The Who at the time. McCullough produced the album with engineer John Jansen. Jansen had worked with Jimi Hendrix and would go on to work with the band Television. *Mind Your Own Business* proved to be a little bit of a Grease Band extension, with members Bruce Rowlands (drums), Neil Hubbard (guitar) and Alan Spenner (bass) helping out. Others on the album included Frankie Miller (who sings co-lead on the song 'I'm in Heaven'), Fairport Convention's Mick Weaver (piano, organ, clavinet), Charlie Harrison (bass, and no relation to George, but he is sporting a Dark Horse shirt in the album's liner notes photographs), Tim Hinkley (piano and organ), Joe O'Donnell (electric violins), Steve Chapman (drums) and future member of The Rutles John Halsey (drums). McCullough and Jansen also arranged a tight, tastefully used horn section, which included Herschel Holden (trumpet), Lionel Kingham (sax) and Lionel Kingham (sax) and finally, Sweedies provided background vocals.

In the 8 November 1975 issue of *Record World*, there is an announcement that the guitarist had signed with Dark Horse. The article is accompanied by a photo of Harrison with McCullough and his touring band. It is noted that McCullough would be touring with Frankie Miller, and promoting the album *Mind Your Own Business* during the tour.

Mind Your Own Business was released in October 1975. In the 15 November 1975 issue of *Record Mirror*, Dark Horse took out a full-page advertisement covering McCullough's album, Splinter's album and Jiva's self-titled album. The three sleeves are shown under the Dark Horse Records logo, alongside a quotation from Harrison: 'New talent is the strength of any label'.

Mind Your Own Business has a number of firsts for Dark Horse Records. It was the first album Dark Horse released that Harrison did not finance or that Dark Horse didn't record. It was not recorded in Harrison's home studio (F.P.S.H.O.T.) or A&M studios. In fact, it is the first (and only) Dark Horse album not to acknowledge Harrison in the credits; indeed, he does not even receive a special 'thank you'. Further, and perhaps most confusing, for the first time, Dark Horse did not release any singles from the album. Finally, the packaging was designed by Paul Jansen (who had created album art for Jimi Hendrix), who also supplied the cover illustration.

Cashbox's review noted that it is an 'easy album' which 'strives for and succeeds on a level of music communication'. Further, they note 'the slow country-blues nature of the music makes for a palatable and pleasing mix to the ear'. High praise indeed.

To promote the album, McCullough, now known as The Henry McCullough Band, filmed an appearance for the German television show *Rockpalast*, filmed on 22 April 1976. His band included Mick Weaver (keyboards), Jeremy Harvard (bass), Neil Hubbard (guitar), Terry Stannard (drums) and Dave Brooks (brass). The show provided McCullough with an opportunity to perform six of the album's ten songs and was later released as a CD/DVD set on Repertoire Records.

But one television appearance aside, the album suffered from a lack of promotion. There is little written about the album. The lack of a single led to a lack of airplay. Given the quality of the album and the music scene at the time, several songs would have made excellent singles, such as 'I Can Drive a Car' and Harrison's favourite, 'Lord Knows'.

The album is a strong mix of blues, country and rock and it should have been a success. One look at the *Billboard* Top 200 album charts for 1 November 1975 shows The Eagles at number four (*One of These Nights*), Linda Ronstadt at number five (*Prisoner in Disguise*), David Crosby and Graham Nash at number ten (*Wind on the Water*), Jethro Tull at number seven (*Minstrel in the Gallery*) and Grateful Dead, The Allman Brothers Band and The Marshall Tucker Band all in the Top 20.

In the UK *Record Mirror* Chart from the same week, one sees Steeleye Span at number 13 (*All Around My Hat*), Dr. Feelgood at number 15 (*Malpractice*) and The Eagles in the Top 30. In other words, there was a market for this album. However, it seems that no one knew it was out, even though at the time of its release, it is noted as being playlisted at WQSR in Tampa for the week of 14 November 1975.

Given that McCullough came to Dark Horse with a proven track record, including being a member of one of the biggest bands in the 1970s, one would have assumed the album would do much better than it did.

Years later, McCullough theorised why the album did so poorly. He blames the lack of promotion on Harrison's plagiarism lawsuit. Harrison was being sued by the publishers of 'He's So Fine' because they felt Harrison borrowed from it, very liberally, for 'My Sweet Lord'. McCullough explained to Saulner:

> ... then he had that problem with the publishing of 'He's So Fine', and he had 'My Sweet Lord', near enough or an exact replica of 'He's So Fine', so when the court case came up, he lost the court case. And what it took him to pay back the amount of royalties he might have gotten from 'My Sweet Lord' to The Chiffons, was part of the money he had laid aside, so to speak, for Dark Horse Records. So, I only had one go at it, and then the company sort of folded. Nice man, too.

In another interview, he added, 'George went to court and lost the case and had to pay at least six or seven million back to the people who had written it. So when he lost that case, Dark Horse folded and that was me at the losing end'.

It was not the lawsuit with the publishers of 'He's So Fine' that caused the problems for Harrison and his Dark Horse artists. There was another storm brewing, this one between Harrison and A&M Records and it would cause a great deal of problems for the artists and the label. But, after one album with Dark Horse, McCullough was set free to find another record label home. Derek Green recalls Harrison bringing McCullough to the label as 'he was very serious about the label' and that he had wanted different styles of music represented on the label, not to mention the fact that Harrison liked the album.

McCullough would not release another solo album until 1994, almost 20 years after *Mind Your Own Business*. He continued performing until 2012, when he was sidelined due to his health. He suffered a heart attack, which blighted his health for the remainder of his life. On 14 June 2016, it was confirmed that McCullough had passed away following a long illness. He was 72 years old. McCartney was quoted in *Billboard* magazine,

> I was very sad to hear that Henry McCullough, our great Wings guitarist, passed away today. He was a pleasure to work with, a super-talented musician with a lovely sense of humour. The solo he played on 'My Love' was a classic that he made up on the spot in front of a live orchestra. Our deepest sympathies from my family to his.

While George Harrison was in Los Angeles signing new bands such as Jiva and Attitudes, he was introduced to The Stairsteps, a band with a very significant past. The Stairsteps became the second most successful band Harrison signed to Dark Horse Records.

In 1975, former Apple artist Billy Preston was working on his 14th studio album, *It's My Pleasure*. By 1975, Preston was a well-established musician and since leaving Apple and signing with A&M, he had a great deal of success, especially on the singles chart. By 1975, he had had five Top Ten singles, two of which ('Nothing From Nothing' and 'Wheel it Go Round in Circles') hit number one.

While he was recording *It's My Pleasure*, Preston introduced Harrison (who also performed on the album under the alias Hari Georgeson) to Keni Burke, noted as 'Kenny Burke' on the album sleeve ... Burke was a member of a well-known rhythm and blues band, The Five Stairsteps. As a result of this meeting, The Stairsteps (they had dropped the 'Five') signed with Dark Horse.

Burke was an established and respected artist, not only as a former member of The Five Stairsteps, a family who have been dubbed The First Family of Soul, but he was also well known for his session work. He had worked with such artists as Sly and The Family Stone, Bill Withers, The Four Tops, Curtis Mayfield, Stargard, Ramsey Lewis, Linda Clifford, Diana Ross, Gladys Knight, and Narada Michael Walden.

In Larry Malone's interesting history of The Five Stairsteps, he notes that Clarence Burke Sr and his wife Betty were raised in Chicago and had six children. Their children, Alohe, Clarence Newton Jr., Dennis, James, Kenneth, and Cubie, grew up in a household where they were surrounded by music. Even though their father was a police detective, he helped the family develop as singers and performers, giving them pointers and helping out where he could. The children developed their own style of singing and formed the band with their name came from their mother, who told them that when they stood in line, they looked like stairsteps.

The family formed a teenage five-member brothers and sister vocal group, officially consisted of Clarence Jr., Alohe, James, Dennis and Kenneth ('Keni'), who was thirteen at the time. Between 1959 and 1964, the group performed at church, school, and talent contests. Keep in mind, in 1959, the eldest, Alohe and Clarence Jr., were 11. Cubie was born in 1964, so he was not a member of the group at this time. In 1965, after the family had won a talent contest at the famous Regal Theatre in Chicago, Fred Cash (a member of The Impressions) got the family to meet Curtis Mayfield, who was instrumental in getting them a recording contract and they signed to Mayfield's label, Windy-C, in 1966. The Windy-C label was distributed by Philadelphia-based parent company Cameo-Parkway, which meant that The Five Stairsteps were no longer just a local group but open to a national audience. In 1967, The Five Stairsteps released their first album *The Five Stairsteps*.

But it was 1970 that was their defining year. They recorded their album *Stairsteps*. Included on that album was their cover of 'Dear Prudence' and 'O-o-h Child'. The latter propelled the band into the *Billboard* Top Ten (peaking at number eight). 'O-o-h Child' was also their only gold record (R.I.A.A.), selling over half a million copies in the US alone. The B-side, their cover of 'Dear Prudence', got as high as number 66 on the *Billboard* Top 100. Once again, even with a Top Ten single, the album failed to make a dent in the charts. And eventually The Stairsteps took a break.

Keni Burke and his brother, Clarence Jr., supplemented their income by becoming session players. It is in this capacity that Keni Burke happened to work with Billy Preston on *It's My Pleasure*. During this time, Keni (known as Kenneth at the time) and Clarence Jr. joined forces with Dennis and James. The Stairsteps, after four years, had reunited and Billy Preston introduced them to George Harrison.

In August 1975, Harrison and Dark Horse announced, through trade magazines, that The Stairsteps had signed to Dark Horse and new music would be released soon. This was big news, as the band had been missed by their fans and their audience was interested in how the band would sound in the 1975 landscape. Fans were not going to be disappointed. The production of the album would be handled by Billy Preston, Robert Margouleff and The Stairsteps.

Robert Margouleff was an important figure in rock history. Along with Malcolm Cecil, Margouleff had developed T.O.N.T.O, which stood for 'The Original New Timbral Orchestra'. T.O.N.T.O. is known for being the first and, still remains, the largest, multitimbral polyphonic analogue synthesiser in the world. It was designed and constructed over several years by Malcolm Cecil, from a Moog modular synthesiser Series III owned by record producer Robert Margouleff. After the duo debuted the technology with the album *Zero Time*, credited to T.O.N.T.O.'s Expanding Head Band, many artists became interested, including Stevie Wonder. Harrison was also interested and had the two work on *Shankar Family & Friends* in 1974.

In 1975, Margouleff became involved with Stairsteps and brought T.O.N.T.O. with him. Cecil does not receive a production credit, but he is credited for programming the keyboard, which Preston plays on the album. Along with Preston, Alvin Taylor performs drums with percussion provided by Ricardo Marrero. The end result was an updated sound for The Stairsteps, with the funk and soul still there, but with excellent use of the then-current technology. When the album was released, *Cashbox* declared it 'the hottest release in February' and would 'put the Stairsteps back on top'. They were not wrong.

The album was recorded at Kendun Recorders in Burbank, California. Billy Preston was heavily involved with the album, providing keyboards and a great deal of support. Preston also brought Robert Margouleff into the project to co-produce and engineer, having co-produced Preston's album *It's My Pleasure*. Margouleff noted to this author that Harrison got involved 'through Billy and through A&M. I was producing Billy, and Billy, of course, is a friend of George's. George asked Billy to work on The Stairsteps album and he brought me along'.

Margouleff remembered the recording as being very straightforward and he also noted the importance of Keni Burke.

Stairsteps is a really interesting record. Keni Burke, the bass player, is commended, because he sort of invented that pop playing on the bassline, where he would slap the strings, more than pluck them. He got that very funky bass sound that way. He was very tricky to record, but I think that record is a good example of that funky style that Keni brought to the table. I think Keni Burke set the stage for very innovative bass playing by popping the strings, which for its time was very revolutionary when it came to playing the bass.

And, Margouleff said, 'he was a really nice man'. Drummer Alvin Taylor, who drummed on the entire album, has very pleasant memories of recording it ('one of my most favourite albums of all time I ever played on'). When discussing Margouleff as the co-producer, he was full of praise:

> What an amazing producer, just so underrated. They talk about George Martin; they talk about Phil Spector. Why don't they talk about Robert Margouleff? Wow, that's the guy. Robert Margouleff was the most amazing producer in the world and I worked with the greatest. I worked with Freddie Perrin, I worked with Richard Perry, I worked with all these great producers that produced records and none of them come close to Robert Margouleff. That guy is just an amazing producer; he is the best.

Margouleff returned the compliment by saying that Taylor was one of the best drummers he worked with. 'We used to call him tick tock because he could keep time with the help of a click track'.

However, Margouleff is very quick to point out that he was not the sole producer. He gives a great deal of credit to Preston. Having worked together previously, Margouleff and Preston made a very strong team and worked very well together. According to Margouleff, it was an excellent partnership, with each being responsible for their areas of expertise. 'Billy was a very big part of it musically, I handled the engineering and technology and the mixing ... Billy handled the songwriting and playing keyboards on it ... I programmed'.

Margouleff also noted that his partner Malcolm Cecil helped. Margouleff added that due to their method of working in the studio and the fact that the band was prepared, he 'tracked the record so I was able to mix it with great ease'.

Taylor agrees: 'Billy Preston was an amazing producer as well. Look at all the stuff he put out'. He agrees that the recording was very smooth and very quick. But he also acknowledges the work put into the record prior to the actual recording.

'These guys knew exactly what they wanted, everything, how to do it; there was no waste of time, no sitting around and trying to figure things out, just to show the musicians what to do', recalled Taylor. 'I did my part in four days ... We rehearsed for maybe a couple of weeks at Billy's house. I was there to learn the songs that were already written and put together. They were going to teach me the parts of the songs, and we went in the studio for four days to cut the tracks'.

According to Taylor, 'the basic track was me, Keni Burke on bass, Billy on keyboards and Steve B on guitar. So it was us four recording the basic track, and we would come back later on and add little guitar parts and other sweetenings. Billy would add keyboards or organ'.

Margouleff also recalled the importance of the rehearsals:

I lived in Alta Topanga Canyon and I had horses, and Billy lived in Topanga Canyon and he had horses, and I used to go to his house. I brought the remote truck from The Record Plant and parked it at his house, which was kind of a ranch ... he had a corral of three or four horses, and ... and I would ride over on my horse in the morning, and Billy would come down from his bedroom in his fire engine red terry cloth robe with a hoodie. He looked like an evil monk, with his hair sticking out in each direction. And we would work there.

And each member had their role to play in the band. Besides their respective instruments, they had other roles as well. According to Taylor:

Clarence was the figurehead for that group, and then Keni was the orchestrator who put it all together musically. Clarence was the writer; he came up with the ideas for the songs, Keni might throw a curveball here and there. They worked real good together.

Taylor enjoyed listening to the brothers harmonise. 'The boys would then do the vocals, angels from Heaven. Those voices. They could sing like nobody I ever heard, open their mouths and nothing but angels. They were so amazing'.

Both Margouleff and Taylor agree that Harrison had minimal contact with the band during the recording of the album. According to Taylor, 'George Harrison was not in the studio. He may have been once, but not when I was cutting the tracks. George had nothing to do with the recording ... The Stairsteps did their thing the way they wanted to do it, no outside influence or hindrance from anybody. Based on a creation these guys already had an idea about, and it was a Stairsteps creation'.

The Stairsteps' debut single for Dark Horse was released first in North America on 3 December 1975 and in the UK on 30 January 1976. The single 'From Us to You' b/w 'Time' was a welcome return for the band,

and they had their highest chart placing on the *Billboard* Soul (the name of the chart was 'Soul Singles Chart' and that is how they will be referenced in this book) charts, getting to number ten on 13 March 1976. Sadly, it failed to make the *Billboard* Top 100, peaking in the 'bubbling under' section at number 102 on 27 March 1976. But this single proved to be second only to Splinter's 'Costafine Town' as the most commercially successful record issued by a Dark Horse artist up to this point.

As far as Taylor is concerned, 'From Us to You' deserved to be a hit and it had a very powerful message. The song was an anthem and very important to the band. For Taylor, it was their manifesto:

> We want people to know that we're not dead, that we are alive. So we want to write them a song, you know, so this is a song from us to you ... just soothe your blues away because you folks have a lot going on here. We are just going to come and bring some joy and happiness to you. That is what that song is all about, soothing your blues away. Musical prophets, that's what they were. They had a message to the world that they wanted to tell. 'We want to soothe your blues away', this is the message they wanted to get out to the world, like 'Give Peace a Chance' ... 'From Us to You', we have a chance.

Taylor remembered the recording of that particular song:

> Keni showed me what parts to play; I didn't think of any of that stuff. Keni showed me note for note. Keni was ruthless, thinking, and extremely descriptive. He simply knew what to do, how long to do it, and what it should sound like. He was amazing. Working with Keni Burke, you better be ready to take instruction; you'd better be ready to take direction. And in the long run, when you hear what he's doing the first two or three times through, you become so familiar with what he is saying that you automatically take on the characteristic of it and you become that part. So with Keni, when it comes to being a director of a movie, he becomes the director of the music; he tells you how he wants you to walk, how to move your hands, when to turn your head, when to open your mouth and what to say out of it. That's Keni Burke.

The album had the clever title, *2nd Resurrection*, and it was released in North America on 6 February 1976 and in the UK on 19 March 1976. In the UK, *Record Mirror and Disc* reviewed the album in their 'Soul

Stirrings' section. Kevin Allen called the album a 'triumphant return' and noted the influence of Stevie Wonder throughout. Overall, they gave the album a good review.

Oddly, the week prior, the same magazine, *Record Mirror and Disc,* were not so kind. David Hancock, in his review, refers to the album as 'at best, second-rate Stevie' and 'second-rate Syreeta'. He does give Billy Preston high marks for his production but ultimately claims 'the major fault lies in the derivative songs that eventually cause a yawn'.

The second track on the album, 'Pasado', was released in the UK as the second single. But with little promotion, the single did not chart. The single was reviewed in *Record Mirror and Disc* and, although the review was an extremely positive one, the single found its way into the 'Misses' section of the singles review. The reviewer noted that the single was perhaps 'much too advanced (or as they used to say 'good') to make the charts'. The reviewer was quite correct.

In North America, attempts to maintain interest in the band and the album failed when the second single was released from the album. Again, it was a great song and a wise choice for a follow-up single, but 'Tell Me Why' failed to have any impact. It was released on 14 June 1976. The single failed to get airplay and did not chart. It peaked at number 106 on the *Billboard* Bubbling Under chart. It was to be the last record released by The Stairsteps, as the group decided to call it a day at this point. There would not be a second Dark Horse album by the band, and its failure remains a mystery.

Margouleff is very clear that the problem lay with A&M and/or Dark Horse Records.

The album really didn't get the promotion it deserved from A&M. They (A&M) did the record as a courtesy to George, to The Beatle. I don't think they really paid attention to it as much as they should have. Their whole promotional thing was kind of laughable in a way ... they should have done another record with those guys.

For Margouleff, A&M and Dark Horse lost a golden opportunity. This band had a lot of life in them and a second album would have solidified their following and fan base. But band problems and other factors got in the way.

There was a certain amount of conflict in the band. A&M and Dark Horse should have stepped up to the plate and done another record with them. And they didn't do it. There was also a certain amount of druginess going on, not by the band but by Billy.

Taylor is in full agreement with Margouleff. And he goes one step further.

There was so much uniqueness and so much amazing music. I don't understand why it is not as big as any other album, including *Dark Side of the Moon* or *Physical Gravity* or any other pop albums. The bottom line is that this was the most amazing album. It didn't catch on like it should have, or I thought it should have.

For Taylor, the problem was squarely on the shoulders of A&M and Dark Horse for not continuing to fund the band to either record a follow-up album or tour. Taylor is very clear that the band was committed to the success of the album, but as Taylor points out, 'It costs money to have a project out on the road and you have to pay the musicians, you gotta pay the stage hands, you got to fly equipment around the world. We don't have the money to do that; that has to be somebody else'.

Taylor went further, expressing his frustration that Dark Horse was not willing to put up the money. As a result, the band simply fell apart.

The company wasn't coming up with the money to move forward and keep them here. They weren't doing anything. These guys came out here from Chicago and different parts of the country where they were staying; one was visiting from New York, we all came together in Los Angeles and there is only enough money to stay for so long, and then after that ... what are we going to do? Rent a hall where we could rehearse, and get a booking agent to book you and put you out on the road. I don't have the answers to what happened.

However, one other factor is that perhaps the album packaging may have hurt the sales. An article in *Billboard* by Nat Freedland stated clearly that poor graphics hampered record sales, and one of the biggest mistakes artists make is using black and white for front sleeves. The Stairsteps' *2nd Resurrection*'s front sleeve was a tinted black and white picture of the band. Yet again, there seems to be very little promotion for the album at the time. Whatever the reasons, it is a shame as the album has sunk into obscurity while at the same time being regarded as a classic.

Unlike other Dark Horse releases, Roland Young, rather than Fabio Nicoli, was the art director. Instead, The album was designed by Chuck Beeson with photography by Fred Valentine. Valentine had made a name photographing albums by artists such as Electric Light Orchestra, Issac Hayes, Ike Turner, and Kinky Friedman. Roland Young was an art director for A&M and had worked with Carole King, Billy Preston and Cheech and Chong, among many others. Chuck Beeson also worked for A&M and had quite a distinguished career, working with such artists as Billy Preston, Carole King, Gary Wright, and Burt Bacharach.

Although The Stairsteps disbanded, Kenneth Burke, now known as Keni, signed a solo deal with Dark Horse. His one solo album on Dark Horse would not be released until after Dark Horse had ended their A&M deal and signed with Warner Brothers. As for the rest of the brothers, they would work together again, but under the name The Invisible Man's Band, and they would have another hit single ('All Night Thing'). But after a second album, the group decided to split permanently. That was the final end of this legendary band.

As for *Second Resurrection*, Taylor has the final word:

They didn't care about the record being a number one record; they really didn't; they couldn't care less about that. They just wanted it to get out to the masses. They had a message. See, these guys are Muslims. They had a message from their God ... speaking and sharing with them to influence and help people be at peace, learn about joy and happiness, love one another and let's clean some of this chaos up. That's what it was; they were messengers, these guys.

Harrison continued to work very hard on his Dark Horse Records. As one can see, 1975 proved to be very busy for him; he had signed three new artists to Dark Horse and it seemed that he was still trying to follow through with the original goal of the label, to promote new acts. By 1976, Harrison would sign one last band to the label and help Shankar with a new project.

The End of The A&M Days

Ravi Shankar's Music Festival From India is an album Harrison loved, but the timing of its release was odd. Despite the fact that the album was recorded at Harrison's home studio in Friar Park (F.P.S.H.O.T.) during August and September 1974, it was not released until 6 February 1976 in North America and in March in the UK.

It is a record that was clearly important to Harrison, as he does identify it as one of his favourite Dark Horse releases. Finally, it is one of only three non-George Harrison albums that has been reissued in its entirety in a physical form. Years after being out of print, the album and the accompanying film were released as part of the Dark Horse Records box set *Collaborations* (2010). Available on CD, the set features both Ravi Shankar albums for Dark Horse as well as the film on DVD.

The roots of this album date back many years before the project was conceived. In 1968, Shankar toured America with his 'Festival From India' orchestra. Harrison said that he had wanted to stage an Indian Festival since 1967 when he was in India recording the soundtrack for the film *Wonderwall*. According to Olivia Harrison, he was inspired by Shankar's orchestral piece 'Nava Rasa Ranga', which he had heard performed at the time. The plan for a larger festival began when Harrison was visiting Shankar at his new home Hemangana, beside the River Ganges at Benares. Harrison suggested to his friend and mentor that he should assemble an orchestra for concert tours across the US and Europe.

Whereas *Shankar Family & Friends* was intended to blend Indian music with western pop, *Ravi Shankar's Music Festival From India* was more a return to type for Shankar, and was full of classical Indian music. Harrison understood the importance of Shankar's music and the need to continue releasing it in the West. Indeed, according to the *Recording Academy Grammy Musician* website, Harrison once called Shankar the 'Godfather of World Music'. Furthermore, the museum entry points out, 'What he most likely meant by the title was that Shankar was one of the earliest and certainly most important non-Western music virtuosos to introduce non-Western music to Western pop and rock fans. Though some American classical music followers might have known of Shankar and the intricacies of Indian music prior to the 1960s, Shankar's ability to draw – and captivate – young listeners in this country was unprecedented'.

It is important to note that this project was the first venture to be funded by Harrison's fund, The Material World Foundation. This was established by Harrison in 1973 to 'encourage the exploration of alternate and diverse forms of artistic expression, life views and philosophies'. The name of the foundation, of course, comes from Harrison's 1973 album *Living in the Material World*. The foundation also supports established charities.

During an interview with Don Eliis on KNET TV, Harrison noted:

> There's a lot of people who still think of it as just a sitar or just two people playing. There has never been an opportunity for people to see an orchestra'. I'm just trying to figure out a way to bring all these people to the West ... to maybe open up the concept that Western audiences have about Indian music.

In the summer of 1974, Harrison and Shankar arranged for Shankar to bring his orchestra to London to begin rehearsals for the tour and to record the accompanying album. Shankar had assembled an impressive 16-piece orchestra for the project. Included in the orchestra were flautist Hariprasad Chaurasia, Alla Rakha (tabla), T.V. Gopalkrishnan (mridangam, khnjira and vocals), L. Subramaniam (violin), Sultan Khan (sarangi), Shivkumar Sharma (santoor, kannon, vocals), Kamalesh Maitra (sarod, madal, tabla tarang, duggi tarang and ek tara) and Gopal Keeshan Veenkar (vichitra veena and vocals). Harihar Rao, who had been a student of Shankar's during the 1950s, provided kartal, manjira, dholak, vocals and gub gubi. Rao also played a huge role in introducing Harrison to one of his collaborators, Tom Scott. Lakshmi Shankar, who sang on the *Shankar Family & Friends* album, provided vocals and was joined by her daughter, Viji and Shankar's wife Kamala Chakravarty, as support vocalists. Sharma, Rakha and Lakshmi had been part of the original 1968 orchestra.

Hariprasad Chaurasia has very fond memories of the recording and the project: 'I fondly remember the recording and my participation. The entire experience was most beautiful and wonderful for all of us. I am a bansuri player. I only played the bamboo flute in the recording'.

While Harrison had arranged a house for Shankar and Chakravarty, the orchestra was housed at the Hotel Imperial in West London. Harrison had arranged for the orchestra to be picked up every day in a limousine, once owned by John Lennon and Yoko, and had them brought to his studio at Henley-on-Thames. Later in his life, he would talk about the amusing sight of traditionally dressed Indian musicians exiting the limousine.

Shankar had composed all-new material for the tour performances and the album, so he would have to teach it to the orchestra. In the book *George Harrison: Living in the Material World,* Harrison is noted as saying how impressed he was watching Shankar teach and arrange the music. 'It was amazing, because he'd sit there and say to one person, 'This is where you play', and the next one, 'And you do this', and 'You do that', and they're all going, 'What?' 'OK, one, two, three ...' And you'd think, 'This is going to be a catastrophe' – and it would be the most amazing thing'.

Harrison further added, 'most of this has been composed right on the spot, and then arranged and then rehearsed for a very short time, because we didn't have much time'. But that does not mean that Shankar came unprepared. In fact, in his autobiography *Raga Mala*, Shankar says that the house Harrison arranged for him was in Belgravia, which would be roughly an hour in a car. This gave him time to compose on the M4.

Chaurasia recalls the recording process was not so complicated, but it did take some time. 'The recording was done in many different pieces, involving many different musicians. I was not present for the entire recording. Hence, I won't be able to tell you about the entire process. I think each musician who was involved will have their own experiences and memories to share'.

Unlike *Shankar Family & Friends*, Harrison did not play on this album but instead sat in the producer's seat. Working with engineers Phil McDonald and Dark Horse F.P.S.H.O.T. engineer Kumar Shankar, Ravi Shankar's nephew, Harrison did a fantastic job capturing the music and performance. Unlike other albums recorded at his home studio, the sleeve of this album notes that it was recorded in 'Ye Drawing Room' at F.P.S.H.O.T., referring to the use of a larger room, literally Harrison's drawing room) doubling as a studio, given the size of the orchestra.

'George Harrison was the producer of this album and he very much wanted to record in India. He loved India and would make a trip once every year to India to meet and collaborate with Indian Musicians and attend concerts. He was in love with Indian Music', recalls Chaurasia. He was equally impressed by Harrison's home and recording studio. 'What a beautiful estate it was! A huge castle!! For us musicians from India, it was a thrilling experience. Meeting so many talented musicians, jamming with them, discussing music with them'.

With the album recorded, it was time to prepare for the tour, which initially had Harrison involved. However, due to many factors, he was unable to participate in the European leg of the tour. At this time in 1974, Harrison was getting Dark Horse Records off the ground, mixing and preparing *Shankar Family & Friends*, recording with Splinter (*The Place I Love* album), writing and recording his own album *Dark Horse* and dealing with the end of The Beatles and Apple. But the tour went on as planned, opening in style at The Royal Albert Hall on 23 September 1974. In the liner notes for the *In Celebration* CD box set, Shankar explained how the concert was organised:

The first part is in the form of a panorama, depicting major stages in the evolution of classical and traditional Indian music, starting with the Vedic hymns and the music of the medieval period, and ending with the present day, touching briefly on all the intermediate forms such as alap, dhrupad, dhamar, khyal, tappa, tarana and chaturanga ... The second part begins with the semi-classical forms, such as the devotional bhajan and the romantic and erotic thumri, ghazal, dadra, etc. and ends with the very lively and earthy folk style.

The show at The Royal Albert Hall was filmed by Stuart Cooper, who also directed the film, *Little Malcolm.* That film would surface on the *Collaborations* box set, released in 2010. The tour moved on to Paris, Brussels, Frankfurt, Munich and Copenhagen. Harrison introduced Shankar in London and was very honest with the audience, stating that he was 'very nervous' and that the show was 'behind schedule'.

For Chaurasia, the tour was part of an incredible experience. 'It was a memorable tour. I met so many musicians. We were touring, giving concerts and recording at Henley-on-Thames. I played with a group of Indian musicians to Pt. Ravi Shankar's compositions'.

Once the European tour was complete, the orchestra was scaled back to only sixteen members to get ready for the lengthy, upcoming American tour with Harrison set to start on 2 November 1974 in Vancouver, British Columbia. As Harrison made clear at the time during press conferences, Shankar and his orchestra were not the opening act, but rather, this was definitely a double bill. It was to be a chance for Western pop music to collaborate with Eastern classical music. The fans of each music would be exposed to the other. However, Shankar and his orchestra's performance in North America was significantly different from the European shows, not only in the size of the orchestra but also in the actual songs performed.

For the North American tour, Shankar played songs from the *Shankar Family & Friends* album. This made sense, since the album had just been released and would hopefully be in the local record store at each stop of the tour. However, the orchestra did include one song ('Naderdani') from the *Ravi Shankar's Music Festival From India* album.

By 1976, the album was prepared and ready for release. A great deal of time and effort went into it, both in terms of sound and packaging. The album's front sleeve picture features a simple yet stark photo of the orchestra with Harrison in Harrison's garden. George sits proudly beside an equally proud Ravi Shankar. The photo, taken by famed photographer Clive Arrowsmith, is, quite simply, brilliant. Arrowsmith recalls on his website that he had met Harrison through Stuart Sutcliffe:

He introduced me to George on a misspent youthful weekend in Liverpool. That's also when I met John and Paul. I'd known George since my art school days when I attended Queensferry School of Art, which was about forty miles from Liverpool. We met via Stuart Sutcliffe. The combined art colleges, Queensferry, Chester and Liverpool, made a deal with the local bus company for art students from the three schools to come down to London for £2.10 on open-top buses that they used at Epsom for the Derby. I first met Stuart Sutcliffe on the top of a bus to London and after the trip, he said to me, 'Why don't you come to Liverpool, we can go to The Crack for a beer' (the art school pub). I used to go to Liverpool at the weekends to meet with Stuart and look for girls with long hair, purple lipstick and short skirts (this being the sixties).

Fast forward to 1974 and Arrowsmith, fresh from working with Paul McCartney on the album *Band on the Run,* received a request from Harrison. 'George Harrison rang me up and said, 'I'm doing an album with Ravi Shankar and there's no one I'd like more than you to take the pictures". Pictures from this session would surface in the future. But for now, the sleeve photo was taken and the album was near completion.

Contemporary reviews of the album are scant. However, *Cashbox* gave it a good review, noting the 'clear production' with the album capturing 'much of the flavour of the music at its purest'. The review also notes that the record should get airplay on 'foreign stations' and that some of the songs were 'FM possibilities'. They single out 'Raga Jait', 'Dehati', 'Naderdani' and 'Tarana'.

The album also served as something of a launching ground for many young Indian musicians who would go on and make a name for themselves, such as Sultan Khan, who played the sarangi (a short-necked string instrument played with a bow), violinist L. Subramaniam (know as Lakshminarayana Subramaniam) and Hariprasad Chaurasia (flutes) all went on to highly respected and successful careers following this project with Shankar.

Whereas *Shankar Family & Friends* made it to number 176 on the *Billboard* Top 200 album charts, *Ravi Shankar's Music Festival From India* failed to chart completely. It deserved a much better fate. Perhaps the lack of a single did not help and *Cashbox* was clear that some of the songs could have gained airplay. Perhaps the fact that the album was released over a year from the original concert series went against it. Certainly, in Europe, the tour was extremely well received, but by the time of the release, perhaps the original concert-goers had forgotten about the project or were not aware of the album's release. Once again, promotion of the album was not very extensive with any interviews concerning the project done in 1974, two years prior to the album release.

Harrison taped an interview with noted jazz musician Don Ellis in 1975, discussing the concert at The Royal Albert Hall and the project. The show was aired on a Los Angeles PBS (Public Broadcasting Service) station KNET. Ellis was able to show scenes from the film of the concert at The Royal Albert Hall, and while it is an excellent interview, it was not enough to propel people into record stores to purchase it. It is worth noting that Don Ellis studied Indian music under Harihar Rao at UCLA, the same programme attended by Tom Scott. Ellis, who had been able to watch the entire film, described the event as 'one of the most extraordinary musical experiences that I've ever heard'.

In the end, although the album was not the commercial success Harrison and the powers that be at A&M Records had hoped for, it was a personal and professional triumph for Harrison. Shankar has spoken very highly of the project, and for one particular musician who participated, he sees the project as a huge success. 'I was very happy with the album. The sound quality, music, composition and everything was wonderful for me and my musician friends who were a part of it', recalls Chaurasia. 'It was very well received by music lovers. People still enjoy each and every piece of the album'. But Harrison and Shankar would not record together again until 1997.

While putting the finishing touches on *Music Festival From India*, Harrison and Dark Horse were also getting ready for a new album by a new band, Attitudes. In 1975, Harrison recorded the majority of his solo album *Extra Texture (Read All About It)* in Los Angeles at the A&M studio. This was the first time Harrison had recorded an album in America. Recording in L.A. also meant that Harrison would be working with local session musicians, some of whom he had worked with before, such as Jim Keltner. But he was also introduced to musicians with whom he had not worked, such as David Foster. According to Foster, it was Keltner who recommended him to Harrison. In his book *Hitman: Forty Years Making Music, Topping the Charts and Winning Grammys*, he recalls receiving a call from Harrison: 'one afternoon the phone rang and a familiar voice said, 'Hullo, David, this is old Harrison here. I was chatting with Jim Keltner, and he says you play all right'. It was George Harrison'.

Harrison also had the chance to work with another respected session player, bassist Paul Stallworth. But what Harrison did not know is that Keltner, Stallworth and Foster had begun playing together in a band that would evolve into the Attitudes. The only future Attitudes member not involved with *Extra Texture (Read All About It)* was guitarist Danny Kortchmar. But, according to Foster, this was not a problem.

Jim introduced me to Danny Kortchmar, a great and unique guitar player, and Paul Stallworth, a bassist, and we called ourselves Attitudes. We did two albums for Dark Horse, George Harrison's label, and, if I remember correctly, we recorded mostly at A&M Records. Harrison was such a low-key guy that he was okay with anything and everything we did.

According to Foster, the group came together with very little effort. Jim Keltner called to ask me if I'd be interested in being part of a band. "You don't have to ask', I said'.

All four musicians were veterans of the music business. David Foster was born in Victoria, British Columbia and had made a name for himself as a member of the very popular pop band Skylark, who had a North American Top Ten hit with 'Wildfire' in 1972. He relocated to Los Angeles after Skylark ran its course following their second album, released in 1974. By then, he did have a great reputation as a session musician and, through Jim Keltner, ended up playing piano, organ, ARP String Synthesiser, electric piano and tack piano on *Extra Texture (Read All About It)*.

It is interesting to note that the ARP String Synthesiser (also known as ARP Solina or the Solina String Ensemble) was just coming into its own, and, up until *Extra Texture (Read All About It)*, was used by many artists, including Pink Floyd and Herbie Hancock. The instrument would go on to feature prominently in disco and 1980s music. Once again, Harrison was using instruments not commonly found in rock radio hits, having used the Moog Synthesiser with The Beatles and on his own album *Electronic Sound* – made up entirely of Moog – released in 1969.

It's is not quite clear how Paul Stallworth came to Harrison's attention. Stallworth got his start in a band, 6ix, who released one single in 1971 ('I'm Just Like You' b/w 'Dynamite'). By 1973, Stallworth was getting a great deal of attention due to his incredible bass playing and his stellar vocals, working with artists such as David Clayton-Thomas, Roger McGuinn, and Keith Moon.

Jim Keltner was very well known to Harrison, and in fact, the two had become very close friends since their meeting in 1969 through Delaney And Bonnie. Keltner would also drum at *The Concert For Bangla Desh,* and work with George on several albums by Harry Nilsson, Gary Wright, John Lennon and Ringo Starr. Keltner had played on Harrison's *Living in the Material World* (1973) and *Dark Horse* (1974). Furthermore, Keltner drummed on *Shankar Family & Friends* and Splinter's *The Place I Love,* both of which were released on Dark Horse. Harrison not only considered Keltner a friend, but he also trusted *him* as evidenced by Foster's account of his conversation with Harrison. By all accounts, Keltner not only considered Harrison a friend but a mentor of sorts. In 2005, he explained to Billy Amendola in *Modern Drummer* the impact Harrison had on him:

Oh, God. He was an inspiration for so many things in my life and my family's life. He was an extraordinary guy. He wasn't like most of your friends. I know it sounds trite, like, 'Well, he was a Beatle, so, of course, he was an extraordinary guy'. But it's so much more than that. He had such a down-to-earth quality. He was funny and bright and loved to share stuff. He was a real people person. He genuinely liked people. And yet, he had a tremendous bullshit metre. He could see through you from a long distance. I saw him do that all the time. My family and I feel very fortunate that we came into his life at such an early time.

By 1975, Kortchmar (known as 'Kootch' and, in fact, on the *Attitudes* album, he is credited as Danny Kootch) was 29 years old and very well established in the music industry. During the 1960s, he was a member of The Kingbees and The Flying Machine, the latter of which also featured another famous alumnus, James Taylor. Furthering The Beatle connection, James Taylor would release his debut album, *James Taylor*, on Apple Records in 1969.

By 1967, Kortchmar was a member of The Fugs, after which he formed The City with fellow members Charles Larkey and Carole King. Although The City failed to make a mark, it helped Kortchmar form a professional relationship with King, who he backed up for her astounding solo career. He would also play on James Taylor records, such as the classic *Sweet Baby James*, in 1971. From then on, he became a much-in-demand guitarist for hire, performing with Warren Zevon, Linda Ronstadt, Harry Nilsson and Jackson Browne, to name just a few. He played guitar on Nilsson's *Pussy Cats*, produced by John Lennon, and featured Ringo Starr and his friend Jim Keltner on drums.

As Harrison recorded his *Extra Texture (Read All About It)* album, something interesting was happening. It seemed weekly jam sessions were happening at the Record Plant in Los Angeles and their sessions were often *the* place to be and attracted many big names. The sessions were known as 'The Jim Keltner Fan Club Hour' and it is from these jams that the Attitudes took form and were later encouraged by Harrison to become a band. He even offered them a record deal with his newly formed Dark Horse Records.

However, it was not Jim Keltner who brought the band to Harrison's attention, who was a little frustrated that his friends did not feel comfortable approaching him regarding their bands and music. According to Harrison:

> Jim Keltner didn't want to tell me about his band because he didn't like the idea of using his friendship to get his band a gig, so I got to sign Keltner's band from meeting his piano player, which is slightly crazy when you consider the friendship between Keltner and me and the fact that all those albums ago I was putting 'Jim Keltner fan club' on my album sleeves. And he's hesitant about coming to see me for a gig.

The band utilised The Record Plant and self-produced the album with Lee Kiefer. Kiefer was best known for his work as an engineer, on albums for The Tubes, America, Howard Roberts, Billy Preston, Keith Moon and John Lennon (his 1975 album, *Rock 'n' Roll*). But he also produced a couple of albums: Rudy Romero (*To The World*, 1973), and Black Pearl (*Black Pearl*, 1969). He also engineered the *Attitudes* album.

Bassist Paul Stallworth remembered that 'The Keltner Fan Club' at Record West Studios was the reason the band came together and their first album was recorded. While being interviewed by Jake Feinberg, he related the story: 'Keltner, Me, Kootch and Foster. We liked what was going on, four kicks at a bucket. We would get the studio time for free, and get in at about two, three in the morning. We had this engineer, Lee Kiefer, who liked to hang out late, put together all these tracks, Keltner brought Harrison down to listen to them, he liked it, signed us and we were Attitudes'.

Attitudes' self-titled debut hit the record shelves in North America on 6 February 1976 in America and Canada. It was released a month later in the UK. The album was promoted with print ads, but, perhaps to its detriment, no live performances by the band. This was clearly a studio band, but a short tour or live performances would certainly have helped it. There was also a severe lack of any interviews, either on the radio or in print.

Once again, it is somewhat of a mystery that the album did not do very well. There seemed to be an unfortunate pattern forming with Dark Horse. It seems there was a problem with the promotion of the records and artists. This album did receive excellent reviews. The reviewer for *Cashbox* was particularly fond of the album, noting 'a wide variety of creative and listenable' music. They also noted that FM radio, easy listening and soul stations would break the album. It did get as high as 21 on *Cashbox*'s New FM Action LP chart, which noted airplay of albums in the US on FM radio stations. In *Billboard*, the reviewer noted, 'Nothing overly original or new, but the material is pleasing'. The reviewer goes on to point out that Kortchmar and Stallworth's vocals are fine and that there is 'No dominant instrument, which works to the advantage of everyone'.

In 2020, talking with *Rolling Stone*'s David Browne, Kortchmar was clear that, although 'soft rock' or 'jazz rock' was much more than those labels imply, the music of *Attitudes,* in his mind, went beyond any genres used to describe their music. 'I don't think you can compare what we were doing to Christopher Cross or Kenny Loggins. And that's not to disparage those people at all. But what we were doing was way rawer and funkier than what you'd play on your yacht'.

Sadly, the album failed to chart on both sides of the Atlantic. It seems, given the *Cashbox* FM chart, that the album received some airplay, mainly in California, but this did not generate sales. As a result, the album, as good as it was – and it *is* a very good album – went unnoticed. A sad way for a band with such promise to make its debut. All the right ingredients were there: strong songwriting, excellent production and a record chock full of excellent songs. By all rights, it should have found an audience, especially in 1976. Kortchmar had hopes of the album doing well, 'I thought maybe it would catch on and people would start digging it'. He had to have been disappointed.

In 2020, Olivia Harrison made the point to Browne that for George, sales were never the driving force behind Dark Horse records: 'You did the music and put it out and tried to promote it. They say, 'Do it and drop it in the well'. That's the reason George did anything, for the pleasure and the need to create'.

In this case, the promotion for the album has something to do with the album not achieving its sales potential. But it was not entirely Dark Horse's fault. David Foster noted: 'Some of the tracks were really pretty good, but we never did anything to promote them. We were just a group of studio guys trying to make good music together, but we were a little spoiled, too: We were making too much money as session musicians to take time off to promote the work'. There is a lot of truth to this comment. In 1979, Harrison agreed with this assessment. In a *Rolling Stone* interview to promote his album *George Harrison*, while talking about the artists on Dark Horse, he pointed out, 'They spend maybe $50,000 more than I'd spend making an album, then they won't do any interviews or go on the road – whatever you'd organise for them, they'd foul it up. It was just too much bullshit'.

Attitudes was the last album Dark Horse released with A&M. The album deserved to do better, but the same could be said for all of the albums released from 1974 – 1976 on Dark Horse. Perhaps Harrison felt that his name would not only attract attention but also sales. But, in fairness to Harrison, he did provide an opportunity for all the artists to establish their careers and in some ways, Dark Horse can be seen as a springboard for the artists it signed.

It is also a sad way for Dark Horse to part company with A&M Records. Attitudes would have the last single released through A&M, but that was months away, and it was a song not on the album *Attitudes*. However, the debut would not be the last we heard from the group. They would have one more album for Dark Horse up their collective sleeve.

Thirty Three & 1/3 at Warner Brothers

In the 6 November 1976 issue of *New Musical Express*, in the section 'News Desk', there is a notice about George Harrison signing to Warner Brothers. 'George Harrison has signed his Dark Horse label, which now includes his own product, to Warner Brothers for worldwide distribution'. The article also mentions that new albums from Attitudes and Kenny (sic) Burke 'will follow shortly'. In the same article, Harrison is quoted, 'after the recent sudden turn of events, we're very excited about our new affiliation with Warners'. An A&M spokesman states, 'we cannot actually confirm a settlement, but it seems likely'.

The Beatles' contract with EMI/Capitol Records ended on 26 January 1976. This meant the four individual Beatles were free to sign with whoever they wished. Paul McCartney signed with EMI to distribute and promote his music. He had formed his own company MPL and maintained ownership of his masters and copyright. Through MPL, he would license his music to EMI/Capitol Records. MPL would also obtain ownership of the Apple albums. Ringo Starr signed with Atlantic/WEA in North America and Polydor for the rest of the world. Previously, in April 1975, Starr had formed his own record label, Ring O'Records, which was distributed by Polydor in Europe and Capitol Records in North America. The name of the label was reportedly suggested by Lennon. Ringo himself never released any records on his own label, which quietly disappeared in 1978.

While McCartney and Starr were forming their own labels, John Lennon did not sign with anyone. His last studio album of the 1970s was 1975's *Rock 'n' Roll*. This was followed by a 'best of collection' *Shaved Fish*, released for Christmas 1975 to fulfil his contract with EMI/Capitol. In 1976, he did help out his old friend Starr by writing and performing on 'Cookin' (In The Kitchen Of Love)' for the *Ringo's Rotogravure* album. After a very busy 1974 and 1975, Lennon quietly stepped away from the spotlight.

As for Harrison, he had already formed Dark Horse Records and had signed an international deal with A&M Records to distribute the label on 15 May 1974. But Harrison signing to Warner Brothers was very disappointing to Derek Green. He looked forward to working with Harrison on his solo projects. Remember, part of the agreement with A&M was that Harrison would release his solo albums on the label once his contract with EMI/Capitol was complete.

According to Green, at the time of signing, it was not well known that Harrison, himself, had also signed with A&M. 'It was to be not announced that George, as a recording artist, was involved in that contract. When we signed Dark Horse, we signed George from EMI. During that time period, he was signed to us. I was working with the head of the label and the superstar recording artist'.

Given that the contract with EMI/Capitol had now ended, A&M expected Harrison's first solo album to be for them, and a deadline of 26 July 1976 was set. However, A&M executives discovered that Harrison had been in negotiations with Warner Brother Records and had arranged for the artwork for *Thirty Three & 1/3* to be sent to Warner Brothers' offices. Needless to say, A&M were not impressed. Derek Green observed, 'It was deeply personal between people'. According to Green, there were some other issues between Harrison's then-manager Denis O'Brien and Jerry Moss (the 'M' of A&M). Green is not aware of what these issues were, but in his own words, 'It got resolved by the courts'.

In 2007, Jerry Moss shed a little light on the relationship between Dark Horse Records and A&M in speaking with David Browne.

> George started hitting the road, and then it was this guy making the record and this guy making decisions, and this guy running up a huge tab that we were paying for, and the records weren't very good. And it got to the point where I couldn't root for this project any more, even though George had charmed a great many people on our lot to do extra work for that label, and we created the whole image for him.

The bottom line was that Harrison did not deliver an album by 26 July 1976. On 26 September 1976, A&M served notice to Harrison in the form of a ten-million-dollar lawsuit, which would end the partnership. They were also seeking an additional $150,000 for not delivering his solo album and a further three million for the international operation of Dark Horse Records. According to reports, the lawsuit was settled with four million being paid to A&M, either by Harrison or Warner Brothers. Harrison commented during an interview that was distributed to radio stations in the US to promote *Thirty Three & 1/3* (making it the first Dark Horse album on Warner Brothers, released on 19 November 1976) on the album *Dark Horse Records Presents A Personal Dialogue with George Harrison at Thirty Three & 1/3*:

> We just settled the thing, and now, I am just happy because I can continue with my life and recording career with Dark Horse Records.

I think it's just best the way it worked out. It's unfortunate it got into a bit of a hassle at one point, but it was resolved, and that's all past now, behind. The future looks really, really good.

But the future did not look so good for the people and artists that had been working with A&M who had hopes of working directly with an ex-Beatle and assisting him with his own music. Working on Dark Horse with other great artists was one thing, but to work with a Beatle was another matter altogether.

In 2020, Olivia Harrison commented on the situation with A&M and Dark Horse. With Harrison taking his album to Warner Brothers, A&M were simply not happy with Harrison being on one label and his Dark Horse label being run through A&M. 'Management and A&M were not happy with the deal. It didn't have much to do with George, but it had *everything* to do with him because he had to sign everything. I don't know the ins and outs, but it was pretty acrimonious and it was very disappointing to George. Being an artist label, he never thought that would happen. It went wrong, and that was really sad'.

Later, Harrison spelt it out. He was able to explain the complicated situation.

What happened was, we had a deal for Dark Horse and I had a deal for myself, which didn't happen until this year because I was with EMI and Capitol. They were trying to get together over the two years to finalise all the details. The attorney who was with them when they made the deal was not the one with them when they were filling in the details. He read the deal and he said they were going to use my money to offset Dark Horse. We said, 'No! No! It's in the contract. It has been there for two years. You don't cross-collateralise me and Dark Horse'. And the attorney said, 'I can't believe the other attorney did this to you'. So, in effect, what happened was they realised that they had not made themselves such a good deal. Instead of phoning me up and saying, 'Now look, George, we made ourselves a bad deal. Let's talk about it and work it out', they found that the only legal grounds they had was that I had had hepatitis, so my album was two months delayed. We had it in the original contract that I would give it to them on the 25th of July. And so they picked up on that legal point and said, 'okay, we'll get him on that'. I arrived in L.A. with my album under my arm, all happy, and I was given this letter saying, 'give us back the million dollars, which was an advance, and give us the album, and when you give us the album, you don't get the million back' ... I couldn't live with that sort of situation, so I left. We backed the truck up to the office and filled it with our stuff and we went off. But, almost overnight, me and Dark Horse Records were transferred from A&M on one side of the Hollywood Hills to Warner Brothers on the other side...

When talking with *Toronto Star* writer Peter Goddard, Harrison was candid about his feelings with A&M. 'I felt really sad about what they did. I thought we had a family relationship, but when they (A&M) said I wanted back all my money, that's crap. That's why I left A&M to go to Warner Brothers. I like the people there'.

Even during the press interviews to promote *Thirty Three & ¹/₃*, Harrison was able to use his wit to express his frustration with the difficulties of 1976. When asked by Tony Wilson on *Granada Reports* in 1976 what he had been doing since *Extra Texture*, Harrison joked, 'Recently, I have been more of a lawyer'.

For Green, the sad part was never being able to work with Harrison on his own release. 'The real prize was to work with George on his own album, which I never got the chance to do; it was never meant to be'.

Many, at the time, felt that Mo Ostin, the then-CEO of Warner Brothers Records, wanted Harrison on that label and it has been reported that Warner Brothers helped out with the lawsuit. The Beatles had split up in 1970, and in 1976, it was still a feather in the cap of any label that could sign an ex-Beatle.

'Mo wanted George on Warner Brothers', states James Strauss. 'Mo was courting George badly; everybody wanted a Beatle, of course, there weren't many of them available. Everybody wanted George, and Mick (Fleetwood) and George were buddies at the time. Best friends'.

The situation may have been settled, but according to court documents reported in an article in *Billboard* magazine, things got very ugly between Dark Horse and A&M. For example, it is reported that all of the office furniture and equipment was removed from the A&M lot prior to Dark Horse signing with Warner Brothers. It was further reported that photographer Bob Cato was directed in August to deliver the film and back covers of all Dark Horse releases to Bob Thrasher at Warner Brothers. Harrison noted in documents that he 'felt the relationship between A&M and Dark Horse had become untenable and that he felt a label must feel a friendly rapport with an artist in order to do a proper job of marketing products'.

Further, the lawsuit with A&M and the move from that label to Warner Brothers had serious consequences for the artists signed to Dark Horse Records. Only three would survive the jump, but the rest of the artists were let go from their contracts.

Strauss of Jiva discussed the complication of the end of Dark Horse's relationship with A&M:

> ... we still had a distribution deal with A&M, which they had no intention of honouring. We met everybody there, and they were just fantastic people. On any given day, I loved to be on the roster. But we were persona non grata within 24 hours. Warner Brothers never showed any interest in Jiva that I ever heard about. I suppose if George was ever asked about a second Jiva album, he would ask, 'who is Jiva?' Remember, this was during the whole Beatle breakup, lawsuits and money problems, so, to be fair, he may have had some bigger things on his mind.

The break with Dark Horse Records also meant a break with Harrison. Strauss recalls:

> I never spoke to George again; I was absolutely brokenhearted until I realised George could not be held responsible for what he did; it is like a tanker running over a little fishing boat. He had no assumption of the careers he had ruined. Splinter, whoever he had, were only interested in him because of his umbrella of being a Beatle.

Years later, Strauss is able to look back on the time and have some perspective:

> There is a baseball term that best describes my experience of those days: When a promising rookie washed out of the big leagues for one of a possible million reasons, it would be said he had 'a cup of coffee' in the Majors. We were a cup of coffee in rock 'n' roll. Roadies with flashlights led us on stages, Margie Kent made our clothes, our guitar strings were changed by a dear boy named Casey Alsbury (who passed away too early). We had a blast, and on a few nights, we were invincible. James is happy.

While the issues with A&M were settled, and the 'My Sweet Lord' case appeared to be coming to an end, Harrison set about to record his new album. Harrison decided not to record this album in Los Angeles. However, the musicians he used from the album were from there. He preferred to be home and have the studio time at his disposal. He assembled a strong backing band and took them to Friar Park Studio,

Tom Scott became more than just the saxophonist on the album. He is given credit as 'assisting with the production' of the album, In effect, becoming Harrison's co-producer, the first person to have that role since Phil Spector. Scott was perfect for the role, with the arrangements on the album being polar opposites to anything found on *Dark Horse* and *Extra Texture (Read All About It)*. The album is less dense and, overall has a much more pleasant vibe to it. That comes not just from the songs themselves but also from Scott's arrangements.

Harrison himself acknowledged that his previous album, *Extra Texture (Read All About It)*, was a darker effort On the interview album, sent to radio stations, *Dark Horse Records Presents a Personal Dialogue with George Harrison at Thirty Three & 1/3*, Harrison is clear: 'It's a very positive album, very up. Most of the songs are love songs or happy songs. It doesn't compare at all to the last album, which was a bit depressing actually, *Extra Texture (Read All About It)*'.

Scott recalls how it came about that he became the co-producer of the album:

I don't think we talked about it much. I was living in Friar Park, and we were just in the studio all day. I guess he grew confident in relying on me as a good sounding board and we just had a real good work relationship. We just sat in a room and said, 'what do you think?' 'I don't know, what do you think about this?' I mean, it is not a science; let's put it that way. It was very casual and very mutually respectful and we tried things that worked or not worked and we would go and try something else, just like two friends getting together.

Scott had done a lot of work with Harrison, who obviously trusted him. Scott invited engineer Hank Cicalo to accompany him to work on *Thirty Three & 1/3*. Cicalo is a prolific and well-respected recording engineer, and one look at his resume tells you all you need to know. Having worked on literally hundreds of albums, including the classic *Tapestry*, Cicalo had the experience and knowledge. 'Tom Scott and I had worked in L.A. and at A&M. I met George at A&M because he had an office at A&M. I had done many albums with Tom. So George wanted Tom to be a producer and to help him with the album, and I came over with Tom'.

He has very clear and fond memories of working with Harrison and the album. 'Tapestry (by Carole King) was one of my great thrills to work on, but this is one of those albums that I would count in my first five albums I have worked on. In my 65-year career, it was one the best times I had working on an album ... so loose and creative at the same time'.

Harrison's talented band were all from the USA with the exception of David Foster, who is Canadian. Alvin Taylor, who Harrison knew from his work on the *Stairsteps* album, drummed on the album, and Attitudes member David Foster (who also played on *Extra Texture (Read All About It)*) provided electric piano and clavinet. Willie Weeks, who had worked with Harrison on *Dark Horse, Extra Texture (Read All About It)* and had toured with Harrison on the Shankar/Harrison tour of 1974, came on board to provide bass. Harrison had wanted Billy Preston, but he was not available as he was working with The Rolling Stones at the time.

Hank Cicalo, who was an engineer for *Thirty Three & 1/3*, recalled that Preston had offered to overdub his part, but Harrison wanted the musicians to be in the same room playing together. Richard Tee would be a suitable substitute for Preston. Harrison had never worked with Tee, but he came highly recommended, so Scott and Cicalo picked Tee up at the airport when he flew over from New York City. Cicalo also recalls the first night Tee was in the studio with Harrison:

... we went back to Friar Park at three or four in the morning, talked a lot and had some food. Tee said, 'let's go look at the studio'. So we went up to the studio. The studio was just gorgeous. At one end of the studio, there was this large stained glass window, it was just beautiful. George's piano was the same piano they had at Apple Studios and it was a German Steinway; they just record beautifully. I had used it on Carole King's *Tapestry*.

Tee sat at the piano and he was playing some tunes, and he and George are bouncing back and forth with stuff and then it started to get light, the sun started to creep, so he went and got some music, and placed it on the piano and asked him to play it. And Tee wove his way through the tune, and the sun came up with the Steinway playing 'Here Comes the Sun'. If you wanted a great moment in music, this was it. Tee was just amazing and George was just smiling, and it was just wonderful.

Billy Preston and Gary Wright would make appearances later and did provide some overdubs. But for the most part, all the musicians performed together in the studio. By all accounts, the recording was extremely pleasurable, and when the sessions started, there were few problems. Cicalo does note that the one hurdle they had to get over was that the studio was not completely ready for recording. He recalled getting to Friar Park a week before recording to help get the studio together. He enjoyed his time there and particularly liked the control room board and console.

Cicalo had some help from Kumar Shankar, who had also been working with Harrison. Besides being a great help in the studio, Cicalo remembered Shankar being a great chef and cooked some great vegetarian meals. Cicalo tuned all the speakers and was pleased to later hear that 'after we left, the guy who was supposed to tune the speakers came in and said, 'I'm not going to touch it; the speakers sound fine'. My ears were ok at the time. Kumar was a great chef as well'.

As far as recording with Harrison, there seems to be agreement that Harrison was not demanding and created a very open and creative environment. Scott recalled during our conversation that Harrison 'never said, 'play this way'. I don't remember him doing it ever'. Scott also recalled that Harrison would play the track and would discuss the structure of the song. According to Scott, Harrison would look for input. 'We would discuss where stuff should go, 'is there a solo somewhere? Are there some background figures?' But I would usually come up with the background figures myself. 'Let's put them in there; if you like them, keep them; if you don't, dump them'. That's the beauty of multi-track recording; it was relatively new in those days'.

Drummer Alvin Taylor had a similar experience: 'He never ever told me anything to play on that album'. In fact, Taylor's memories of the album are similar to Scott's:

He would give you the storyline and the concept as to why he wrote the song; what it was about and he would begin to play it, show you where the verse was and where the chorus was and why the chorus is doing what it is doing, and he would play the song and say 'have you got an idea?', 'What do you think?' 'What do you feel?' I remember asking him a couple of times, what do you want me to do, George? And he would say, 'hell if I had known, I wouldn't have to call you. I called you because this is your expertise and you know what to do, just do it'. That was George's attitude, lay aside his own preferences and thoughts and he would encourage me to be me, and what I thought and what I thought would be best.

Taylor also remembers it being very important to Harrison that the musicians understood what the song was about and what Harrison was trying to achieve. Taylor recalls Harrison telling him about a song that he had written, 'Learning How to Love You':

George said, 'Let me play this for you, and I want you to envision what you would be playing on it'. Before he would play the song, he would tell you about it; he would give you a storyline. 'I met this guy named Georgy Grief... and this is what happened'. That became 'Crackerbox Palace', or he would say, 'I was working with A&M Records, and I had a deal going with Herb Alpert, who was the A of A&M, A was Moss's partner. He would say Moss is pretty good, but Alpert was running stuff, and he would make all the main decisions, no matter what Moss wanted. Alpert was the guy who made the final decision and judgement about things. And I wanted certain things to go a certain way, and I figured Alpert would understand that because he is a musician and he would be sensitive to other musicians, but when it came to me having an idea about certain things, Alpert disagreed and would let Moss ok what I wanted. I am learning how to love him; I am learning how to love this guy. He would say the song 'Learning How to Love You' is based on that.

Cicalo agrees with both Taylor and Scott and talked about the collaborative nature of the album, even though it had been thoroughly planned out prior to recording:

They worked on the tunes before we even got there. They knew the material. They would talk before we got there; they were close to doing the things they wanted to do on the album. When you get started and sit down in the studio like that and you are creating at the same time, things change, and you have to jump on those changes because those are the changes that make the record work. A little thing here and a little thing there. That is how you build a record. Even though you do all the things you have to do before you get to the studio, that input has to come from guys playing and George was always open to those things. Everybody contributed.

The recording seemed to be going well, they worked hard on the album and there was a very positive feeling in the studio. Cicalo recalls, 'There were times when you were just on the song. It was a wonderful atmosphere; we worked, got on a tune, and everybody just thought, let's keep going. Sometimes we worked late, and sometimes we didn't. It depended on what the tune was. For me, it was a very, very easy kind of operation, very relaxed'. This type of work translated to the finished product and can be heard on the record. And then, just as everything seemed to be on course, Harrison got ill.

'Then I got sick, I got Hepatitis, hippietitus, which laid me off for two months, and then I recovered and I went into the studio, finished all the overdubs and the mixing of the album, and came here to be sued. And here I am!'

'We recorded most of it in two weeks, then George was ill', says Cicalo. 'Tom and I had to go back to L.A. There was some stuff done after we left and someone else mixed the album. I would say we were 90% done by the time we left. As I said, I did not mix the album, but it came out all right'.

This is the illness that caused the delay for Harrison in completing his album for the original deadline. Initially, he thought he had food poisoning, but when he didn't get any better – he lost weight and started noticing yellow skin (a sign of jaundice) – he realised that he was ill. He was diagnosed with Hepatitis B. Rather than turn to medicine alone, Arias assisted Harrison in getting better by encouraging him to seek alternative treatments, such as acupuncture and natural remedies. And he got healthy again. Alan Clayson, in his book *George Harrison*, noted that Harrison later noted that 'I needed the hepatitis to quit drinking'.

Once well, Harrison was able to finish the album. Billy Preston and Gary Wright also visited Harrison and provided some overdubs for the record. The overdubs and the mixing were handled by old friend and engineer Phil McDonald.

'The guy (Phil McDonald) who mixed it did a nice job', observes Cicalo. 'He was listening to the rough mixes and he stayed pretty close.

George was happy with those rough mixes, so he stayed close to those rough mixes, it came out nice'.

The album was completed and a release date was set. *Thirty-Three &* $^1/_3$ was released on 19 November 1976 in the UK and North Americans had to wait for a week when it was released on 24 November 1976, the first album to be released on his new deal with Warner Brothers. From here on, with few exceptions, George Harrison records would appear with the Dark Horse logo.

The album was preceded by a single, 'This Song' which was released worldwide in November 1976. It was accompanied by a very funny promotional film directed by Michael Collins (who would go on to make music promo films for Toto), and featured cameos from Olivia Arias, Ronnie Wood and Jim Keltner (who did a brilliant job as the Judge). Since these were the days before MTV, the promo film was not shown all that often at the time of release, but it did receive its North American television debut when Harrison was the musical guest on *Saturday Night Live* on 20 November 1976.

As noted earlier, promotional copies were sent out to radio stations for all Dark Horse singles. In the US, mono/stereo copies were sent out until the mid-1980s. However, in Canada, the singles were identical to stock copies, with one exception. The label had a white background, as opposed to the brown background. In the UK, as usual, the promotional singles were similar to the stock copies, notated that it was a promo copy.

As part of his European promotion for the album, Harrison mimed the song on the German television show *Disco '77*, which aired on 5 February 1977. Harrison seemed to understand that his name alone would not simply mean a Top Ten record. By 1976/77, The Beatles were no longer the commercial force they were in the 1960s and early 1970s. He had to promote the album fully.

Billboard magazine favourably reviewed the single. In the 20 November 1976 issue of the trade magazine, they suggest that the song was Harrison's 'most commercial in some time', calling the tune 'cheerful' and the words clever – overall, the end result is 'irresistible'. Meanwhile, *Cashbox* highlighted the track in their 'Single Reviews', stating that it takes off with the 'piano and organ' at the beginning. They also refer to Scott's saxophone as 'fiery'.

Confusingly, the single proved to be only a minor hit, peaking at number 25 on The *Billboard* Top 100, while Leo Sayer sat at number one with 'You Make Me Feel Like Dancing'. The same week on the *Billboard* album charts, *Thirty Three & ¹/₃* was at number 12. The album would peak at number 11, failing to crack the Top Ten. For one of the weeks that Harrison peaked at number 11, his old friend, McCartney, took the top spot with his album *Wings Over America*. *Thirty Three & ¹/₃* became Harrison's first studio album to not make the Top Ten since his experimental album *Electronic Sound* released in 1969. 'This Song' failed to even make the charts in the UK, and the album peaked at a disappointing 35.

Perhaps if the singles released from the album had been hits, the album would have done much better. It is somewhat confusing as to why the singles did not achieve the success they deserved. Perhaps the lack of radio play didn't help, but again, 'This Song' was really custom-made for radio play.

But it is important to put *Thirty Three & ¹/₃* into context. 1976 was the year that interest in The Beatles started to gather pace again. Kicking off the year was an interview album, *The Beatles Tapes,* released by Polydor in the UK – Harrison and Starr both failed to prevent the release via court in 1975. Elsewhere, much to The Beatles' dismay, Capitol released a new compilation *Rock 'N' Roll Music* on 26 June 1976, complete with a sleeve design that raised the ire of Lennon and Starr. Cheaply designed cover aside, the album still reached the number two spot in America and Canada, kept out of number one by Paul McCartney and Wings' *Speed of Sound* album. It reached number eleven in the UK. McCartney also had massive hits in North America with two singles ('Silly Love Songs' and 'Let 'Em In'). While they were charting, a ten-year-old song from the *Rock 'N' Roll Music* album, 'Got to Get You Into My Life', was a Top Ten single in the US. In the UK, 'Back in the U.S.S.R.' was the chosen single, which made number 20, but then EMI re-released The Beatles singles collection, and six Beatle singles recharted. Beatlemania was in full swing, and ironically, Harrison was now competing with himself.

And he was truly competing with himself when EMI/Capitol exercised their right to release a George Harrison compilation. As The Beatles' contract expired with EMI/Capitol, the company had the rights to release the material they owned in the form of compilations. First, the album *Shaved Fish* by John Lennon was released in October 1975 – a Top Ten success. Ringo got the treatment next with his album *Blast From Your Past* one month later and earned gold status in the US.

Two weeks prior to the release of *Thirty Three & ¹/₃*, while Harrison was beginning the promotion trails, Capitol/EMI released their compilation of George Harrison's solo career. *The Best of George Harrison* was released on 9 November 1976. The UK sleeve featured a nice photo of Harrison, while the North Americans were treated to a cover that rivalled *Rock 'N' Roll Music*. Thankfully, when the album was finally reissued on CD, EMI/Capitol made the UK cover the international standard. On *The Best of George Harrison,* side one of the album consists of songs with The Beatles, while side two sampled his solo records without including all of his singles.

During one interview to promote *Thirty Three & ¹/₃*, Harrison addressed *The Best of George Harrison*. Harrison made it clear that, as Lennon had done, he prepared a suggested track listing, which EMI/Capitol ignored.

'What they've done is taken a lot of ... my songs, which were Beatles songs, when there was really a lot of good songs, they could have used by me separately. Solo songs. I don't see why they didn't do that. They did that with Ringo's *Blast From Your Past* and John's *Shaved Fish*'.

Thirty Three & ¹/₃, was met with very good reviews. *Billboard* made it a 'Spotlight album' (along with the soundtrack to the movie *A Star is Born*) in its 4 December 1976 issue. They refer to the production as being 'top-notch' and call Harrison's writing 'spectacular', believing that such talent is 'on display here'. They sum up the album as 'a sunny, upbeat album of love songs and cheerful jokes that is his happiest and most commercial package, with least high-flown postures, for perhaps his entire solo career'. Jon Parles, writing in *Crawdaddy*, was less enthusiastic about the album. While praising the musicianship, he states that 'Most of the time, the music saves Harrison'. He seems to struggle with Harrison's lyrics, referring to songs such as 'Crackerbox Palace' and 'Pure Smokey' as 'silly'. He sums up his review with a backhanded compliment. 'This LP gives hope that George can produce a full-fledged sequel to *All Things Must Pass*', he writes. 'He just has to figure out what he's trying to say'.

In the UK, Barry Cain wrote in *Record Mirror*, 'the ride is fun' and cites 'This Song' and his cover of 'True Love' as highlights. Ray Coleman, in *Melody Maker,* referred to it as a 'fine' album and compared it to The Beatles' *Rubber Soul*. The *New Musical Express* critic Bob Woffinden was somewhat harsher both on the album and on Harrison as an artist. His review is very lukewarm, criticising Harrison as a lyricist and calling the album bland. However, he concluded, 'while it is an album of no particular merit in itself, it is one which leads me to believe that his best work may not necessarily be behind him'.

Rolling Stone magazine was much harsher. Reviewer Kurt Tucker complained of Harrison's 'persistent preaching' and placed a lot of blame on Tom Scott. Scott's influence, in his opinion, left the 'music with the feeling and sincerity of cellophane'. Steve Simels was downright mean in his review by comparing *Thirty Three & ⅓* to the then-current *The Best Of George Harrison*. In *Stereo Review*, he writes that because half of the album features Beatle music while Starr and Lennon's 'best of' collections did not, it 'says more than enough about the declining state of George's creative powers'.

Harrison made himself available to promote *Thirty Three & ⅓*, participating in interviews for television, radio and magazines. Although he was not prepared to undertake another tour, he did a five-day promotional tour of major American cities, talking to local press about everything from The Beatles to his new album. He worked his way across the United States, the UK, Germany, and the Netherlands, where the album did extremely well.

Harrison recognised the need to promote the album to as many people as possible. Much like The Beatles appearing on Ed Sullivan, Harrison appeared on a very popular live television show *Saturday Night Live,* on 20 November 1976. He performed two songs with the host of the evening, Paul Simon. They performed many songs, but only 'Here Comes the Sun' and 'Homeward Bound' were broadcast. He also brought along two promotional films: 'This Song' and 'Crackerbox Palace'.

Monty Python's Eric Idle directed the video for 'Crackerbox Palace', which features cameos from Eric Clapton, Neil Innes (future Rutles member) and, once again, Olivia Arias. It is an extremely well-made promotional film, and when the song was released as a single in 1977, it no doubt helped it to greater success than 'This Song' and developed renewed interest in the album. The promo was filmed at Harrison's home. A third promotional film was for the UK/Europe single 'True Love', a cover of the classic Cole Porter song made popular by Bing Crosby and Grace Kelly in the film *High Society*. It wasn't shown on *Saturday Night Live*. It was also directed by Eric Idle. Harrison had been a fan of *Monty Python's Flying Circus* since the show debuted in 1969, even helping them with their single 'Lumberjack Song'. In the years to come, *Monty Python's Flying Circus* would play a huge role in Harrison's life.

The second single released from the album in North America was 'Crackerbox Palace'. It was released on 24 January 1977 and, interestingly, contained the same flip side as the previous single, 'This Song', 'Learning How to Love You', which, at the time, seemed unusual.

'Crackerbox Palace' was a North American hit, making the Top 20, and giving the album a boost. The second single in the UK was Harrison's cover of 'True Love', released on 18 February 1977 in the UK, with the promo film to accompany the release. *Record Mirror* placed the song in the 'Maybe' section of their singles reviews, where reviews are split 'Hits', 'Maybes', 'Misses' and 'No Hopers'. The reviewer Sheila Prophet was kind and stated that the song is 'quite jolly, but it doesn't exactly set the eardrums buzzing'. She notes it 'could make the charts, but I don't see it being a big hit'. She was correct; it was not a hit. The flip side to the single was another album cut, 'Pure Smokey', Harrison's tribute to Smokey Robinson.

The cover of 'True Love' was an odd choice for Harrison. Harrison joked at the time, 'Cole Porter got the chords wrong'. It is another example of the impact of American music on Harrison, who claimed that The Beatles may have done it when they were playing in The Cavern and Hamburg in Germany, citing 1959, when The Beatles may have attempted it. Harrison noted the simplicity and beauty of the song, musically and lyrically. Author Gary Giddens noted in his biography of Bing Crosby that Harrison, later in his life, complemented Crosby: 'He had a lovely voice, a presence that sort of crackles. He always remained popular over here [i.e. England]. I like his stuff very much'.

In the article of March 1977 in *Record World*, there is a mention of plans for Dark Horse to get into films and soundtracks. They note that Dark Horse is launching 'Dark Horse Goes to the Movies'. The first project under that banner is the release of 'Crackerbox Palace' and 'This Song' on stereo 35 mm film to theatres to run with the film *Winter Equinox*. The article also notes that there will be tie-ins with local radio stations. It sounds like a great idea, but there is no evidence of this project getting off the ground. It is also interesting to note that it predates Harrison's creation of HandMade films by two years. The article also talks about new releases forthcoming from Attitudes, Keni Burke and Splinter.

While North America only had the two singles released from the album, in the UK, Dark Horse released a third single, 'It's What You Value', on 31 May 1977. Robin Smith, writing for *Record Mirror*, is particularly unkind in his review: 'It sounds reasonable until Harrison attempts singing'. Nevertheless, the single, as with the first two singles from the album, failed to chart.

Given all that had happened in 1976, Harrison was able to still go into a studio and create an incredibly strong album, arguably one of his best. Harrison, much like the other three Beatles, responded well when working with other producers. In this case, he did not rely on the heavy-handed production of Phil Spector but instead went with a producer and arranger who helped create a loose, spacious sound. Tom Scott was an excellent choice to assist with production. The album touches on different styles of music; from the opening funky bass and drums of 'Woman Don't You Cry For Me', to the closing of the very mellow and melodic 'Learning How to Love You', the album never sags or lets you down. It is a complete, cohesive album that holds together.

The album *Thirty Three & $^1/_3$* is now regarded as a classic and is much loved. Why did it not do as well as hoped in 1976? First, it must be made clear the album was far from a flop. Although it was Harrison's first album to not reach the top ten in the United States since *Electronic Sound*, it narrowly missed. Perhaps the timing of the album was wrong. Harrison and Dark Horse released the album for the Christmas market, and he was competing with Elton John, Led Zeppelin, Barbra Streisand and himself. The sales of *The Best of George Harrison* must have had an impact on the sales of *Thirty Three & $^1/_3$*, and one wonders if the album would have had the sales to boost it into the Top Ten had it not been for that release.

In the UK, Harrison was battling greatest hits packages. One look at the Top Ten, when Harrison's album peaked at number 35, over half of the albums were 'greatest hits' packages (Glen Campbell was at number one with *20 Golden Greats*). Given the economics in the UK at the time, greatest hits packages were the best value for music fans, and that is clearly reflected in the charts.

The album achieved Gold status in North America, and it was a success, perhaps not the success Warner Brothers had hoped, but again, chart positions are just one part of the story. The album stayed on the charts well into 1977 and continued to sell steadily. Harrison did an excellent job promoting it. In terms of sales, it was the largest-selling Dark Horse album up to that point, so Warner Brothers must have felt it to be a wise investment.

Although *Thirty Three & $^1/_3$* proved to be a success and was a positive transition to Warner Brothers, Dark Horse artists would not have the same good fortune.

'Good News'. Attitudes, Keni Burke and Splinter On Warner Brothers

On 23 July 1976, Dark Horse Records released a single by Attitudes, 'Sweet Summer Music', with 'If We Want To' on the B-side. Two months after the release of the single, A&M served notice to George Harrison that he had not met the terms of their contract. The result was that on 26 September 1976, Harrison was given notice of the lawsuit A&M was filing against him. This meant the end of the relationship between Harrison's Dark Horse Records and A&M. It would appear that once the lawsuit was filed, A&M stopped any work with Dark Horse Records.

In the 7 August 1976 issue of *Billboard* magazine, 'Sweet Summer Music' is listed in the 'Top Single Picks' under the recommended section. On 9 October 1976, the single had made it to number 43 on the *Billboard* Soul Charts (as they were titled then) and was at number 96 on The *Billboard* Top 100. 'Sweet Summer Music' was Attitudes' biggest hit and was on its way to being one of Dark Horse Record's biggest successes. One week later, the single dropped to number 94 and then the single was off the charts. By this time, the bands signed to Dark Horse were caught in the crossfire of the lawsuit between A&M and Harrison. Attitudes were one of the bands.

The next Dark Horse record released would be a George Harrison single and that would be distributed through Warner Brothers.

When Harrison signed his deal with Warner Brothers, only three Dark Horse Records artists went with him: Splinter, Attitudes, and Keni Burke, with Burke, of course, member of The Stairsteps. However, an advertisement was taken out by Warner Brothers on 5 March 1977 in *Cashbox* stating that Stairsteps were part of the roster remaining with Dark Horse, while Jiva, Ravi Shankar, and Henry McCullough did not make the transition. However, by 1977, Shankar had signed with Guardian Records in North America and EMI's His Master's Voice label in Europe.

The first band to release music with the new Dark Horse/Warner Brothers deal were Attitudes, who released their album *Good News* in North America on 5 May 1977 and in the UK, the album was released on 3 June 1977.

Very few specifics are known about the album *Good News*. It was produced by Jay Lewis, who had engineered the *Jiva* album and the band's debut album, *Attitudes*, but specific dates as to when the album was recorded are unknown. What is interesting about *Good News* is that, although Harrison is thanked, he does not appear on the album, but Jim Keltner's good friend Ringo Starr does play drums on the title track 'Good News'. The only studios noted in the credits are 'Let's Talk Turkey', which was recorded in Sunswept Recorders by Lee Kiefer (who co-produced their debut album) and 'Foster's Frees', which was recorded in London, England and engineered by Keith Olsen.

Bob Cato did the photography and designed the cover art. By this point, he had been retained as a consultant to Dark Horse Records. It is noted in a *Cashbox* article from 15 May 1976 that Cato was brought on to assist with 'special projects in the areas of creative services, advertising and marketing'. Cato had a very strong career. He had won a Grammy for the sleeve photography and design of Barbra Streisand's *People* (1965, Columbia) and for Bob Dylan's *Greatest Hits* (1968, Columbia). He also worked on albums by Johnny Cash, The Band and George Harrison, to name just a few.

In the same article regarding Cato, there were other changes at Dark Horse. Harrison announced that Dennis Morgan was now director of operations. Morgan, who had worked at Elton John's Rocket Records label, would be responsible for sales, promotion and marketing. Pattie Wright, who had worked at Capitol Records as national publicity manager, was named director of artist development. She would be responsible for artist relations & development, publicity and corporate public relations. It was further reported in the article that Morgan, Wright and Cato would report directly to Denis O'Brien, George Harrison's manager.

For an album with such star power, one might assume that it might have received a great deal of coverage upon its release. This is not the case. *Good News* received very little attention when the album hit radio and retail. One of the few reviews for the album comes from *Record World* on 14 May 1977. In the review for *Good News*, they note that the band is composed of 'four seasoned west coast studio musicians' and that they create a 'light, soulful sound, reminiscent, at times, of War. They also make note of the guests: 'Ringo Starr, Tower of Power and Booker T Jones help maintain a crisp groove'. The only other mention of the album could be found in the 7 May 1977 issue of *Billboard*, where the album is listed as a new release.

Once again, there do not seem to be any interviews with band members at the time of release. This seems odd, given the stature of these four musicians. There is also a lack of television and radio appearances. There are no promotional films and the band did not tour or perform live. Perhaps some live appearances and media exposure would have assisted in the album getting some attention. The album failed to make the charts in the UK or North America. It was, for all intents and purposes, ignored.

One look at the Top Ten in America at the time does little in helping to understand why this album failed to strike a chord. The Top Ten for the week the album was released featured: The Eagles (*Hotel California*), Fleetwood Mac (*Rumours*), *A Star is Born* (Soundtrack), Kansas (*Leftoverture*); Jethro Tull (*Songs From the Wood*), Boston (Boston), Marvin Gaye (*Live at the London Palladium*), and Stevie Wonder (*Songs in the Key of Life*). It is not hard to imagine songs from *Good News* being slotted in with these artists, yet radio ignored the album. With little or no radio exposure, the album did not stand a chance.

Warner Brothers assisted Dark Horse in promoting the album. Posters, frisbees, and banners with the slogan, 'Good News is Attitudes', were distributed. But that just didn't seem to be enough. On 13 June 1977, a month after the album was released, Dark Horse re-released 'Sweet Summer Music' as a single, with hopes of continuing the success of the single from the previous year and generating interest in the album.

But a year is a long time and any excitement the previous single gained in 1976 had disappeared in that year. Radio, it is fair to say, has a short memory. In the end, few seemed to care. This includes radio, where there is no evidence of the song receiving much airplay. However, in the 18 June 1977 issue of *Billboard* magazine, the single is listed in the 'Recommended' section of the magazine.

The second and last single to be lifted from the album was 'In a Stranger's Arms', with the album's title track, 'Good News', on the B-side. The single was released in North America on 5 September 1977. It was to be their last single released on Dark Horse Records, and, for now, it marked the end of Attitudes as a band.

Again, *Billboard* did like 'In a Stranger's Arms' and, although they did not review it in their 'Top Singles Picks', they did list the single in the 'Recommended' section of Soul Singles. Although the magazine was (and is) an industry standard, their recommendation of the single did little to help.

In his book, David Foster is honest about the success of Attitudes: 'unfortunately neither of the albums created so much as a ripple'. Given the success of other bands that are formed by studio musicians (Toto comes to mind), the lack of success for these albums is very puzzling. All the right ingredients were there, including two extremely good-sounding albums. There is no reason that these albums did not find an audience with the jazz/middle-of-the-road audience. And yet, for reasons unknown, they did not.

However, it was not the end of Attitudes and Dark Horse. Foster writes in his book, '30 years later, I ran into Harrison's widow, Olivia, and she couldn't stop talking about those recordings. 'We should get those tapes', she said. 'The band was so good. We should dig them up and put them out again. It was really great stuff'. Olivia Harrison was correct in her assessment, and she did follow through with getting some of their music out into the public once again.

In 2018, Foster and Stallworth looked back on the experience with a great deal of fondness. In discussing the band in *Broadwayworld*, they were positive about their time with Dark Horse: 'I didn't realise how great an experience it would end up being for me, how much I would draw on that for my whole life, being with those guys', David Foster said. Paul Stallworth further added, 'We were just four completely different people. As it says in 'Turning in Space', 'Attitudes of the points of view from different points'. We all had four very different attitudes. And, amazingly, they worked together very well'.

All four members of Attitudes went on to bigger things in the music industry. Jim Keltner remained one of the most sought-after drummers in the industry. Along with his recordings with Harrison, he would drum on albums by The Traveling Wilburys, Little Village, Bob Dylan, Neil Young, Ry Cooder and The Pretenders, to name very few. Paul Stallworth would establish himself as an in-demand session musician. His bass can be heard on albums by Harry Nilsson, Ringo Starr, Yvonne Elliman and even fellow Attitudes member Danny Kortchmar. Kortchmar would continue with his own solo music, continue to play with Carole King and perform with such artists as Jackson Browne, Bob Dylan and The Fabulous Thunderbirds. David Foster went on to a successful career as a writer, producer and performer. Although he had success with his own music ('Love Theme From St Elmo's Fire (Instrumental)', he is perhaps best known for his work with Celine Dion, Barbra Streisand, Josh Groban and Chicago. He would also record with Harrison, Starr and McCartney.

Three months following the release of *Good News*, Dark Horse was ready for its next Warner Brothers release. This came in the form of Keni

Burke, former member of the Stairsteps. Although trade ads for the Dark Horse Records label signing with Warner Brothers listed the Stairsteps as one of the bands signed, the band had split up and would not record under that name again.

His self-titled debut album was officially released on 16 August 1977. It came out only in North America. Although it had been mentioned in numerous articles in music magazines in the UK as a future release, it was never issued in the UK. It would seem that Warners UK did not think there was a market for it in that market, especially since *2nd Resurrection* and the singles released from it did so poorly there.

'I had too much creativity to be contained within the confines of a five-man group', Burke stated in an interview with *Cashbox* magazine. 'I would have been lost if I could only have contributed two or three songs to an album'. In the *Cashbox* article, it is noted that Burke came to Dark Horse after Harrison met him through Billy Preston, and Harrison was impressed with the instrumental 'From Me to You'. There is no mention of The Stairsteps having been signed to Dark Horse specifically.

The breakup of The Stairsteps in 1976 is not well documented. Robert Margouleff, who co-produced the album, remembers, 'There was a certain amount of conflict in the band'. The exact nature of the conflict is not specified, but Alvin Taylor, who played drums on the Stairsteps album and Keni Burke's record recalls a lot of issues revolving around money, or lack thereof.

As for Burke going solo, drummer Alvin Taylor was not surprised that he made that move. Taylor worked with The Stairsteps and was impressed with Burke's musical ability. 'Keni Burke, he is the genius of geniuses. He is Curtis Mayfield; he's Sly Stone; he's Jimi Hendrix; he's Paul McCartney, John Lennon, all in one body. He is the most amazing creative creature on the face of the earth'.

Burke also commented that it was important for him to keep the album positive. He is quoted in the *Cashbox* article, 'Well, on this album, I wanted to stay away from getting too heavy with people. I didn't want to talk about anything down. Even my lost love song is to an up-tempo beat. Even when I sing about depressing things, I like to put in a happy vibe because it's not all over; life goes on'. He succeeds on all fronts, as the album is extremely positive.

Billboard, in reviewing the album for 'Top Album Picks', comments that it demonstrated Burke's 'multi-faceted sides' and that he plays 'riveting bass/guitar'. They compare his music to Stevie Wonder and oddly refer to the album as his second solo album, while It is actually his first. For *Billboard*, the standout tracks are 'Give All the Love You Can', 'Shuffle', 'Something New (Like a Sweet Melody)' and 'You Are All Mine'.

Meanwhile, *Cashbox* was very kind with their assessment of the album. They refer to him as a 'tenor vocalist' who plays a 'clean guitar'. They also note that 'if 'From Me to You' doesn't totally knock you out, you need to get your stereo fixed'. High praise indeed. And they do note that it is his debut album.

As for singles, Dark Horse Records released two. The first was a coupling of 'Shuffle' (a song noted by *Billboard* magazine as a 'standout song') with an instrumental on the B-side, 'From Me to You'. This is not a cover of The Beatles' song, but rather an instrumental version of the Stairsteps' hit 'From Us to You'. Once again, *Billboard* magazine listed the single in recommended 'Soul Singles' in their Top Singles Picks.

The second and last single released by *Keni Burke* on Dark Horse Records was 'Keep on Singing', with the instrumental 'Day' on the flip side. It appears to have been released on 30 January 1978 and as with his debut single, *Billboard* magazine listed it in the Top Singles Picks as a recommended 'Soul Single'. Both singles, 'Shuffle' and 'Keep on Singing', failed to make any impact on radio or with the record-buying public, with neither reaching the charts in North America. Both songs deserved much better fates as they are excellent songs and the ideal choices as singles.

George Harrison does not appear on the album, but he does receive a special credit on the sleeve: 'Special thanks to George Harrison and Dennis Morgan for making this album possible'. Bob Cato, who was now overseeing all the art direction of the albums, took the stylish photos and did a fine job with the overall design.

Given that disco was dominating radio and riding high in the charts (Emotions and Commodores were both in the Top Ten album chart the week *Keni Burke* was released), it is somewhat perplexing as to why the album failed to register with record buyers. It didn't get a lot of attention from radio, which resulted in poor sales. As with *Good News*, there is very little press coverage and there is no indication of any live appearances. Even though *Keni Burke* received very strong notices from two industry magazines – *Billboard* and *Cashbox* – Dark Horse Records could not parlay that into radio play and sales.

Keni Burke was the end of Burke's dealings with Harrison and Dark Horse. Burke would continue to make music as a solo artist and as a member of the short-lived band The Invisible Man's Band. He is also a very respected studio musician, working with many classic artists on many classic albums. In the 2000s, some of his solo work became popular to sample. In fact, 'Keep on Singing' was sampled by LB feat. Goburin and Ohral for their song 'Woowee Day'. Later, Burke tried to cash in on his Dark Horse connection when he released a single on Expansion Records in 2011. One look at the single 'So Real' and one would be forgiven for thinking it was a Dark Horse release. The design and colour of the label were very reminiscent of Dark Horse.

This left Splinter as the only other act to transition from the A&M Dark Horse years to the Warner Brothers.

Splinter's second album, *Harder to Live,* had been released in October 1975. Throughout the remainder of that year and much of 1976, the duo worked very hard to promote the album. They also caught the attention of the Japanese market, thanks to a friendship they struck up with Masatoshi Nakamura (who had translated their song 'Lonely Man' into Japanese for the duo to record and release in Japan). This friendship led to other opportunities, including their involvement in the Yamaha World Popular Song Festival, which was performed at Nippon Budokan in Tokyo, Japan. The festival, organised by Yamaha Music Foundation in Tokyo, ran from 1970 until 1989. It was very much like the Eurovision Song Contest and attracted artists such as Celine Dion, Bryan Adams, Bucks Fizz, Erasure, Bonnie Tyler and Cissy Houston. Splinter performed the song 'Love is Not Enough (To Stay Alive)'.

Although Splinter did not win the festival (Franco & Regina from Italy won with their song 'Amore Mio'), their participation and the 'Lonely Man' single helped the band develop a large and loyal following in Japan. Dark Horse and Warner Brothers in Japan released the single 'Love is Not Enough (To Stay Alive)' following the festival. This was Splinter's first product to be released with the new deal with Warner Brothers. Although the single was not released outside of Japan, the song 'Love is Not Enough (To Stay Alive)' would be re-recorded with a different producer in 1977.

On 6 September 1977, a new Splinter single, 'Round and Round' hit the shelves in America. Although they did not review it, *Billboard* lists the single in their 'recommended' of the 'Top Single Picks' in the 10 September 1977 issue. Fans in the UK had to wait almost a month for it to be released on 1 October 1977.

'Round and Round' was not written by either Purvis or Elliott. In fact, the song was written by Parker McGee, who also played on the song. McGee was a very popular songwriter at the time and had written hits for England Dan and John Ford Coley ('I'd Really Love to See You Tonight' and 'Nights Are Forever Without You'). Other artists, such as Seals and Crofts and Tanya Tucker, also recorded his songs. He even had his own solo career, and had his own hit, 'Just Can't Say No To You'. But his music was strictly easy listening, middle-of-the-road, smooth pop music and up until this point, Splinter had written (or co-written) all of their material.

McGee's involvement was Harrison's idea. Harrison also brought in the famed session musician and producer Norbert Putnam to produce the album. Putnam had achieved a great deal of fame and respect for being Elvis Presley's bass player and playing in sessions with artists such as Roy Orbison, Tony Joe White, Ian and Sylvia and The Nitty Gritty Dirt Band. He went on to produce artists such as Jimmy Buffett, Joan Baez, Dan Fogelberg, John Stewart, John Hiatt, The Flying Burrito Brothers and Donovan, to name just a few. It's also worth noting that he (along with David Briggs) built the famous Quadrafonic Studios in Nashville, where Keni Burke remixed his album.

There's no doubt that Harrison wanted this album to be a success. He had been a supporter of Splinter from the very beginning and one could say that it was his love of the band that was the reason he established Dark Horse in the first place. Although Harrison had the best of intentions in asking Putnam to produce, the sessions were not easy and there were some issues between Putnam and the band. Elliott's memory of Putnam was not overly positive. He looked forward to working with Putnam but felt that the producer was not a fan of their music, as Elliott noted in a 2020 conversation with the author: 'He wasn't a striking, appealing character as far as I was concerned. I think also, with having so much success with the whole Elvis thing, I think we weren't looked on as anything other than a George Harrison signing. I don't think he liked our material, actually. But, that's all down to personal taste'.

Bringing McGee and Putnam on board for Splinter's third album demonstrates a few things on Harrison and Dark Horse's part. Firstly, Harrison was still very invested in Splinter and wanted them to have another hit. It appears that he felt responsible for their career and tried to assist them. Secondly, Harrison was aware that the band was not doing well and achieving the success they deserved. He had to have been aware of the record sales for *Harder to Live*. Thirdly, now that Dark Horse Records was with a new record company, Harrison wanted to prove that Dark Horse was a viable label. He was hoping for some of the non-George Harrison releases to have a strong commercial impact. Fourthly, with a reduced roster, Harrison and Dennis Morgan could put more money and time into the individual albums. Also, while Harrison had more of a 'hands-off' approach with *Harder to Live*, he was very involved with *Two Man Band*. Besides acting as 'executive producer', he also played guitar on the album and sang backing vocals. In fact, their first single from the album, 'Round and Round', has a very stylish solo from Harrison. Bob Purvis recalls being there with Harrison when he came up with the solo for the song 'Round and Round'. In 2017, Purvis went so far as to say he 'loved it. Briggs on piano, Argent on synth. I was there when he (George Harrison) composed the lead guitar part for 'Round and Round'.

The single was not well received in the UK. Tim Lott, in *Record Mirror*, states it is 'as stimulating as a cowpat'. Lott even manages to run down Dark Horse Records in the same review. The single did not chart in either the UK or North America. It failed to make an impact on radio or get the album the attention it deserved. By all rights, it should have been a massive hit. Splinter themselves, may not have been fans of the song, but given air time, it should have caught on with pop music fans in 1977. There is no doubt that the song would have been a perfect fit alongside acts such as Electric Light Orchestra, Fleetwood Mac, Stephen Bishop, Rita Coolidge, and James Taylor, all of whom were doing very well on the charts at the time. But, for some strange reason, the single did not get the airplay it deserved.

For the album, Putnam and Harrison pulled together a very strong backing band, including Rod Argent on synthesiser – Argent was, of course, famous for his band Argent and The Zombies. The backing band also featured Putnam on bass, Parker McGee on guitar, George Harrison on guitar and David Briggs on keyboards and the string arrangements. Briggs, a long-time friend and collaborator with Putnam, made his name playing with such artists as Waylon Jennings, Elvis Presley, Dean Martin, The Monkees and Todd Rundgren. He also had a successful solo career in the 1960s and was a member of the band Area Code 615. Finally, included in the band was drummer Kenny Buttrey, who started playing professionally at age 11 for Chet Atkins. He also drummed for Bob Dylan, Bob Seger and was a member of Neil

Young's band, The Stray Gators. Finally, Putnam brought along another Nashville Cat, Steve Gibson, a very popular and in-demand session guitarist who had played on records by Tanya Tucker, Guy Clark, B.J. Thomas and Olivia Newton-John, to name just a few. Harrison and Putnam put together an incredibly strong, talented backing band, most of which came out of Nashville.

Once again, it is worth noting that, aside from Rod Argent and Harrison, this was an American band recording in England. Even though Splinter did not record in America, it is for all intents and purposes, an American album.

Two Man Band was released in October 1977. Of the ten songs on the album, Purvis and Elliott wrote one song together (the opening track, 'Little Girl'), Purvis wrote seven songs, and two were written for the band by Parker McGee – the first single, 'Round and Round', and 'Motions of Love'. Purvis, in his discussion with Tom Brennan, was clear that he did not like this song at all: 'I can't remember anything about 'Motions Of Love'. I disliked the song'. However, 'it would be the second single released in North America. Splinter had not had other writers on their other albums, and they were not pleased. Bill Elliott remembers:

> I think they thought we were drying up material-wise, so they wanted us to sit down and write songs with Parker McGee. I was kind of half and half. I can state this categorically. Bob was not very happy at all, because he is very guarded about his songwriting. At the time, he was having hits with England Dan and John Ford Coley and people like that. I think they thought he was going to be the saving grace. When, in actual fact, they should have just let us carry on acoustically. It was running in a different direction. It is water under the bridge.

Bringing Parker McGee in and having him write 'hit' songs had shades of The Beatles being given 'How Do You Do It' as a surefire hit single after 'Love Me Do' failed to make the Top Ten. Harrison must have had some sympathy for the band.

Purvis, when he spoke to Brennan, was very clear that *Two Man Band* was not the album Splinter wanted to make. For Purvis, the album was a disappointment and he said as much:

> I felt the project was a non-starter. As soon as they said we have two hit songs for you, we had to forget about our own creativity. I only liked a

couple of tracks overall. I had a great song called 'Rush of Daily Life', which had to be sacrificed for the two non-Splinter songs. I lost interest halfway through. I've no idea about the intrinsic stuff – it was taken out of our hands. Everything went wrong – I hated it. We just didn't get it right – we should have had a different feel to the whole album. It was all taken to America (mastering in Nashville). I wasn't happy with the way the LP was mastered. We weren't consulted on anything.

According to Simon Leng, at one point during the sessions, recognising that things were not going well, Harrison suggested that the duo cover 'Don't Let Me Wait Too Long' from Harrison's 1973 album, *Living in the Material World*. The song was intended as a single in 1973, so Harrison obviously felt it had commercial potential. Splinter covering that song would have been interesting, especially with Harrison playing on it.

In 2020, with the ability to look back, Elliott viewed the whole situation with *Two Man Band* in this way:

It wasn't the easiest time. Bob and I were an acoustic duo. We didn't need Elvis Presley's backing band, and we didn't need high-flying producers, and people like that. That's one of the reasons why we did the radio station tour of America. The actual radio jocks loved us; it was just one guitar, singing live in the studio. We have had some amazing, amazing musicians ... but I always preferred to go back to the acoustic roots, always. It was never discussed. We would have, obviously, preferred it, but then again, when you think, at the time, there were a lot of good acts ... there was us, Stealers Wheel, McGuinness Flint.

The band had other complaints about the album. Both agree the front sleeve was terrible. According to Purvis, 'It was done in a studio in London. When we saw the final cover, we shook our heads in disbelief. Worst album cover ever. If we had had a better design, then it may have had a better chance'.

Elliott agrees, 'Didn't like the album cover. Well, it was too much like *Sgt Pepper*. Two guys, standing there in bandsman uniforms, come on, what genius thought of that?' The 'genius' who designed the album sleeve was Bob Cato. Cato had designed the last few Dark Horse releases and was a gifted photographer in his own right. He had the very talented Clive Arrowsmith photograph the album cover.

'Motions of Love' is the second McGee song on the album. When
it was released as a single on 1 February 1978, *Billboard* once again
highlighted it in the 'recommended' of their 'Single Top Picks' section.
Cashbox included it in their 'Singles To Watch' and gave the single a
positive review. They refer to the song as a 'smooth ballad'. They note
the 'uncluttered instrumentation' and note that it has middle-of-the-
road (MOR) or pop radio potential (February 4, 1978). The single sank
without a trace. 'Motions of Love' would be their last single in North
America. It was also the last non-George Harrison Dark Horse Records
single to be released in the territory.

As for Elliott, he does not hate the album. 'I was never drastically
disappointed with any of the recordings we've ever done', he said in
2020. Reviews of the album were not bad, either. *Cashbox* referred to
the band as a 'dynamic duo'. While the review makes note of the session
players, the reviewer is clear that 'focus should rightfully belong to the
pair who sing ... together'. Phillip Hall, in his review for *Record World,*
notices, 'the American influence is felt throughout', but does not give
the album a negative review. He is somewhat cutting about Harrison's
involvement: 'By the way, George Harrison is reputed to play guitar
on the album, but there is nothing here to distinguish him from any
hundred session musicians'.

Sadly, *Two Man Band* repeated the success of *Harder to Live*. Even
the presence of a Beatle was not enough to sell an album. A great deal
had changed since 1974 and a Beatle was no longer as bankable as he
had been. Unlike their debut album, *Two Man Band* did not find an
audience. It failed to chart and it disappeared over time. This is a shame,
as it is a strong album and truthfully, Dark Horse Records and the band
did all they could do to promote it. Posters and paper ads appeared.
Singles were sent to radio stations. Splinter were made available for
radio appearances and they toured. In October 1977, they opened for
The Kinks in the United States. In November, the band opened for Cher
and Greg Allman throughout Europe and the UK. As Elliott points out, '...
we supported The Kinks on three tours. We did part of a tour with Cher
and Greg Allman. Both ends of the spectrum. It was just easy for these
people. We were a good opening act; as far as costs are concerned, we
kept everything down to a minimum'.

If Splinter's December 1977 live broadcast is any indication, their
setlist favoured their then-new album, performing 'Love is Not Enough',
'Silver', and 'Baby Love'. They also played songs from their first album,

including their hit 'Costafine Town' and 'Drink All Day (Got to Find Your Own Way Home)', a song from their second album 'Half Way There' and an obscure Japanese only B-side, 'White Shoe Weather'. According to Elliott, they had their live set down to almost a science: 'Just Bob and I and one guitar and a little bit of harmonica to highlight certain songs', said Elliott. 'That's basically, once again, how we would get the support we need. For us, it was just like a two-minute sound check, 7.30, go on, 45 min spot, and that was it, finished'.

The band also toured in the US in the early part of 1978. By then, any interest in the album was gone. And no amount of touring was going to generate air time on the radio or increase sales of the album. Also, by then, Warner Brothers did not seem quite as invested in the label and in 1978, there was no new music from any other artists on the label. Aside from a couple of singles in North America, there was very little released from Dark Horse. The band have since been very clear that their true artistic vision was never achieved beyond their first album.

Purvis has said, 'Don't get me wrong, I know George was doing what he thought was right and I have always had the highest respect for him. I would have kept our friendship going. We had the wrong producers on the last two albums with Dark Horse. No one really captured the music'.

On 3 March 1978, Splinter released their last single on Dark Horse, 'New York City (Who am I)', only in the UK and Europe. Sadly, the UK did not take any notice of the last non-George Harrison single to be released in the country.

Perhaps by the time *Two Man Band* was released, Dark Horse were trying to make Splinter into something they were not. Dark Horse saw the potential in the band and had a vision for the duo. Splinter, it seemed, wanted to release an album much like that acoustic promo album released in 1974. The truth is Splinter wrote and recorded lovely songs, with lyrics that ranged from nostalgic to romantic but which were always heartfelt and honest. Their three albums with Dark Horse Records have stood the test of time and still sound fantastic.

By 1978, Dark Horse Records had moved on from Splinter. Elliott sums it up very clearly:

We weren't having any commercial success. We were actually the only band that Dark Horse signed that had any kind of commercial success at all. Shankar, Henry McCullough, none of them had success at all. I think George was tired of ploughing money in and getting nothing out.

It was just a natural progression. If records companies cease to make a profit, they don't renew your contract. One minute you are flavour of the month, the next minute, you go off the boil and start to go down a little bit ... if you are not flavour of the month, and you are not selling albums and not having hits, the public loses faith in you.

But by 1978, Splinter were well established and, although they were no longer signed to Dark Horse Records, they continued to make music. They released three more albums, but by 1981, the band called it a day.

However, in 2020, Splinter returned, launching their official website (*www.splinterlegacy.com*). It provided Splinter with the opportunity to tell their story in their words. The website also announced the first Splinter album in 39 years, *Never Went Back*. It was a purely acoustic album from the duo, composed of rehearsal tapes from 1981. It was a wonderful surprise and a brilliant album.

Elliott looks back on the band with a great deal of fondness, 'Bob and I were like two dolphins, swimming alongside each other. We just knew each other's every single move. That's why the sync was spot on; the harmonies were spot on; we didn't have to think ... it was absolutely natural. Because you didn't have anyone else to think about, and it was so simplistic, it just fell into place. It was easy to sing together'.

As for Purvis, he looks back at his time with Dark Horse Records affectionately, especially recording at Friar Park. Splinter never achieved the status they deserved, but it was clearly not due to a lack of trying by Harrison. Purvis noted, 'I just wish I could have let him know that I was grateful and sorry for not seeing what he was trying to do for us. He was an absolutely sincere man'.

Bill Elliott passed away on 6 June 2021.

George Harrison in 1979

On 17 December 1977, two articles of interest appeared in *Cashbox*. The first focused on WEA (which stands for Warner Elektra Atlantic and was the umbrella company of Warner Brothers Records) and changes in the company, naming new people to executive posts. A shake-up in a record company usually means some things are going to change.

Directly below that article, there was a much shorter piece. It announced that 'Warner Drops All Acts on Dark Horse Except For George Harrison'. There is not much more information, but they do note that Attitudes, Keni Burke, Stairsteps and Splinter will no longer be associated with Warner Brothers. There is no other information given.

.Despite this, Splinter and Keni Burke released singles in 1978 from their 1977 albums. None of the singles were successful,and one wonders how much effort Warner Brothers put into the acts and their current singles, knowing that they had now been dropped by the mothership company.

Although the news was harsh to read and may have come as a surprise to the artists on the label, it was not entirely unexpected. Harrison had spent much of his time between 1973 and 1977 working with artists on the label, using his own studio. Although the music produced by these artists, for the most part, was outstanding, outside of very few exceptions, the artists had not become established. While a handful of singles managed to find their way onto the music charts, with two exceptions, the albums had not made a dent.

This had to have been disappointing for Harrison. Although he was clear from the outset that he was not looking to create a huge record company, he also seemed to be building a cottage industry designed to sustain itself. He had his own studio, which could be used, and he had the popularity to have the music made available to a large market. Unlike Apple, Harrison played it very safe with his choice of artists, not expanding too quickly. He also kept the roster small in order to provide attention to the artists and find audiences for their music.

Although, by all accounts, Harrison let the bands get on with their music without interference, he remained very involved. He assisted with the choice of songs to become singles and he offered support and the ability to bring in talented, big names. He did not let the company merely exist; he took a very active role in the records. From the beginning with Splinter and Ravi Shankar until the last non-George

Left and below: George Harrison promoting *33 and* $1/3$ in Paris, France in Europe 1 Studio, February 1977. (*Photos by and courtesy of Jean Helfer*)

Wonderwall Music by George Harrison

Left: *Wonderwall Music,* the first Harrison album released on Apple (1 November 1968). As of February 2023, it is now on Dark Horse Records. (*Dark Horse Records*)

Right: *Electronic Sound* (9 May 1969), originally released on the Apple subsidiary label, Zapple. It is also now on Dark Horse Records. (*Dark Horse Records*)

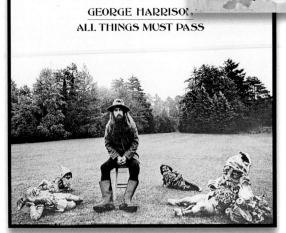

GEORGE HARRISON
ALL THINGS MUST PASS

Left: *All Things Must Pass* (27 November 1970), George Harrison's worldwide number one album. It is now also a Dark Horse album. (*Dark Horse Records*)

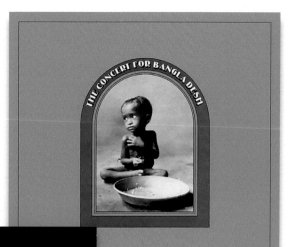

Right: *The Concert For Bangla Desh, released* 20 December 1971. (*Apple*)

Left: *In Concert* by Ravi Shankar and Ali Abkar Khan. Originally released on Apple on 13 April 1973, it is now available on Dark Horse Records. (*Dark Horse Records*)

Right: *Living In The Material World* (30 May 1973). Another number one album re-released on Dark Horse Records in February 2023. (*Dark Horse Records*)

Left: *Dark Horse*. Originally released on Apple on 9 December 1974, it was re-released on Dark Horse Records in 2023. (*Dark Horse Records*)

Right: *Shankar Family & Friends* by Ravi Shanker. The second album released on Dark Horse Records on 20 September 1974. (*Dark Horse Records*)

Left: 'I Am Missing You' single by Ravi Shankar released 13 September 1974. This is the French picture sleeve with its own, unique b-side. (*Photo by Linda Badgley, Dark Horse Records*)

Right: Splinter's debut album, *The Place I Love* released on 20 September 1974 in the UK and five days later in the US. The North American cover has Bob Purvis's index finger removed. (*Photo: Linda Badgley/Dark Horse Records*)

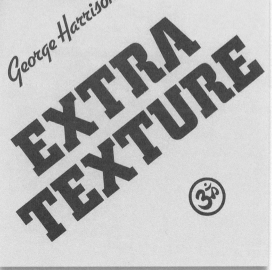

Left: Splinter's 'Costafine Town' US single with picture sleeve, released 7 November 1974. It was their debut single. (*Photo: Linda Badgley/Dark Horse Records*)

Right: *Extra Texture (Read All About It)*. George Harrison's last album on Apple Records (22 September 1975). It has since been reissued on Dark Horse Records. (*Dark Horse Records*)

Above: George Harrison with Ravi Shankar in 1969.

Below: Ravi Shankar pictured in 1965.

Above: Splinter with George Harrison. The photo was taken during the photo session for the front sleeve of *The Place I Love* and was used in the press kit for the album. The photo was taken by Terry O'Neill. (*taken by and courtesy of Jean Helfer*)

Right: Splinter with their producer at F.P.S.H.O.T. studios in November 1973. Note Bill Elliott's t-shirt featuring Ringo Starr's *Ringo* album.

Left: *Jiva* by Jiva on Dark Horse Records, reoleased on 31 October 1975. (*Dark Horse Records*)

Right: Splinter's *Harder To Live*, their second album, released on 24 October 1975. (*Dark Horse Records*)

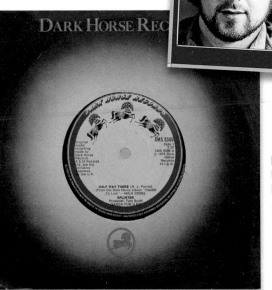

Left: Splinter's 'Half Way There' UK single, released on 21 May 1976. (*Photo by Linda Badgley, Dark Horse Records*)

Right: *Mind Your Own Business* by former Wings and Grease Band member Henry McCullough, released on 24 October 1975. It was his only release on Dark Horse Records. (*Dark Horse Records*)

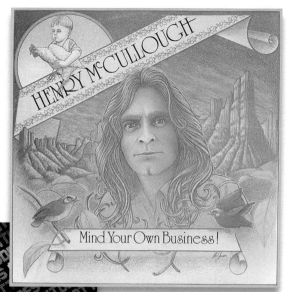

Left: Attitudes' debut album, *Attitudes* released on 19 March 1976. Their first of two for Dark Horse Records. (*Dark Horse Records*)

Right: Attitudes' US single with picture sleeve for 'Ain't Love Enough' released on 3 December, 1975. It was their debut single for Dark Horse Records. (*Photo: Linda Badgley/Dark Horse Records*)

Above: George Harrison with Attitudes during the recording of their debut album in 1975.

Below: Attitudes promotional photograph, used in their press kits. Top left to right, Jim Keltner and Paul Stallworth. Bottom left to right, David Foster and Danny Kortchmar. (*Courtesy of Jean Helfer*)

Left: A Jiva publicity photo from their press kit (*Courtesy Jean Helfer*)

Right: A print ad for Jiva's debut album. (*Courtesy of Jean Helfer*)

Left: *Ravi Shankar's Music Festival From India, released on* 19 March 1976. Produced by George Harrison, it was Shankar's last album for Dark Horse Records. (*Dark Horse Records*)

Right: Stairsteps' only album for Dark Horse Records, *2nd Resurrection,* released on 19 March 1976. (*Dark Horse Records*)

Left: *33 and* ¹/₃. George Harrison's first commercial album for Dark Horse Records, and their first album to be released via their new deal with Warner Brothers on 19 November 1976. (*Dark Horse Records*)

Right: Splinter's last album for Dark Horse Records, *Two Man Band*, released on 7 October 1977. They did not like the front sleeve. (*Dark Horse Records*)

Left: Keni Burke's self-titled solo album *Keni Burke*. It was not released in the UK but was released in North America on 16 August 1977. (*Dark Horse Records*)

Right: Attitudes' *Good News*. Their second and last album for Dark Horse Records, was released on 29 April 1977. This rare alternative sleeve was released for a brief time in the US. (*Photo: Linda Badgley/ Dark Horse Records*)

Left: *George Harrison,* released 20 February 1979. The album did well in Canada and the USA. Less well in the UK. (*Dark Horse Records*)

Right: *Somewhere In England* released on 1 June 1981. It features George Harrison's return to the top five in the US and Canada, with the hit single 'All Those Years Ago', a tribute to John Lennon. (*Dark Horse Records*)

Left: George Harrison's *Gone Troppo,* released on 5 November 1982. Harrison did not promote the album, although it is brilliant and should have been a hit. (*Dark Horse Records*)

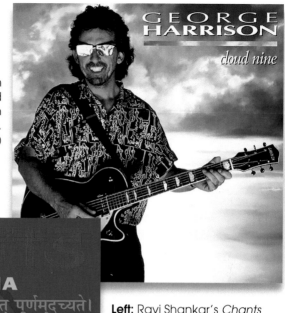

Right: *Cloud Nine,* released on 2 November 1987. It marked Harrison's return to the top ten on both sides of the Atlantic. (*Dark Horse Records*)

Left: Ravi Shankar's *Chants Of India was* released on 06 May 1997. Although produced by Harrison, it was not initially released on Dark Horse Records but found its way onto the label on August 29, 2020. (*Dark Horse Records*)

Right: *Brainwashed* by George Harrison. It was released posthumously on 18 November 2002, after it was completed by Dhani Harrison and Jeff Lynne. (*Dark Horse Records*)

Left: *Collaborations* by Ravi Shankar and George Harrison, released on 18 October 2010. (*Dark Horse Records*)

Right: An advertisement for *33 and 1/3* in *New Musical Express*. (*Photo by Linda Badgley, Dark Horse Records*)

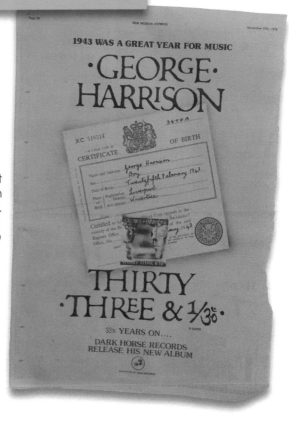

Harrison album (Splinter, *Two Man Band*), Harrison tried very hard to help the artists, sometimes to a fault.

Splinter, for example, were not happy with their third Dark Horse album and, at that time and later on, were very vocal about producers not understanding them and trying to mould them into something they were not. In some regards, this led to conflict between Harrison and the artists he was trying to help. This was their third album and third producer. Other than their debut album, produced by Harrison, they had very little say in the choice of producers and material, but by the time of the third album, that had shrunk to almost nothing.

As Bob Purvis recalled in 2017, when discussing 'Motions of Love': 'I said to George: 'Do you really want us to sing this, are you serious?' I got upset about how we had to get Parker McGee in to save the day. That was a mistake. We had no say in anything, and I wish they had listened to us a bit more instead of treating us like they did and getting producers who weren't right for us'.

By 1978, it seemed to be the end of Dark Horse Records. The label would be an imprint or logo for Harrison's records. It would be almost a further 20 years before Dark Horse released any music not by George Harrison. In 1996, the label partnered with Angel Records to produce the box set, *In Celebration*, by Ravi Shankar. Harrison produced that album for Shankar's 75th birthday.

Warner Brothers dropping all of the Dark Horse artists except Harrison marked the end of an era for the label. To be fair to Warner Brothers, the three non-George Harrison albums failed to register with the record-buying public. Business is business, and Warner Brothers did not want to invest more money and work into something that was not showing any return. While promotion was an issue, it would be unfair to lay the blame entirely at the door of Warners, because Attitudes' *Good News* was actually nicely promoted. It's probable that some of the issues with those three albums lie with the material itself. They are all good albums, but some of the issues may also have been to do with the changing times and finding a marketplace for them. Keni Burke's self-titled album has many fine songs on it, but by 1977, the Rhythm and Blues and Funk genre was changing. The Commodores, The Emotions and Rose Royce were all examples of how the music was evolving and attracting larger audiences. Prince released his debut with *For You* around this time, and artists like Stevie Wonder were able to be part of this change, but other artists, like Keni Burke, did not grow with the times. The songs on his solo album are well-produced and played but do not stand out in the genre's arena. 'From Me To You', which is an instrumental version of The Stairsteps' big hit, has a feel of filler about it.

However, the album has found a small but loyal following. The same can be said for Attitudes. There is no question these four studio musicians could play and were technically fantastic musicians. Their album is full of great songs, but, as with the first album, they did not establish a clear sound. The albums are tonally inconsistent, offering up a mixture of jazz-flavoured instrumentals – rarely a commercial move – and slick pop/soul songs. The Harrisons obviously loved Attitudes, with good reason, but others may not have been so enthused. The music possibly lacked the general appeal to produce hits. Even the addition of Ringo Starr drumming on *Good News* and other musicians (Tower of Power, for example) could not help the album get the attention it needed. As good as the songs are on both of their albums, they had a limited audience.

By 1977, Splinter seemed to have lost their focus, which was not their fault. Working with three different producers on as many albums did not allow them to establish their sound. What if Tom Scott had remained their producer; how would the band have grown? His production for *Harder To Live* seemed to capture the right balance in creating an album of commercial folk-pop music. The truth is that Splinter saw themselves as part of the British 1970s folk scene and felt more comfortable in that format. However, when given more pop-oriented songs, such as 'Round And Round', on their third and final Dark Horse album, which they did not even write, they lost sight of their original goal. As a result, the music is good but not convincing. As with the other two albums, Warners did promote the album, but as good as the songs are (and in some cases, they are outright brilliant), they sounded a little dated by 1977. As with R&B, the singer/songwriter genre was changing by 1977 and Splinter (and their producer) was trying to tap into a mid-1970s style. It just didn't work. The result was an album that failed to attract the attention that it and the duo deserved.

Once Harrison had completed his promotion blitz for *Thirty Three & ¹/₃* in mid-1977, he had the chance to stop and catch his breath. 1978 was both difficult and celebratory for Harrison. His father, Harold Hargreaves Harrison, passed away at the age of 68 on May 3 1978. Harrison was very close to his father, who had joined Harrison on the tour with-Shankar tour in 1974. While mourning the death of his father,

Harrison's girlfriend, Olivia Arias, gave birth to Harrison's first and only child, a son, Dhani Harrison. He was born on 1 August 1978. Harrison would marry Arias on 2 September 1978. They married in a private civil ceremony at Henley-on-Thames registry office.

During all of this turmoil, Harrison continued to write songs, but not with any clear intention of recording. His last studio album, 1976's *Thirty Three & $^{1}/_{3}$*, had been received very positively but did not have the same sales as his previous albums of the early 1970s. In 1978, when Harrison decided to record the follow-up, he made a couple of decisions. The first was that he did not want to produce the album on his own. *Thirty Three & $^{1}/_{3}$* was 'produced by George Harrison, assisted by Tom Scott'. But for all intents and purposes, Scott co-produced the album with Harrison. However, when *George Harrison* was released, there was no mention of Tom Scott. Of course, this could be due to scheduling conflicts, as Scott did work with Harrison on his next album, but it did seem that Harrison was looking for a new sound.

Before he could record, he needed the songs. In an interview with *Rolling Stone* magazine in 1979 to promote *George Harrison*, Harrison admitted: 'all of 1977, I didn't write a song'. He went on to say that he had been 'skiving', which is British slang for avoiding work, for most of the year. He also noted that the record business was starting to get to him. 'Just sick of the whole thing. If you look at the trade papers, everybody's changing companies'.

Later in the interview, he talked about Dark Horse Records and the fact that it had been scaled down to just him: '... that was another reason why 1975 wasn't so good ... why I was so wiped out and it resulted in me saying, 'sod it, I don't want a record company'. I don't mind me being on the label because, all right, I can release an album and it makes some profit, and I don't phone myself in the middle of the night to complain about different things. But artists are never satisfied'.

During a press conference in February 1979 promoting the *George Harrison* album, Harrison repeated his opinion about not running a label: 'Now all I'm interested in is having peace, 'cause all they ever do is ask for your money and phone you all night long, you know'. This sentiment was echoed during a short interview with CBS News, 'I enjoy going home and being with the family'.

Clearly, Harrison was no longer so enthused by working with the artists on his label and he was content to wind down that aspect of Dark Horse. It is also clear that Harrison was somewhat frustrated with, and even resentful of the artists he had signed to Dark Horse. Could it be that he felt a little betrayed? The years 1974 to 1976 did take its toll on him. He was invested in making the label successful and he spent a great deal of time away in Los Angeles trying to sign and establish artists. He did this while maintaining a solo career and dealing with many legal issues, both personal and professional.

But it is interesting that he does not complain about A&M or Warner Brothers, but rather he notes that working with the artists became exhausting. However, it was not all negative for Harrison. He did acknowledge that some very good music came from the label. 'But, nevertheless, there were some good things that came out of it: the Attitudes album, *Good News,* is really good. And I'm happy about the Indian music we did – The Ravi Shankar's *Music Festival From India* and the *Shankar Family & Friends* albums. But generally, the record company was too much of a problem'.

So, he singles out albums made by his friends rather than any of the artists that he signed to the label. It is also odd that he does not mention Splinter, given the amount of work he put into their albums, especially their debut. Perhaps he was still hurting from the falling out he had with Purvis over the third album, *Two Man Band.* But Harrison is clear: from this point, Dark Horse would only exist to release his own music.

By 1978, Harrison had had a break, probably his first proper break from everything in his career. For the most part, 1977 and 1978 allowed Harrison to dabble in his hobbies, such as gardening and F1 racing. But losing his father and becoming a father himself and a husband (for the second time) also prompted Harrison to look to the past and appreciate it more than he had previously.

Of course, Harrison was not completely absent from the pop world during 1978. He helped out fellow Beatle, Ringo Starr, with Ringo's 1978 television special, *Ringo,* a television show to promote his album, *Bad Boy.* Harrison also appeared in the film, *All You Need is Cash*, a brilliant parody of The Beatles from his friend (and member of *Monty Python's Flying Circus*) Eric Idle, a mockumentary about the fictitious band The Rutles.

When it came time to complete the writing of *George Harrison,* author Eliot J. Huntley notes in his book *Mystical One: George Harrison – After the Break-up of the Beatles* that Harrison reportedly listened to *All Things Must Pass* for inspiration. Harrison also looked to The Beatles and revived 'Not Guilty', a song written for *The Beatles* (aka *The White Album*). It was actually recorded by The Beatles and finally released by them on *The*

Beatles Anthology 3. But in 1978/1979, the song was the 'Holy Grail'. Fans had read about it, but few had ever heard the song. Harrison very kindly (and smartly) recorded it for *George Harrison*. And he also revisited his classic, 'Here Comes the Sun'. Here, he created the sequel (of sorts) with 'Here Comes the Moon'. 'I wrote the song and it turned out really nice, so it stands up in its own right', Harrison said in 1979.

In 1978, Harrison demoed a number of songs, some of which would be recorded for *George Harrison*. The presence of a producer would take some pressure off him and allow him to do what he did best: write the songs. Also, a producer would help him sort through his material and record the best tracks available.

He approached Warner Brothers, and three names were proposed: Ted Templeman, Larry Waronker and Russ Titelman. 'I decided I'd work with Russ Titelman. He did the first Little Feat album, and with Lenny Waronker, he co-produced Randy Newman, James Taylor and Ry Cooder. And he's a nice, easy person to get along with'. In the same interview, he pointed out that Titelman '... helped me decide what sort of tunes to use, encouraged me to actually finish certain songs and helped lay down the tracks'. Once again, his co-producer was American and Harrison name-checked American artists he liked. He seemed to be more enthused about such artists and perhaps was looking to have an album that would fit into the musical climate and market of that country.

Harrison and Titelman assembled a great backing band at Friar Park Studios. Harrison had some familiar faces: Andy Newmark on drums, Willie Weeks on bass, Emil Richards on marimba, Eric Clapton on guitar and Gary Wright on Oberheim synth. But there were some new faces to Harrison as well, many of them British, such as Neil Larsen (Minimoog, Fender Rhodes and piano), Gayle Levant (harp), Steve Winwood (Polymoog, harmonium, backing vocals), Del Newman (string and horn arrangements, who had worked with Elton John and Cat Stevens to name just two and played a large role in Harrison's life, professionally and personally) and Ray Cooper (percussion).

Strings recorded at AIR Studios, which was owned by old friend and mentor George Martin and recording took place between March and November 1978, and the first single from the first new album, 'Blow Away', was released on 4 February 1979 in North America and ten days later in the UK. A promotional film was also released on television.

The promotional film for 'Blow Away' was directed by Neil Innes (Ron Nasty of The Rutles). It is an amusing film, with Harrison showing his fancy footwork and some very whimsical scenes, including Harrison alongside large toys (such as a duck, toy swan, and dog). It is fun and it demonstrates Harrison's unusual sense of humour.

It had been three years since Harrison's last album and a lot had changed in that time. Disco was still a force, punk was morphing into different genres, and new wave was starting to make inroads on radio. Artists such as Blondie and Ian Dury were top of the charts in the UK, while Rod Stewart and The Village People were doing the same in the US. However, Harrison's favourite, Nicolette Larson, was sitting at number ten with 'Lotta Love'. The question is: where would Harrison and his music fit in 1979?

Billboard was very positive about the single and its chances of being a hit, saying at the time that they '..find the ex-Beatle in top form vocally and lyrically' while noting that his 'guitar paces the cut' and the song has a 'catchy melody'. They were quite correct. The song has hooks, a strong melody and is very positive. But the single did not perform as hoped in the UK, where it peaked at number 51, but it was a Top Ten in Canada, reaching number seven. And it made the Top 20 in the US.

On 14 February 1979, Dark Horse Records released the album in the USA. It was released two days later in the UK. *Billboard* raved about the album, referring to Harrison as a 'consistently top-selling album act'. It was the 'spotlight' album that week in *Billboard*'s Top Album Picks. They are very complimentary of the 'top-notch session musicians' and said the album contained music that 'continues the somewhat lighter, less serious mood'. They single out 'Love Comes to Everyone' as being a highlight. *Cashbox* agreed, referring to the album as 'assured (and) polished' with 'understated acoustic ballads and light rockers'. They refer to his vocals as 'fluid and expressive'. While referring to the 'all-star cast', it is Harrison's 'own singing and his ten compositions that make the LP a winner'.

Stephen Holden, in *Rolling Stone*, wrote that *George Harrison* was his best work since *All Things Must Pass*. In the UK, some critics were favourable, such as E. J. Thribb (clearly a pseudonym for another writer, possibly Barry Fantoni or even Peter Cook) in *Melody Maker*. He wrote a very kind review and commented on the album's lightheartedness. In the *New Musical Express* (*NME*), Harry George went so far as to compare the album to Dylan's *New Morning* and Van Morrison's *Tupelo Honey*. Of course, not all reviews were positive. *Smash Hits* in the UK gave it six out of ten, and *People* magazine were not overly kind in their assessment of the album.

In terms of promotion, Harrison did not do as much as he did for *Thirty Three & ¹/₃*. There was the promo film for for 'Blow Away', a press conference in Los Angeles, appeared on Jim Ladd's syndicated radio show, *Innerview*, did an interview with *Rolling Stone* and a radio 'Round Table' for the BBC with radio presenter David 'Kid' Jensen. During the show, Harrison freely admits, 'To tell you the truth, I've no idea what is a hit and what isn't a hit these days'.

The album did well, peaking at number 14 in the US on the 28 April 1979 *Billboard* Top 200 Charts. In Canada, it reached the same peak of 14 on the national R.P.M. charts. In both countries, The Doobie Brothers were at number one. This also marked the second time since *Extra Texture (Read All About It)* that Harrison could not crack the Top Ten. In the UK, the album fared worse, peaking at a low 39. However, it did achieve Gold status in the US (meaning it sold over 500,000 copies) and, in the 2000s, found a whole new audience, becoming one of Harrison's most popular solo outings.

The album deserved a much better fate. In a just world, it would have made number one; it certainly was full of strong songs, good melodies and beautiful lyrics. As with *Thirty Three & ¹/₃*, *George Harrison* has an overall optimistic vibe. Harrison wanted a positive feel and commented on Jim Ladd's show, 'it felt very positive in the late 60s, and then it just disappeared. I don't know where it got to...' Harrison was also aware of the pressure of having a hit album or single: the 'Concept of success is ringing up the cash register perpetually; if you are not a success, if your records don't get into the Top 20, you are not a success. That is true as far as the music business goes'.

Once the album was released, and 'Blow Away' began its decline down the charts, Dark Horse Records and Warner Brothers felt a second single was necessary. It would, in theory, breathe new life into the album. 'Love Comes to Everyone' was chosen in the spring of 1979, but failed to chart. As noted, 'Love Comes to Everyone' was a song that many critics cited as being an obvious single. *Billboard* agreed, listing it in their 'Top Singles Picks' on 26 May 1979 in the 'Recommended' section, although there was no accompanying review.

Cashbox went one step further, reviewing the single in their 'Singles Reviews'. The writer of the review states: 'Harrison's soothingly melodic follow-up to 'Blow Away'. Electric piano blends in perfectly with tambourine and a nicely mixed synthesiser. Harrison's vocals are top notch and the inspirational message of the lyrics will surely appeal to Top 40 and A/C stations'. In May, *Cashbox* listed George Harrison in the Top Ten of FM Rotation. It looked like a surefire hit. But the single failed to chart with the one exception of *Billboard*'s Adult Contemporary charts in the US, where it peaked at 38.

A third and final single from *George Harrison* would be released in Europe. 'Faster' was released in the UK on 30 July 1979. The proceeds of the single went to the Gunnar Nilsson Cancer Fund. A promotional film was also released using footage Harrison shot at The Brazilian Grand Prix in San Paulo in February 1979. Other footage was later shot with racing driver Jackie Stewart in Monaco following the Monaco Grand Prix. The 'Faster' promotional film was directed by Harrison himself, but sadly, the single failed to chart.

As with 'Love Comes to Everyone', 'Faster' deserved to be a hit and, in later years, gained favour with fans. But these singles may have suffered due to Harrison not keeping up with trends. Harrison was not willing to 'play the game'. He was not a fan of disco or punk and made the decision not to jump fads as Rod Stewart had. He wanted to create his own music. As he said to Jim Ladd: 'In the 70s, it was one fad after another, nothing long-lasting. People probably thought it was a fad for me, too, Indian music, India, the spiritual thing. But I'll tell you, that is stronger for me than it ever was. The first Indian raga I heard, I can play that tune today and I can enjoy it twice as much as I did in 1965'.

Collectors should take note that it is quite fun collecting the singles from this album, as B-sides differ from place to place around the world and the promo copies (which feature mono mixes) are always fun to try to track down as well.

As Harrison entered the 1980s, his focus went from his record company to a new fledging film company. His goal was not a number-one album, although that would have been nice. Harrison had other questions to answer, especially given the last half of the decade. During the interview with Jim Ladd, he said he was interested in 'the purpose of life, who am I, what are we doing here?' That question would continue to be present in his work throughout the next decade.

George Harrison – The Later Dark Horse Albums

Harrison entered the new decade with a continued interest in recording and making music. But he also had another project that was beginning to take up a great deal of his time. Harrison had become the owner of a film studio, HandMade Films. The name, Handmade Films, is typical of Harrison's humour and his memory and love of nostalgia. 'The name of the company came about as a bit of a joke. I'd been to Wookey Hole in Somerset ... [near] an old paper mill where they show you how to make old underpants into paper. So I bought a few rolls, and they had this watermark, 'British Handmade Paper' ... So we said ... we'll call it Handmade Films'.

Harrison became involved with filmmaking due to *Monty Python's Flying Circus*. Harrison had been a fan since the show debuted on British Television in 1969. He was quoted in the *Monty Python's Flying Circus* autobiography about the spirit of The Beatles being passed on to *Python*, as the comedy group was starting up as The Beatles were ending. There is something to that, though, as the troupe did for comedy what The Beatles did for music. In fact, Harrison sent a congratulatory letter to The Pythons via the BBC following the debut of the show, and McCartney was known to stop recording when *Monty Python* was on television.

Terry Gilliam of *Monty Python* noted that:

George was always convinced that the spirit of the Beatles went into the Pythons. The year they broke up was the year we came together – 1969. George was our patron. When Bernie Delfont read the script of *Life of Brian* and pronounced it blasphemous, just as we were getting on the plane to film in Tunisia, he rescued it. After that, we formed HandMade Films and produced *Time Bandits,* which is still the most famous film we've done.

The topic of HandMade films is a book in itself, and although Harrison had once said that Dark Horse Records would release soundtracks (they never did), HandMade Films and Dark Horse Records were two very separate entities. Although the offices for HandMade films were initially in Dark Horse's London office in Cadogan Square, Ray Cooper remembers, in speaking with author Robert Sellers in his book about

Handmade Films, *Always Look on the Bright Side of Life: The Inside Story of HandMade Films*: 'The office was Dark Horse Records and all that sort of stuff and HandMade squeezed in'. Terry Gilliam added, 'Handmade got bigger; suddenly Dark Horse was getting smaller and George's little bit of the office'.

The fact that Dark Horse Records never released soundtracks seemed like a lost opportunity for the label. Several of the HandMade films had soundtracks, but none appeared on Dark Horse Records. Warner Brothers released the soundtrack of *Life of Brian* (titled *Monty Python's Life of Brian*), which charted in the UK and Australia. It would have been a great bonus for Dark Horse to have had that album released with the Dark Horse logo.

Although from 1979 until 1989, the film company kept Harrison busy. But it did not mean Harrison was done with music, far from it. With the release of *George Harrison* in 1979, it seemed that Harrison was once again in the spotlight. It made sense then that he would go back to the studio. In March 1980, he did just that; he started recording what would become his third album for Dark Horse Records, *Somewhere in England*, although some of the songs had been written for his *George Harrison* album and some recording was done in 1978 ('Flying Hour' for example). He assembled a brilliant backing band, which included old friends Jim Keltner (drums), Willie Weeks (bass), Neil Larson (keyboards and synthesisers), Tom Scott (lyricon and horns), and Alla Rakha (tabla). And there were newer friends, such as Procol Harum's Gary Brooker (keyboards and synthesisers), Ray Cooper (keyboards, synthesisers, percussion, drums), Dave Mattacks (drums), Herbie Flowers (tuba, bass), Mike Moran (keyboards and synthesisers) and Al Kooper (keyboards and synthesisers).

The album was recorded at Friar Park, with old friend Phil McDonald engineering. McDonald, of course, had worked on several Harrison albums, as well as recordings by solo Beatles, The Beatles and other Apple artists. Harrison worked on the record throughout 1980 and presented it to Warner Brothers in September of that year, although the content was much less optimistic than the last two by Harrison. It had a darker edge to it, tied in with more material about spirituality than previous offerings. The sleeve was also somewhat darker, with the map of England seemingly emerging from Harrison's head.

Then the unthinkable happened: Warner Brothers rejected the album. They felt that there were no obvious hits and that the album was too mellow for the current marketplace. They asked him to remove songs, add new ones, and change the album cover. One supposes that, although his first two albums for Dark Horse's new partner, Warner Brothers, had done well, especially in North America, they did not meet sales expectations, especially in international markets.

The original album, which made it as far as test pressings (and then into the hands of bootleggers everywhere) was a ten-track album, and from all indications, produced by Harrison. Four of those songs were to be removed, and Harrison was to provide four new songs that were more in keeping with the time. The four songs identified to leave were 'Flying Hour' (a song he wrote with Bad Company guitarist Mick Ralphs), 'Lay His Head', 'Sat Singing' and 'Tears of the World'. He was asked (or ordered) to remix the remaining songs to give them a more 'contemporary' feel. Although *Somewhere in England* was scheduled for release in 1980, it did not make it out onto record store shelves until June 1981.

The songs selected to be excised from the album are somewhat puzzling, as they are all quite good and are, in some respects, lost gems. The four songs cut from the album would be released in various methods over the years.

Harrison returned to F.P.S.H.O.T. to reassess the album and record new tracks while remixing the surviving songs. He also reached out to a trusted friend to help him. Ray Cooper recalls, 'George rang me and said he needed some help producing his next album, *Somewhere in England*. So, I co-produced the recut version, which really involved the recording of about four alternative tracks'.

One can only imagine the impact of having an album rejected on Harrison. He had not self-produced an album since 1975's *Extra Texture (Read All About It)*, and when he does, the album gets returned for an upgrade. Harrison, who since 1975 had not played the 'rock star' game, just wanting to make his own music, must have been very frustrated with this turn of events. Warner Brothers had already dropped the other Dark Horse artists, and now they were rejecting his own albums.

For the new tracks, Harrison recruited Dave Mattacks (drums), Herbie Flowers (bass) and Mike Moran (keyboards). With Cooper and Harrison producing, Harrison responded with three very pointed songs; the most obvious song was 'Blood From a Clone', a song that surprisingly made the cut by Warner Brothers and opened the album. Perhaps the executives at Warner Brothers were not listening as Harrison, very clearly and quite angrily, pointed a finger at the record company for not being interested in music but more concerned with the marketplace. It is a clever, sometimes very funny song that has the feel of catharsis for it's composer. The song has feels like a ska/new wave song that sounded very contemporary. Harrison was obviously aware of the music being made at the time; he simply wasn't interested in that style for himself. But, here, he uses the current fads to make fun of the current fads.

While promoting *Cloud Nine* in 1987, Harrison commented on the song:

> Yeah, 'cause that was all the stuff they were telling me: 'Well, we like it, but we don't really hear a single' and then other people saying, 'now, look, radio stations are having all these polls done in the street to find out what constitutes a hit single and they've decided a hit single is a song of love gained or lost directed at 14 to 20-year-olds'. And I thought, 'Shit, what chance does that give me?' So anyway, I went in and wrote the song just to shed some of the frustrations.

Harrison was also helping out his old bandmate, Ringo Starr, with an album he was recording in 1980. One of the songs he wrote for Starr, 'All Those Years Ago', didn't suit Ringo's vocal range, so author Robert Rodriguez notes in his book, *Fab Four FAQ 2.0: The Beatles' Solo Years, 1970 – 1980,* after recording the backing track with Harrison, that Starr passed on it, claiming the song was too high for him to sing. He also did not like the original lyrics, so Harrison kept the track for future use.

On 8 December 1980, everything changed for the world and for Harrison. Harrison woke to the news that John Lennon had been assassinated the night before in New York City. Harrison released a prepared comment to the media:

> After all we went through together, I had and still have great love and respect for him. I am shocked and stunned. To rob a life is the ultimate robbery in life. The perpetual encroachment on other people's space is taken to the limit with the use of a gun. It is an outrage that people can take other people's lives when they obviously haven't got their own lives in order.

Beyond his comment to the press, Harrison also responded by rewriting the lyrics of 'All Those Years Ago', turning it into a tribute to Lennon, and using the backing track, which featured Ringo, to record his own version. He also enlisted Al Kooper, who provided the electric piano, while Harrison played guitar, synthesiser, organ and lead and backing vocals. He also received some help from McCartney, his wife Linda and Wings member Denny Laine, who provided backing vocals to the song. According to Chip Madinger & Mark Easter in their book, *Eight Arms To Hold You: The Solo Beatles Compendium.*, McCartney had gone to Friar Park with George Martin in order for Harrison to provide a guitar solo for 'Wanderlust', a song from McCartney's 1982 album, *Tug Of War.* Harrison did not play on 'Wanderlust', but the McCartneys and Laine did sing on 'All Those Years Ago'. It was the first time the three Beatles (Harrison, Starr, and McCartney) had appeared together on a song since 'I Me Mine' in 1970. It was a brilliant, honest and loving tribute to his friend, John.

Harrison delivered a new version of *Somewhere in England* to Warner Brothers in early 1981. This version included a new cover design, courtesy of Ray Cooper, featuring a picture of Harrison in front of Mark Boyle's 'Holland Park Avenue Study' (1967). The photo was taken by Caroline Irwin. Gone was the original sleeve by photographer Basil Pao (who, ironically, had provided a great many sleeves for Warner Brothers). The new sleeve was brighter and more inviting.

Warner Brothers accepted the new version and prepared to release it on 1 June 1981 in North America and 5 June 1981 in the UK and Europe. The first single released from the album was the Lennon tribute, 'All Those Years Ago'. This time, it featured the same B-side around the world, another album cut, 'Writings on the Wall'. It was released with a picture sleeve that was a variant of the album cover of *Somewhere in England*. The single was released worldwide in May 1981.

When *Billboard* reviewed the single in the 16 May 1981 issue, they made no mention of 'All Those Years Ago' being a tribute to Lennon. Instead, they focused on McCartney and Starr being on the single and described the song as 'light' and 'frolicsome'. They further noted that the hook is 'very infectious' and that it is 'bound to be an immediate hit'. *Cashbox*, on 16 May 1981, listed it in the 'Hits Out of the Box' section.

It proved to be Harrison's biggest hit since 'Give Me Love (Give Me Peace on Earth)', peaking at number two on the American *Billboard* Top 100 Singles Chart. Kim Carnes' 'Bette Davis Eyes' kept it from number one for three weeks. However, it did make it to number one on *Billboard*'s Adult Contemporary charts. While in the UK, when it peaked at number thirteen, number one was Adam and the Ants' 'Stand and Deliver'.

With the single tearing up the charts, a video was necessary, which were not only commonplace by 1981 but essential to ensure the success of a single. A video was prepared by Warner Brothers using Beatle footage, and it appears that Harrison had little, if anything, to do with it. In fact, according to Chip Madinger and Mark Easter, the video was put together by Ron Furmanek for Warner Brothers. He used items from his own collection in the video. This is interesting, given that The Beatles pioneered promotional films and, up until 'Love Comes to Everyone', Harrison embraced the practice. Nevertheless, 'All Those Years Ago' became a very popular video and went into heavy rotation when MTV debuted it on 1 August 1981

Somewhere in England received some very good reviews. *Billboard*'s review of the album highlighted the single 'All Those Years Ago' but added that there are '... additional treats such as his cover of Hoagy Carmicheal's 'Hong Kong Blues' and 'Baltimore Oriole''. The review also noted that some of Harrison's own songs are 'very polished' and other ones are 'very spiritual', such as 'Life Itself'. They also highlight the 'superb playing from a cast of stellar players including Gary Brooker, Tom Scott and Jim Keltner'.

Cashbox refers to Harrison as the most 'reserved and spiritually conscious' of all The Beatles and states the album is another 'subtle and introspective' album. They compliment the backing musicians and credit Ray Cooper for his production. The reviewer refers to the album as 'the latest subdued renderings' from Harrison (whom they refer to as 'one of rock's most loved figures'). They identify the wacky 'Blood From a Clone' and 'Life Itself' as highlights. *Billboard* had singled out 'Life Itself' as well.

While *Rolling Stone* was far from kind, Harry Thomas had a few positive things to say about the album but mainly remained somewhat ambivalent, with a leaning toward downright negative. He admits that Harrison can write incredible tunes, but often, the dour lyrical content does not match the music. Further, he adds, 'Throughout *Somewhere in England*, he's apt to throttle an attractive melody with mouthfuls of excess verbiage or stretch a word several syllables out of recognition to meet the demands of a tune'. He sums up his review with the non-committal 'As it stands, *Somewhere in England* is neither here nor there'.

One of the main problems at the time was that Harrison flat outright refused to do any promotion or interviews for the album. It is understandable, given the circumstances of 8 December 1980, but one cannot help but wonder how the album would have been received if Harrison was able to contextualise the album via interviews. Also, the lack of music videos or presence in the music world did not help the album in terms of sales or reception. There was a backlash; if he is not going to make himself available, we are not playing the album. While 'All Those Years Ago' achieved a great deal of airplay, the rest of the album did not. The album peaked on *Billboard*'s Top 200 album charts at number 11 on 11 July 1981. Although the album did very well on the album charts, peaking just outside of the Top Ten, it did not achieve gold status, his first album not to go gold since *Electronic Sound*. In England, the album peaked at number 13.

While the album was at its peak, Dark Horse Records and Warner Brothers released the second single from the album, 'Teardrops', which was well-reviewed by radio and record insiders. *Billboard* magazine gave it a favourable notice, referring to it as a 'lifting midtempo tune'. *Record World*, in its 1 August 1981 issue, listed it as the top single on 'Hits of The Week', noting that the 'mellifluous keyboards and a resounding title chorus' make it a 'natural for pop radio'. And yet, the single missed the charts, peaking at 102 on *Billboard*. Perhaps the lack of a video or other media exposure killed it. By 1981, it was not good enough to simply release a brilliant song as a single. One had to promote it rigorously.

But one year later, Harrison returned with a new album and single. On 27 October 1982, George Harrison released a new single, 'Wake Up My Love', and an album, *Gone Troppo*. It saw Harrison turning to synthesisers and keyboards for a slightly different sound. Working with Ray Cooper and Phil McDonald as co-producers, Harrison seemed interested in trying new styles and sounds. Harrison had not released albums one year apart since 1975 – 1976.

Cashbox referred to 'Wake Up My Love' as a 'colourful cut' while noting that Harrison 'rouses his love with one of his most aggressive pop productions', giving credit to Ray Cooper's percussion and Henry Spenitti's drumming and use of hi-hat. Harrison's single was not the spotlight single (it was a feature pick); in the same issue and section of 'News and Reviews', Yoko Ono was given the spotlight with her single 'My Man' (Polydor). It is also interesting that they do not suggest that 'Wake Up My Love' has hit potential, as they had with previous Harrison singles.

Upon release, the single was added to a number of radio stations in America. In the 5 November 1982 issue of *Radio and Records*, a half-page advertisement from Dark Horse Records lists 26 radio stations that had added the single in the first week. But the single did not do well, peaking on *Billboard*'s Top 100 at number 53 on 4 December 1982. It failed to chart in England or Europe. Once again, Harrison refused to promote the single in any way. No interviews, no video, no personal appearances, nothing. There were print ads, but Harrison would not assist in promotion. Although it was a good song, it still needed a push to get airtime and sell singles. There was no picture sleeve for it in North America or England (although there are many sleeves throughout the world that are quite nicely done), and it sadly did not achieve the chart status the quality of the record deserved.

Harrison began recording *Gone Troppo* on 5 May 1982. Once again, Harrison assembled old friends (Billy Preston, Jim Keltner, Willie Weeks, Ray Cooper, Neil Larson) and some new friends (Herbie Flowers, Dave Mattacks, Alan Jones, Jon Lord, Gary Brooker, Mike Moran, Joe Brown), a number of backing singers (Willie Greene, Bobby King, Vicki Brown, Pico Pena) and three singers who performed with Preston, all recording stars/artists in their own right (Syreeta, Sarah Ricor and Rodina Sloan). He enlisted the help of Phil McDonald, who not only was the recording engineer but was noted as a co-producer and Ray Cooper, who was the other producer. At this point, Harrison trusted Cooper and looked to him for sound advice. Cooper was now also appointed Head of Development and Production for Handmade Films.

The album was released in North America on 27 October 1982 and on 9 November in the UK. The front cover was designed by former Bonzo Dog Do-Dah Band member 'Legs' Larry Smith. Legs had been immortalised in a song on Harrison's *Extra Texture (Read All About It)* album with the closing track, 'His Name is Legs (Ladies and Gentlemen)', on which he also guested. *Gone Troppo* was the first album by Harrison on Dark Horse Records to be released in the then-new format, QUIEX II, which was used for promotional albums. The idea was that the vinyl was thicker and heavier than stock albums one would buy in the store; thus, the sound was better – a product for the audiophile of the time. And for the most part, they did sound better. Warner Brothers used this format a great deal in the 1980s, and *Gone Troppo* was one they must have felt would benefit.

Upon release, *Cashbox* gave the album a very good review, commenting that Harrison 'Delivers one of his most delightful albums in years'. The reviewer goes on to identify the title track as 'especially appealing' and the title track being 'calypso flavoured, which refers to hanging out in the tropics'. Finally, they sum up the review with the observation that *Gone Troppo* is 'possibly Harrison's best release since 1977's *Thirty Three & ¹/₃*. In *Billboard*, they compare his music with Ry Cooder, pointing out Harrison's sunny lyricism and, as with *Cashbox*, they identify the title track as a highlight with its 'playful island mood'.

Rolling Stone was very harsh with their review of the album, referring to it as being 'So offhand and breezy as to be utterly insubstantial', and that 'the LP is made up of throwaway ditties, instrumental fragments and formulaic love songs'. The author, Steve Pond, goes on to write that, 'Tired of battling the temptations of the material world, Harrison sings about hanging out in the tropics (hence the title). But with the exception of the jaunty 'Wake Up My Love', writing (a) good song clearly wasn't on George's agenda'.

For the record, 'Gone troppo' is an Australian slang term for 'going crazy'. It is common knowledge that it comes from 'stories of the tropical heat in the northern parts of Australia driving people crazy'. Harrison had spent a great deal of time in Australia and, given the circumstances of the last five years, there is no doubt he felt he was 'going troppo'.

When the album was released, it did not do well. It failed to reach the charts in the UK and peaked at 108 on the *Billboard* charts. In America, while *Gone Troppo* was struggling at number 108, number one was held by an Australian band, Men at Work (*Business as Usual*). One can only hope that the irony was not lost on Harrison. A follow-up single, 'I Really Love You', was released and failed to chart.

The single was ignored by radio, magazines and record buyers. On a personal note, the College Radio Station (located in Toronto, Ontario, Canada) in which I worked, played the record quite a bit and it did make the Top Ten of Centennial College's playlist. But other than some college/university radio play, the single did not help to promote the album. By the time the single was released, *Gone Troppo* was off the charts for good. Again, one wonders: if a video had been released alongside the single, would there have been a difference? Harrison did not do any promotion, just as he had not promoted the album.

Gone Troppo was the last album for George Harrison for five years, although no one knew it at the time. Warner Brothers was well aware that times had changed since the 1960s and 1970s. A great album and fantastic commercial songs were no longer enough. America changed the game considerably with the invention of MTV. While music videos (or promo films) had been around since the 1950s, and The Beatles

145

changed them in the 1960s, artists such as Harrison could not predict or know how much influence such promotional vehicles would have on the buying public. For all intents and purposes, if the video is not on MTV, the song did not exist. A simple look at the Top Ten in 1983, any week, one will see that every song in the Top Ten had an accompanying video. It stayed that way for the next three decades.

Perhaps it was more that Harrison had to learn the new business model of the recording business rather than him not wanting to promote an album. A number of artists from the 1960s and even the 1970s were being forced to deal with the music business very differently by the early 1980s. One simply looks at McCartney, who, in 1982, scored two top ten singles from his *Tug of War* album (which also made number one), with one of the singles ('Ebony and Ivory') making it to number one. While *Tug of War* is a great album, *Gone Troppo* is, in every way, its equal. The difference was that the record-buying public was well aware of McCartney's album, while many people were not aware of Harrison's album.

This is by no means meant to put the blame on Harrison and Dark Horse Records. But, in all honesty, Dark Horse Records seemed to matter less and less to Harrison. His time was now being occupied by gardening and movies. And while he was not out of touch musically, he was not up to date on the way records were marketed in the 1980s.

Cloud Nine

From February 1983 until November 1987, Dark Horse Records were relatively quiet. While George Harrison albums remained in print and were still available, Dark Horse was a shadow of its former self. However, Harrison was keeping quite busy with other projects. A 'five-year hiatus' makes for great press, especially when he launched his comeback in 1987 with one of the most successful albums in his career, but he was no recluse.

After *Gone Troppo*, Harrison focused on other activities, such as HandMade Films. From 1983, starting with the film *Bullshot*, until the end of 1987 (with the release of *The Lonely Passion of Judith Hearn*), HandMade Films produced and released eight films, two of which Harrison was quite involved in. He was still making music, but this time, however, it was all on his own terms. He worked with friends and contributed, albeit, in the background. This would include concert appearances with Deep Purple and other shows.

During 1984 and 1985, Harrison continued to write and demo songs. Harrison actually released one single, 'I Don't Want to Do It', a song written by Bob Dylan in March 1985. The song was recorded for a film (*Porky's Revenge*) and was not released on Dark Horse but rather on Columbia Records. It failed to chart.

Next up for Harrison was work on a film for HandMade named *Shanghai Surprise*. Harrison agreed to score the film and write and perform songs for it. Harrison ended up collaborating with Michael Kamen and composed and performed five songs, including the title track. He even had a very small role as the band leader in the club.

Fans must have been excited to see that in the credits, it is noted, 'Soundtrack available on Dark Horse Records and Tapes', as the songs featured in the film were the first new Harrison compositions since 1982's *Gone Troppo*. Even more importantly, the songs were the best part of the film, while the score was also excellent. A soundtrack album featuring the songs and score would be welcomed by fans and a single featuring the title track, 'Shanghai Surprise', was even prepared and a very small number of promotional copies were sent out to select radio stations. The songs and score were all registered with BMI Music on 17 December 1986. Music titled '12 Bar Bali' and 'Shanghai Surprise 1', are all copyrighted.

The only problem was that the film, which starred Madonna and then-husband Sean Penn, was not well received, was crucified by critics, having become nothing more than tabloid fodder during its making. Once the film died a quick and painful death at the box office, all thoughts of a soundtrack album and single went out the window and the album was pulled from all media listings. This is a pity because there have been examples of films not doing well, but the soundtracks finding an audience and Harrison came up with incredible and diverse songs for the film.

Thankfully, over the years, all of the songs have been released in re-recorded or remixed form. The score music has not been released, despite being, for the most part, recorded at Abbey Road Studios, making it the first time Harrison worked there since 1970. Harrison kept busy working with Shankar (on his album, *Tana Mana*), Duane Eddy, and working on Mike Batt's adaptation of Lewis Carroll's *The Hunting of the Snark*.

In January 1987, Harrison began recording what would become his eleventh studio album, *Cloud Nine*. It would seem that he had learnt his lessons from *Gone Troppo* and was willing to promote his music differently. The media and many people suggested that Harrison had disappeared for five years, and this was his comeback. Indeed, perhaps, commercially, it was indeed a comeback, but as evidenced by the amount of musical work he had done from 1983 until 1987, he was not exactly coming out of retirement. Harrison had not disappeared; he was just not releasing solo albums. But he had been busy.

He asked ELO's Jeff Lynne to produce the album. He had met Lynne over the years and, most recently, performed with him at *The Heartbeat '86* concert. According to Gary Wright, Harrison was interested in working with Lynne, and while Harrison was in Los Angeles in 1986, he asked Wright to host a dinner party. Harrison cooked the meal, and Wright, his family, and Lynne enjoyed a lovely dinner. Wright writes that the three retired to his studio, where they jammed for a few hours. 'I could tell George was enjoying himself and that the chemistry was working between him and Jeff'. Wright was a very big part of the recording of *Cloud Nine* in the upcoming months.

The first single from Harrison and Dark Horse since 1983 was released on 3 October 1987 in North America and 12 October in the UK. The song is a cover version of a song originally released by James Ray in 1962. 'Got My Mind Set on You' was written by Rudy Clark (a postal carrier turned songwriter), but it was the James Ray version with which Harrison was most familiar. When Harrison visited his sister in Illinois in

1963 (months before The Beatles made their historic performance on *Ed Sullivan*), he visited record stores looking for The Beatles' single (which had been released on Vee Jay) and ended up buying a few albums, one of which was the eponymous *James Ray* on Caprice Records. The song (known as 'I've Got My Mind Set on You Pt. I and Pt. II) was on that album and stuck with Harrison.

The B-side of Harrison's single was one of the four tracks removed from the original *Somewhere in England* album, 'Lay His Head'. That song seeing the light of day on Warner's must have given George some satisfaction.

Harrison produced two music videos for the song, both directed by Gary Weiss, and both extremely well-made and full of humour and originality. The second video (Harrison sitting in an easy chair with his house coming alive around him) won three MTV Music Video Awards. Warner Brothers had to be happy; Dark Horse Records had embraced the second half of the 1980s and was doing things properly. *Cashbox* loved the single, stating that the 'long awaited return of Harrison is spearheaded by this advance single' and, in the same review, they note that the record is 'released on Harrison's revived Dark Horse label'. Finally, they predict that the pop/rock tune will 'saturate Top 40 and AOR radio'.

In the UK, the single peaked at number two (for three weeks), unable to knock T'Pau's single 'China in Your Hand' on 21 November 1987. Still, peaking at number two was his biggest hit in the UK since 'Give Me Love (Give Me Peace on Earth)' had peaked at number two and it became his second largest single (behind 'My Sweet Lord', his only number one in the UK).

In America, the single spent 22 weeks on The *Billboard* Top 100, peaking at number one on 16 January 1988, Dark Horse Records' first number-one and Harrison's first US number one since 1973's 'Give Me Love (Give Me Peace on Earth)'. Harrison was ahead of artists such as George Michael, Michael Jackson, INXS and The Bangles, all in the charts at the time.

The album *Cloud Nine*, was highly anticipated and was finally released on 2 November 1987. It was the first Dark Horse album to be released on CD worldwide. By 1987, CDs had become an industry standard since their debut in 1982. Soon, vinyl would be phased out, for a while, in favour of CDs.

Right out of the box, the album was a success, commercially and critically. Harrison also promoted the album with interviews, television appearances, music videos and radio appearances. The fact that it was preceded by a number one single helped sales a great deal as well. Harrison and Dark Horse embraced promoting this album and he was rewarded with one of the biggest albums of his career.

Billboard magazine called the music 'wonderful' featuring a 'glittering assemblage of backup talent'. They further add that the album is 'deep in follow-up hits' and predict that *'Cloud Nine* looms as Harrison's biggest since *All Things Must Pass'*. Meanwhile, *Cashbox* wrote 'that this ex-Beatle still has the ability to write and play captivating, intriguing pop/rock'. Again, the supporting cast is named and it is a positive review. *Rolling Stone* even gave it a great review. Danny Wild wrote, 'It is in fact an expertly crafted, endlessly infectious record' and further noted that the production team of Lynne and Harrison was a winning combination: 'Throughout *Cloud Nine*, Harrison and Lynne add layers of inspired production touches that make undeniable aural confections'. *Creem* even gave it a good review. Writer Bill Holdship, in his review, says *'Cloud Nine* is plenty good'.

Harrison called upon friends, old and new, to play on the album. Besides producing the album, Lynne, a very talented musician and composer in his own right, provided bass, acoustic and electric guitars, keyboards and backing vocals. Jim Keltner and Ringo Starr were back to provide the solid drumming throughout, and Eric Clapton provided some very tasteful solos. Gary Wright returned after an absence from *Gone Troppo*, and for the first time on a Harrison record, Elton John played piano. This means Elton John had worked with three Beatles in the studio. Ray Cooper was also back providing percussion and drums, while Jim Horn played baritone and tenor saxophones. Finally, Bobby Kok provided cello on the album. Kok, a well-respected and well-known session musician (and member of the Philharmonia Orchestra), had previously played on the soundtracks for *Life of Brian* and *Time Bandits* and also worked with Paul McCartney on his album *Give My Regards to Broad Street*. He also played on The Beatles' 'Hey Jude'.

Harrison also went for a slightly different look for this album and accompanying singles. Harrison hadn't used the design staff of Dark Horse Records, headed up by Bob Cato since *Thirty Three & ⅓* in 1976. Here, Gered Mankowitz's photography and David Costa's design presented Harrison in a contemporary style, with a nod to the past. In fact, prior to the release of the album, Dark Horse Records and Warner Brothers released a cassette to radio stations of Harrison talking about the guitar he is holding on the sleeve of the album. Titled *George Harrison: George Harrison speaking about his first American guitar as pictured on Cloud Nine*, it was a very unique promotional release and a highly sought-after collector's item today. Harrison talks about his old Black Gretsch and how he 'Bought it from a sailor in Liverpool' in 1960. He says it was his 'first real decent guitar' and his first American instrument. Further, he reveals that he had 'given it to Klaus Voormannn ... and could I have it back ... for nostalgia'.

Not long after the album was released, and it was steadily climbing the charts, a second single appeared on radio stations. It is not clear if 'Devil's Radio (Gossip)' was ever intended to be the second single from the album, but promotional copies of the song were released to American radio stations. Although not a single, the song did chart on *Billboard*'s 'Album Rock Tracks', peaking at number four on December 26 1987. While this was getting saturated airtime on 'album rock' stations, 'Got My Mind Set on You' was still climbing the Top 100, as was the album. It made it to number four on *Billboard*'s Mainstream Rock chart, denoting songs most played on 'mainstream' rock radio (*Billboard* – Chart History). Indeed, Dark Horse, with assistance from Warner Brothers, was actually targeting markets with various songs from the album. 'Devil's Radio (Gossip)' became a radio hit and one wonders if it could have been a hit single.

The second single that Dark Horse lifted from the album was the very Beatle-esque 'When We Was Fab'. The song was written by Harrison and Lynne and was George's tribute to The Beatles, featuring Starr on drums, providing his best Beatle fills. Harrison made one video for the song, directed by Kevin Godley and Lol Crème. At one time, the duo were one-half of the heavily Beatles-influenced band 10CC and went on to become very famous and well-respected music video directors. This video features Starr as Harrison's helper and a person in a walrus costume playing bass. No, it was not McCartney, as was rumoured at the time, but many fans had hoped that was the case. It was a brilliant music video that was played a great deal on *MTV* (and *MuchMusic* in Canada). The B-side was from the *Shanghai Surprise* days, a remake of 'Zig Zag'.

The song was released in the UK on 1 February 1988 and 30 January 1988 in North America. While the picture sleeve for 'Got My Mind Set on You' was directly connected with the *Cloud Nine* sleeve design, Harrison went for modern nostalgia with this sleeve. For this sleeve, old friend Klaus Voormannn created new art incorporating his drawing of Harrison from The Beatles' *Revolver* with a drawing of Harrison from the present. It was a stunning picture sleeve and once again, collectors had a field day.

The single was met with great anticipation and did very well. *Cashbox* reviewed it in their 30 January 1988 issue, noting that Harrison and Lynne 'unveil a historical re-creation of The Beatles' career' and comparing the song to a 'Beatles song circa *Magical Mystery Tour*'. It was the second Top 40 hit from the album.

Cloud Nine did very well for Harrison and Dark Horse; their biggest album to date. On the *Billboard* Top 200, the album peaked at number eight and it did make it to number one on the Compact Disc *Billboard* sales charts. It also went on to earn Platinum status in America, selling over one million copies.

There was one more single to be released from the album, 'This is Love', one of three songs Harrison wrote with co-producer Jeff Lynne, and one highlighted by critics. It is a commercial, upbeat, love song for his wife – a beautiful song. The line-up for the recording was quite small, Harrison on guitars, Keltner on drums, Cooper on percussion and Lynne playing bass, keyboards, guitar and backing vocals. Released in the summer of 1988, the song was a radio hit and further promoted the album.

Harrison actually recorded a new song to be a B-side for the single. He recorded the song with help from Tom Petty, Jeff Lynne, Roy Orbison and Bob Dylan. The new song, 'Handle With Care', was recorded at Bob Dylan's studio in Santa Monica and was co-written between the five musicians. When the executives at Warner Brothers heard the song, they, quite rightly, thought it was too good to be buried on a European B-side of a 12" single. Up to this point, 12" singles were not commonplace in North America, so the song would have only been released in Europe as the previous mixes and bonus tracks on Harrison's last two single releases in Europe.

Harrison was in Los Angeles to oversee the production of the HandMade film, *Checking Out* (in which he has a cameo as a janitor and features 'End of the Line' by The Traveling Wilburys during the end credits), when he received a request from Warner Brothers for a track for the 12" single. The song was actually recorded in April of 1988, but as early as February 1988, Harrison was floating an idea of a band with his friends during interviews. According to Jeff Lynne, Harrison introduced the idea of forming a band with him roughly two months into recording

Cloud Nine. The name Traveling Wilburys was originally Trembling Wilbury, a term Harrison had come up with during the recording of *Cloud Nine* for any small errors in a recorded song.

When the five received the feedback, they made a decision, with encouragement from Warner Brothers, to record an entire album. They recorded the album over a ten-day period at Dave Stewart's (of Eurythmics) home studio in Los Angeles. The songs were all credited as joint compositions and the band adopted pseudonyms to suggest that the Wilburys were a family. For *Volume 1*, their names were Nelson Wilbury (Harrison), Otis Wilbury (Lynne), Lefty Wilbury (Orbison), Charlie T. Wilbury (Petty) and Lucky Wilbury (Dylan). They were assisted by Keltner on drums.

But given that the band members were signed to different labels, it is a miracle that the album was released, but it was on 17 October 1988 on vinyl, CD and cassette on the newly formed label Wilbury Records, through Warner Brothers. Although Harrison was the primary holder of the rights for this (and all future Traveling Wilbury recordings), it was decided that the music not be released on his Dark Horse Records label as to promote the idea of band unity. Hence, a new label, Wilbury Records, was established. The album would go on to be a worldwide Top Ten hit.

As it turned out, *Cloud Nine* would be Harrison's last solo studio album released in his lifetime.

Dark Horse in the 1990s

Following the success of *Cloud Nine* and The Traveling Wilburys, Harrison continued to work with other musicians and appeared on their albums, such as Sylvia Griffin (an opera singer and a member of the alternative band Kissing the Pink), old friend Jim Capaldi (a former member of Traffic), Gary Wright and fellow Wilbury, Roy Orbison, with his album *Mystery Girl*. However, one month before the album was released, on 6 December 1988, Orbison passed away from a heart attack. The album was released on 31 January 1989 and it became the best-selling album of his career.

While Dark Horse lay quiet, Harrison was helping other members of the Wilburys. He worked with Tom Petty and later on albums by Jeff Lynne and Bob Dylan. Not only did Harrison play guitar on Tom Petty's *Full Moon Fever*, but also also helped Petty with health issues. In a 2010 interview with *Mojo*, Petty recalled the story of the day they recorded the song and was ill with a cold. 'George went to the store and bought a ginger root, boiled it, and had me stick my head in the pot to get the ginger steam to open up my sinuses, and then I ran in and did the take'.

As for Dark Horse and his own solo career, Harrison's follow-up to *Cloud Nine* was to assemble a 'best of'. Usually, in the rock industry, a 'best of' or 'greatest hits' is often released to fill in the gaps between albums, and *The Best of Dark Horse, 1976–1989,* (A George Harrison best of, not one covering all the artists on the label) was released on Dark Horse Records on 17 October 1989 in the United States and on 23 October 1989 in England and Europe. This was Harrison's second 'best of' compilation and the first one in which he had total control.

Harrison included three 'new' songs, one of which, 'Cheer Down', was actually started in 1987 during the *Cloud Nine* sessions, having also featured on the soundtrack album *Lethal Weapon 2* and released as a single. It was George Harrison's last single released in the US for that decade and his last on Dark Horse Records during his lifetime. Dark Horse was winding down. In the US *Billboard* Top 100 singles chart, it failed to chart, thus becoming his second single since 'When We Was Fab' to miss the charts. But it did well on other charts, getting to seven on the Mainstream Rock chart.

Harrison included two other songs which he had recorded in 1989 at his home studio, 'Poor Little Girl' and 'Cockamamie Business'. 'Poor Little Girl' was chosen as the single in Europe but failed to chart.

The album had a couple of purposes. Harrison had not released a solo album since 1987's *Cloud Nine* and furthermore, it was an excellent chance to advertise his back catalogue. His *Thirty Three & ¹/₃* album, released thirteen years before, seemed like a lifetime ago. A lot had changed since Harrison brought his Dark Horse Records to Warner Brothers. The way music was sold, marketed and advertised had all changed.

Harrison chose the songs for the compilation himself. Curiously, he did not put all of his singles released via Dark Horse on the album ('This Song', 'When We Was Fab', 'I Really Love You', 'Dream Away' and 'This is Love' were not included) instead he favoured album tracks that he had said he loved, such as 'Life Itself'. It was odd, in hindsight, that he did not include all of his hits. But, he was clear in the title; this was a 'Best Of', not a 'Greatest Hits' package.

The Best of Dark Horse, 1976–1989 was largely ignored by critics and the record-buying public. It failed to chart in the UK. On 4 November 1989, while Tom Petty was sitting at number nine with *Full Moon Fever* (featuring Harrison), Harrison entered the *Billboard* Top 200 at number 132. There was very little promotion, which was intruiging at the time as it was released during the pre-Christmas record blitz. If the public is not aware of the album, they will not buy it. It should have been under a lot of Christmas trees that year.

For the first time at Dark Horse, an outside company was brought in to design the sleeve. Trendy album and single designers, Wherefore Art?, created it, and it could be one of the reasons the album was not successful. It is a rather dark and complicated sleeve. It is interesting to note that Dark Horse Records and Warner Brothers in Italy took matters into their own hands and revised the cover art and title for a reissue in 1991. The album title was shortened to *The Best of George Harrison*, and the cover featured a bright colour photo of Harrison circa 1987. It was released on CD, vinyl and cassette on Dark Horse Records.

While *The Best of Dark Horse, 1976–1989* was struggling in the charts, Harrison kept busy, working with artists such as former Go-Go, Belinda Carlisle, former Thin Lizzy guitarist Gary Moore, and old friend Eric Clapton with his album *Journeyman*. Harrison also contributed his live duet with Paul Simon ('Homeward Bound', recorded for *Saturday Night Live*) to an album that Olivia Harrison was instrumental in putting together. It was an all-star record to assist the orphans and neglected children of Romania: *Nobody's Child: Romanian Angel Appeal*. Romanian

Angel Appeal Foundation, a charity founded by the Beatles partners
Olivia Harrison, Linda McCartney, Yoko Ono and Barbara Bach, were
given a brand new Traveling Wilburys song, 'Nobody's Child' (the first
without Orbison).

Also, in 1990, a second Traveling Wilburys album (the comically titled
The Traveling Wilburys Volume 3) was recorded, and, this time around,
the four adopted new names. Here, they are known as Spike Wilbury
(Harrison), Clayton Wilbury (Lynne), Boo Wilbury (Dylan) and Muddy
Wilbury (Petty). Much of the album was recorded at F.P.S.H.O.T. and,
once again, Jim Keltner was on drums. Gary Moore even made a guest
appearance on the first single, 'She's My Baby'. As with the first album, it
was released on Wilbury Recordings.and was dedicated to Roy Orbison.

Although Dark Horse Records was not signing new artists, Harrison
continued to demonstrate his desire to assist other artists. In 1990,
Harrison helped out vocalist Vicki Brown, who had helped with *Gone
Troppo* and 'Shanghai Surprise' and a Canadian guitarist, Jeff Healey, on
a cover of 'While My Guitar Gently Weeps' for his album *Hell to Pay* on
Arista Records.

In June 1991, there was some activity from Dark Horse. On 11 June,
Dark Horse Records released, for the first time, *Somewhere in England*
and *Gone Troppo* on CD. *Thirty Three & ¹/₃* and *George Harrison*
were released two weeks later, on 25 June 1991. They were released
worldwide and, at this point, all of Harrison's Dark Horse albums were
now available on the current format of moment. The tracks had to be
digitally remastered for compact disc, but the original versions of all
songs were used so that the music mirrored the original vinyl versions
of the album. In terms of packaging, the original artwork and inner
sleeves were left largely intact, although there were some alterations
to the front sleeve. Most noticeable were *Somewhere in England* and
George Harrison.

Perhaps most surprising was Harrison's decision to tour in 1991.
Eric Clapton convinced him to tour Japan and a short, twelve-date
tour, utilising Clapton's backup band, was scheduled. It consisted of
Andy Fairweather Low (guitars, backing vocals), Nathan East (bass,
backing vocals), Chuck Leavell (piano, Hammond organ, keyboards,
backing vocals), Greg Philinganes (keyboards, backing vocals), Steve
Ferrone (drums), Kate Kisson (backing vocals), and Tessa Niles (backing
vocals). Clapton provided guitar and vocals and took the spotlight for
four songs midway through the concert. Ray Cooper was also there to

provide support as well as percussion and backing vocals. Harrison handled acoustic and electric guitar as well as slide guitar. Once it was announced, the tour sold out immediately. Just beforehand, he took time to help out British vocalist and actor Jimmy Nail with his album *Growing Up in Public.*

Harrison shortlisted about 35 songs to rehearse prior to the tour. Some considered were 'Just For Today', 'This Guitar (Can't Keep From Crying)', 'Wake Up My Love', 'Beware of Darkness', 'Don't Bother Me' and 'It's All Too Much'. This was eventually pared down to 19, although two additional songs were performed at the beginning of the tour that were dropped. 'Fish on the Sand' was played at the first two shows (1 and 2 December 1991) and 'Love Comes to Everyone', which was performed only on 1 December 1991.

The tour, officially titled 'Rock Legends: George Harrison and Eric Clapton and His Band', took place from 1 December through to 17 December 1991. Listening to the recordings now, Harrison was in good humour and seemed to be enjoying himself, with his voice and guitar playing in top form. The announcement of the tour was unexpected and attracted a great deal of international attention.

The concerts were filmed and recorded and on 13 July 1992, a double album was released. *Live in Japan,* is credited to George Harrison with Eric Clapton. The material on the live album was recorded during three shows in Osaka (December 10 – 12) and three dates in Tokyo (December 14 – 17), with the songs split pretty evenly between Beatles classics and solo material. The production of the album is credited to Nelson and Spike Wilbury, the two identities Harrison adopted for The Traveling Wilburys. Harrison reasoning was that 'it sounded kind of boring when you just keep putting your name on everything' The concerts were recorded by John Harris.

During an interview with Scott Muni on WNEW, Harrison noted, 'A lot of songs I have done, I wrote them and then I recorded them. I sang them one time on the records, and never, ever done them since. So to me, they're like new songs'.

The album, *Live in Japan,* was released on the now standard CD, cassette and on vinyl, but only in Europe, although Dark Horse Records did release a CD single in France, featuring 'Here Comes the Sun' and 'My Sweet Lord'. In 1993, Dark Horse Records released a deluxe version through Genesis Publications, the same publishing company that had put out the limited edition books by Harrison. Genesis Publications put together a lavish version, complete with a full-colour book (with 500 never-before-published photos) and an essay written by engineer John Harris on working with George Harrison. It came bound in a nice box, which included a laminated 'after-show pass', and Harrison and Clapton's guitar picks. The set was autographed by both and was limited to 3500 copies. It sold out immediately.

Billboard gave the album a positive review: 'Goosebumps are guaranteed from the electrifying opening riff of 'I Want to Tell You' onward', and noting: 'it's tough to pick favourites in a collection this compelling ... A portable, utterly fab house party'. High praise indeed. The review even states that this recording of 'While My Guitar Gently Weeps' is 'more stirring' than The Beatles' version. Parke Puterbaugh gave the album four stars out of five in his review for *Rolling Stone* magazine. He refers to Harrison's performance as 'rocking and extroverted' and that Harrison and Clapton 'bring out the best in each other'.

The album peaked at number fifteen in Japan, while in America, it reached a disappointing number 126, making it the second Harrison album in a row not to crack the Top 100. Interestingly, in that issue of *Billboard*, Doris Troy's self-titled Apple album received a rave review in the 'Vital Reissue' reviews, and gives credit to Harrison for producing the album's 'smokingest song', 'Ain't That Cute', referring to it as 'stormy'.

As with *The Best of Dark Horse*, this is another mystery. *Live in Japan* should have been a huge album. Harrison did radio promotion, (*Rockline, Scott Muni,* and *In the Studio*) and yet, the album failed to register sales in record stores. There are a few potential reasons for its failure. By the early 1990s, live albums were not the big sellers they were in the late 1970s (*The Song Remains the Same, The Beatles at The Hollywood Bowl, Frampton Comes Alive* and *Kiss Alive* as just four examples of very popular live albums in the latter half of the 1970s) but had been replaced by the new marketing tool: the live video. There have been exceptions. The 'Unplugged' albums by Eric Clapton, Bob Dylan, Nirvana and Paul McCartney all proved to be very successful live albums, but they offered very different versions of very well-known songs.

Perhaps the failure of the album was down to Warner Brothers. With the release of this double live album, Harrison's contract was done with them. Perhaps, since Dark Horse was moving on, Warner Brothers did not give it the attention it needed or deserved. Regardless, Warner Brothers and Dark Horse were no longer a partnership.

While Harrison was working with other musicians and preparing for this tour of Japan with Eric Clapton, he was having some difficulty with his film company, HandMade Films, who were running into financial difficulty by 1991. The last film that Harrison had direct involvement with, *Nuns on the Run*, was released on 16 March 1990.

In 1991, it ceased producing films and three years later, it was sold to a Canadian company, Paragon Entertainment. The company that he had built was gone. Not only did he lose Handmade Films, he also lost his manager, Denis O'Brien someone he had trusted. O'Brien had been instrumental in helping Harrison establish Dark Horse Records, so it was a considerable loss. It also meant that Harrison was involved with yet another lawsuit when he sued O'Brien for fraud and negligence, a lawsuit Harrison would eventually win. But he still lost the company.

Even with all of the disappointment and legal issues, Harrison ended 1992 on a very positive note. On 8 December 1992, during the *Billboard* Music Awards, George Harrison received *Billboard* Magazine's first Century Award, presented by Tom Petty. The award is presented to an artist 'whose career and body of work continues to evolve and influence new generations of musicians'. The music he had released on his Dark Horse label certainly contributed to this award, acknowledging Harrison's part in the development of 'World Music'.

On 13 October 1992, Harrison performed at Madison Square Garden in New York City. He joined the all-star salute to Dylan, titled *The 30th Anniversary Concert Celebration* (or as Neil Young called it, 'Bobfest'). Harrison performed two songs with the band, 'If Not For You' and 'Absolutely Sweet Marie'. He also took part in the all-star ensemble performing 'My Back Pages' and 'Knocking on Heaven's Door'.

Other than this appearance, Harrison, once again, seemed to disappear from public view during the first half of the nineties and with him went Dark Horse. In fact, his contract with Warner Brothers ended in 1994 and he did not seek to renew it. This meant that, for the time being, Harrison was not signed with a label, nor was Dark Horse with a distributor. By 1995, the entire Harrison catalogue on Dark Horse records had been deleted and was no longer available.

Harrison was kept busy in the early 1990s with two very big projects. The first was working with The Beatles. Harrison contributed a great deal to *The Beatles Anthology* project, which would see the release of three double CDs, two singles, a television mini-series, a VHS box set (which later became an expanded DVD box set) and a book. The project would also include two new songs by The Beatles. Harrison, Starr, and McCartney added content and their instruments to four demos Lennon had recorded in the late 1970s. Only two of these songs were released: 'Free as a Bird' and 'Real Love'. The original idea was for the three Beatles (nicknamed at the time in the press as 'The Threetles') to record incidental and background music, but this was expanded to recording new songs. Yoko Ono has stated that it was Harrison and Aspinall who came up with the idea of using Lennon's demos to record new Beatle music.

While *The Beatles Anthology* was taking the world by storm on television, radio and record stores, Harrison was keeping busy preparing another anthology. He was working with Alan Kozlowski, in association with Ravi Shankar, on *Ravi Shankar: In Celebration*. The four-CD set (there was also a single CD consisting of highlights from the box set version) was released on Dark Horse Records in North America on 20 February 1996. This was the first new product from the label since Harrison's contract had ended with Warner Brothers. Alan Kozlowski had made a name for himself as a photographer, filmmaker and musician and had worked on the restored 1999 *Yellow Submarine* film as an executive producer. In 1978, he started studying under Ravi Shankar and he performed with Shankar on many occasions, participating in the 1993 Royal Albert Hall performance. Along with documentaries of other musicians (Lionel Richie, Jackson Browne, Michael McDonald, Kenny Loggins), he carefully documented Shankar's career starting in 1978.

Harrison and Kozlowski, with assistance from Shankar, decided to celebrate Shankar's 75th birthday in 1996 by putting together a comprehensive collection of his work, which would include never-before-released material. Harrison and Kozlowski also involved another student of Shankar's, Harihar Rao, to assist with research. The CD box set was released in conjunction with Shankar's autobiography (*Raga Mala*), published through Genesis Publications.

Not only was this the first Dark Horse Records project since *Live in Japan*, but it was also the first time that Dark Horse Records worked on a joint project, as the box set was released as Angel/Dark Horse Records. Angel Records had been owned by EMI since it was founded in 1953 and was known mainly for classical recordings but would release soundtracks and operettas as well. By the 1990s, they branched out to release world music as well.

Although Harrison was working on *The Beatles Anthology*, which was on the Apple label, via EMI, *Ravi Shankar: In Celebration* is the first time Harrison worked directly with his old label since 1975. EMI was to play a large role in the Dark Horse story in the future.

The set was a chance to bring Shankar's music together from various sources and labels. Songs originally released on World Pacific Records, Apple Records, Private Music, Gramophone Co. of India, EMI, Chandra Dhara, Angel Records, and, of course, Dark Horse Records are all on this compilation. Rather than presenting the music in chronological order, his music was divided into four sections: 'Classical Guitar', 'Orchestral and Ensembles', 'East-West Collaboration' and 'Vocal and Experimental'. This was a very wise move in that it allowed the music to exist within a context other than simple release dates.

Billboard magazine featured the album in an article in their 23 December 1995 issue. In the article, written by Heidi Waleson, Kozlowski singles out the cuts from the out-of-print Dark Horse albums as being the prizes in the set. The article notes that Harrison will be travelling to India with Shankar to record an album set for an April 1996 release featuring Indian Chants. That, of course, would turn out to be *Chants of India*, which was to have an interesting history on the Dark Horse label.

Ravi Shankar: In Celebration allowed fans to hear music which had been out of print for many years and was hard to find. For example, it was nice to hear 'Oh Bhaugowan', originally only available on the Apple EP, *Joi Bangla*. It was equally an excellent chance to hear songs from *Shankar Family & Friends* and *Ravi Shankar's Music Festival From India*, both albums at least 20 years out of print at that point. The set even included a previously unreleased song recorded for *Ravi Shankar's Music Festival From India*, 'Ta Na Nom'. A beautiful piece that would have been lost had it not been placed on this collection. From *Ravi Shankar's Music Festival* came 'Jait' and 'Vandana'and from *Shankar Family & Friends* came 'Supané Mé Ãyé Preetam Sainyã.

Billboard magazine gave the set a rave review, referring to Shankar as 'an icon of world music', and noting that the set was a 'labour of love for producer George Harrison, who ably documents Shankar's adventurous spirit and versatile talents'. It was the 'Critic's Choice' for the week. In the same issue of *Billboard*, that 'Real Love' by The Beatles received a rave review.

Ravi Shankar: In Celebration was the most elaborate album/package with which Dark Horse Records had been involved. Along with the four CDs, *Billboard* magazine writer/editor Timothy White provided very thorough liner notes, while Shankar himself provided commentary on the songs. Harrison wrote the introduction: 'To have been able to produce many of the tracks within and to have had a hand in the selection and preparation of this collection, is for me an honour ...'

The package was designed by Rick Ward and The Team Design Consultants. The cover was beautiful and the whole set was given the care it deserved. Rare photographs throughout and the White essay/liner notes made it quite perfect. It sounded wonderful, too. Bruce Botnick and Larry Walsh, CD Mastering Engineers, had the task of taking analogue music, some of which was very old, and making it sound good without losing the warmth and beauty of the original recordings. They achieved this task due to the fact that the music had been so well and carefully recorded in its original form.

At the same time, *Ravi Shankar: In Celebration Highlights* was released through Angel/Dark Horse Records in March 1996. It featured 'I Am Missing You' and 'Supaney Mein Aye'. The highlights CD was an excellent idea for those who could not afford the lavish box set and just wanted a nice, albeit short, overview. These two releases proved to be the last two releases from Dark Horse Records in George Harrison's lifetime.

Waleson, in her article for *Billboard* Magazine, accurately notes that Harrison and Shankar returned to India to record an album. When the pair were working with Angel Records on the *Ravi Shankar: In Celebration* box set, they worked out an arrangement with Angel Records to release a new Shankar album, which would be made in collaboration with Harrison. They agreed and the two began work on the album. Shankar recalled the decision to make it:

> Steve Murphy [the president of Angel Records] said, 'I would like you to do some of those chantings from India because they had great success with those Spanish monks'. George Harrison was very enthusiastic and he wanted to take charge of the production. These chantings are very old, from the Scriptures. Some I composed. 'Mangalam' came to me while I was walking in Friar Park, George's place, where we were recording. I was looking at the trees and the sky, and feeling very elated all of a sudden, wishing everything would be good for everyone, and it just came to me.

Shankar is, of course, referring to the album *Chant (Benedictine Monks of Santo Domingo de Silos album)*, which went on to hit number three on the *Billboard* charts. However, *Chants of India* was not an album trying to cash in, as Harrison and Shankar had been down this road before with the Dark Horse album *Ravi Shankar's Music Festival From India*. This was Harrison and Shankar exploring the roots that brought them together in the first place. It was a very personal album for both of the artists.

The pair began recording the album in Madras, a city in the south of India at Sruthilaya Media Artists Studio, working there in January and April 1996 and Shankar noted in his liner notes that they finished the album in Harrison's home studio, F.P.S.H.O.T. in July. The album was released on 6 May 1997 on the Angel Records label; however, it might have been on Dark Horse Records. Upon careful inspection of the CD packaging, one notes that the copyright of the recording is under Harrison's name. In other words, he had the copyright of the recordings and licensed the album to Angel Records. This explains why the album would be reissued twice by Dark Horse Records. It was released on vinyl on the Dark Horse label, in 2020.

Chants of India was very well received by critics and by the record-buying public. On the *Billboard* Top World Music Albums charts, it peaked at number three on 21 June 1997, kept out of number one by two albums benefiting from the *Riverdance* phenomenon at the time. Number one was Bill Whelan's *Riverdance* and number two was Ronin Hardiman's *Michael Flatley's Lord of the Dance*. But the album stayed on the charts for over five months. When Dark Horse re-released it in 2010, two songs charted on *Billboard*'s World Digital Song Sales chart. On 6 November 2010, 'Sahanaa Vavatu' reached number four, while 'Vandanaa Trayee' made it to number eleven. Furthermore, in 2020, when the album was reissued on vinyl (by Dark Horse), *Chants of India* made it to number one on *Billboard*'s New Age Music chart.

In 1997, Harrison acted as Shankar's editor for his book *Raga Mala*, which was released through Genesis Publishing. Harrison also wrote the foreword. Said Harrison: 'back in 1994, we were thinking of ways to mark Ravi's 75th birthday. I asked Brian Roylance if he wanted to publish a book, and he said 'yes'. Ravi liked the idea too, and then we started to prepare'. The original first edition came with two CDs featuring rare and unreleased music. Dark Horse was represented with a version of 'I Am Missing You' (featuring Harrison and Starr) along with tracks from *Chants of India*.

Harrison and Shankar were more than willing to promote the album. They were interviewed in print, and radio and even made an appearance on America's other music television channel, VH 1, where on 24 July 1997, a pre-recorded interview with Harrison and Shankar was broadcast. They came on to talk about *Chants of India*, but the interview turned out to be so much more. Although the interview lasted 150 minutes, only 22 minutes were broadcast as *George & Ravi – The Yin & Yang*. Harrison performed three songs, only one of which was televised, 'All Things Must Pass'. The other songs Harrison performed were The Traveling Wilburys' 'If You Belong to Me' and a song he was working on, 'Any Road'. The duo also performed 'Prabhujee' (featuring Shankar's wife, Sukanya, on vocals).

The show was taped in May 1997. Shortly after the taping, Harrison was diagnosed with throat cancer. He was treated with radiotherapy, which initially seemed successful.

Harrison was kept busy with his health, Shankar, and, surprisingly, more Beatles projects. He helped promote the relaunch of the classic 1968 Beatle film *Yellow Submarine* in 1999 and he was on hand to help his former bandmate and friend, Ringo Starr, with his 1998 album *Vertical Man* (Mercury, 1998).

On 17 April 1998, Linda McCartney died after a short battle with breast cancer. Harrison, although not entirely healthy himself, did provide support for his old friend through his grieving. as this was also a huge loss for the Harrison family.

Over a year later, further unfortunate events affected the Harrison family. On 30 December 1999, Harrison and his wife, Olivia, were attacked in their home. Harrison suffered over 40 stab wounds and part of his punctured lung had to be removed. And yet, Harrison continued to record, helping new bands, such as an Irish band, Rubyhorse, and old friends, such as Bill Wyman, Jeff Lynne, Albert Lee and Jim Capaldi.

While Harrison was helping other artists, he continued writing and recording for a potential new solo album. Although he continued to have health issues due to the attack and cancer, Harrison continued by working on a reissue of his classic *All Things Must Pass* album. In 2000, the album would celebrate its 30th Anniversary. He remastered the album and had the original front sleeve colourised. He also added five new tracks to the album. Going through his archives, he found a brilliant, previously unreleased song, 'I Live For You', as well as the acoustic demo of 'Beware of Darkness'. He also added an alternative backing track for 'What is Life' (featuring a piccolo trumpet and oboe) and an alternate version of 'Let it Down'. Finally, he created a new version of one of his most famous songs, titled, 'My Sweet Lord (2000)'. The original backing track was hardly noticeable, with new instrumentation from Harrison, his son, Dhani (on guitar), Ray Cooper and Sam Brown on vocals.

The original album, *All Things Must Pass*, was originally released on Apple. This version was released on GnOM Records, a new label for Harrison, and distributed by EMI. Although Harrison's health was not good, he still promoted the album.

On 2 October 2001, George Harrison recorded a song for inclusion on the upcoming Jools Holland's Rhythm and Blues Orchestra album. Holland had been the keyboardist for the band Squeeze and was an accomplished musician with his own band. He had recorded with George previously in 1991. Holland had a television documentary *Mr. Roadrunner*, on which Harrison made a surprise appearance, performing a cover of the Cab Calloway song, 'Between the Devil and the Deep Blue Sea'. He wrote a new song with his son, Dhani, called 'Horse to Water', which was finished on 2 October 2001 when Harrison recorded the vocal (with backup from Sam Brown). It proved to be Harrison's last recording.

The song was released on the album *Small World Big Band* on 23 November 2001 on Warners Music. The publishing company noted on the credits was R.I.P. Music. On 1 December 2001, Jools Holland had his first solo Top Ten album in the UK at number eight.

On 29 November 2001, George Harrison lost his battle with cancer and passed away.

Brainwashed in the 2000s

Dark Horse Records continued past 29 November 2001. There were, however, differences. Loka Productions and Ganga copyright notations were replaced by a new publishing and copyright owner, Umlaut. Dark Horse Records was now owned by Umlaut Corporation (*trademarks. justia.com*). For the average record buyer, this change meant very little, but it did signify a new era for the label, with Olivia Harrison taking over the responsibility.

Dark Horse Records also had a new partner. After leaving Warner Brothers in 1994, Olivia Harrison signed with Parlophone/EMI. It was good to see Harrison's music connected with his old label Parlophone. Paul McCartney had also partnered with Parlophone, so it was heartwarming to see two Beatles signed with their original record company. Keep in mind that Harrison himself, had worked with Parlophone/Emi/Capitol for his reissue of *All Things Must Pass.*

The first order of business was a new George Harrison album. Throughout the 1990s, Harrison had worked on new music. But he was never able to turn that work into an album. He had been kept busy with *The Beatles Anthology* project, Traveling Wilburys, working with Ravi Shankar, the *All Things Must Pass* reissue, his business issues with his former manager/business manager, the collapse and sale of HandMade Films and his health. Dark Horse Records took a backseat and the last album released was *Live in Japan* in 1992. However, while promoting *All Things Must Pass*, Harrison did mention that a new album was forthcoming.

In 1999, he reported the album was to be called *Portrait of a Leg End.* Interviewed in 2001, he said that the album was going to be called *Your Planet is Doomed – Volume One*. Harrison had the songs recorded, for the most part, by 1999 and from 1999 until 2001, he worked on what would become *Brainwashed,* calling on his friend Jeff Lynne, and his son, Dhani, to help complete the album. Dhani worked very closely with his father, and the two came up with the track listing and a release schedule.

Brainwashed was released on 18 November (UK) and 19 November (North America) 2002. It was released worldwide on CD, a limited CD box set with a DVD, vinyl, and cassette. This was the last Dark Horse release to be available on cassette.

By the 2000s, record and album promotion had changed. Vinyl sales, especially singles, were at an all-time low, cassette and CD singles never really took off and the definition of 'single' had been altered. The numbers speak for themselves; in 1973, the first year that all record sales were tracked by the RIAA, vinyl singles sold 228 million copies. That was the peak year. Vinyl album sales peaked in 1978 with 341.3 million sold. By the mid-1980s, total vinyl shipments were cut by more than half. By 1991, total sales of vinyl were down to 22 million.

In order to promote *Brainwashed*, Dark Horse Records and the Harrisons had to keep up with the times and act accordingly, which they did. Most importantly, they used the internet. It was announced that America Online (AOL) service would be premiering the song, 'Stuck Inside a Cloud', on AOL Music's first listen on 28 October 2002. This would be the world's first opportunity to hear the brand new George Harrison song.

The song helped the album do very well in terms of sales. *Brainwashed* earned gold status in the US and on 7 December 2002, *Brainwashed* went to number eighteen on the *Billboard* Top 200. This was Dark Horse's (and Harrison's) best showing on the *Billboard* Top 200 since 1987's *Cloud Nine*. In the UK, the album peaked at 29, also his best showing since *Cloud Nine*. The album did achieve gold status in the UK as well.

One single was released in Europe, featuring 'Any Road' on the A-side. The single made it to number 37 in the UK charts. Harrison can be seen singing 'Any Road' in 1997 while promoting Ravi Shankar's *Chants of India*. 'Marwa Blues', from the album, was placed on side B of the single. It is a rare Harrison instrumental, his first since 'Hari's on Tour (Express)' released in 1974 on *Dark Horse*. Peter Lavessoli, in his book, *The Dawn of Indian Music in the West,* says that the title refers to 'Raga Marwa', which is a traditional classical Indian piece, usually played at sunset. 'Marwa Blues' won the 2004 Grammy Award for Best Pop Instrumental Performance, with Paul McCartney saying that 'Marwa Blues' is one of his favourite songs of all time, and he included it on a CD he put together for *Uncut* Magazine (*Something For the Weekend: Paul McCartney's Glastonbury Groove*).

David Fricke, writing in *Rolling Stone*, wrote: '*Brainwashed* is a warm, frank goodbye, a remarkably poised record about the reality of dying, by a man on the verge. Fear and acceptance run together in these songs, anger as well as serenity. Most importantly, there are lots of guitars'. He gave the album four stars out of five and concluded his review with, 'It is a fine, enchanting epitaph for a man who, to the end of life, believed rock 'n' roll was heaven on earth'. Adrian Zupp, in *Billboard*, raved about the album and Harrison, stating that there is 'not a flat moment on the disc' and that the album 'further confirm(s) Harrison's importance to The Beatles, as well as his individual brilliance'. Chris Jones, writing on the BBC Website, gave the album a good review, noting that it 'turns in a bunch of lovely, sad, love songs, tinged with regret yet lifted by his trademark slide guitar' and 'This is, without doubt, the way we should remember this dark horse'.

The album ends with the title track, 'Brainwashed'. Another scathing, sometimes amusing, but overall dark song, counterbalanced by prayers to God. The song was written, most likely in 1997, and it is the cornerstone of the record. The song ends with a prayer, 'Namah Pavarti', which Harrison sings with his son, Dhani. 'Brainwashed' also features more musicians than any other song on the album. George Harrison (vocals, slide and acoustic guitar, bass, background vocals), Lynne (electric and twelve-string guitar, keyboards, backing vocals), Dhani Harrison (acoustic guitar, backing vocals), Bikram Ghosh (tabla), Jon Lord (piano), Sam Brown (backing vocals), Jane Lister (harp), Jim Keltner (drums) and Isabela Borzymowska (reading from *How to Know God (The Yoga Aphorisms of Patanjali)*)

'I don't think that there should be politicians. They seem to be the ones who mess everything up', George Harrison once said. 'Brainwashed' gave him the opportunity to vent and express himself. It is an angry song, but it ends with a realisation that God is going to get us through this, not money or elected officials and by ending the song with a prayer, the song is actually quite hopeful. The album ends on a positive, albeit sad, note. The work Dhani Harrison and Jeff Lynne did on the album was remarkable and unlike other 'unfinished' albums that are released posthumously, *Brainwashed* sounded like a complete, cohesive album created by the artist. It was (and is) difficult to listen to the album knowing that he had passed away, but as an album, it stands on its own and is a magnificent artistic success. Dark Horse and The Harrisons had every right to be proud.

Eleven days after the release of the album, *Concert For George* took place on 29 November 2002 at The Royal Albert Hall, London. The concert marked the first anniversary of George's passing. The event was organised by Olivia and Dhani, with Eric Clapton as the musical director. The intention of the show was to have Harrison's family and friends perform his music rather than random artists who may have been influenced by Harrison. By having friends and family on stage, the show had a very intimate tone and proved successful both in attendance (it sold out very quickly) and critical reception.

The show was divided into two parts, with Indian music comprising the first part and rock music occupying the second half. Anoushka Shankar (daughter of Ravi) opened the show with Ravi Shankar's composition, 'Your Eyes'. This was followed by a performance from *Monty Python's Flying Circus* (which also featured Tom Hanks in the 'Lumberjack Song' Mountie choir) before the rest of the concert featured artists such as Tom Petty, Gary Brooker, Jeff Lynne, Eric Clapton, Joe Brown (who performed the deep album cut, and one of Harrison's favourites, 'That's The Way it Goes'), Sam Brown and Billy Preston. Also featured were his old Beatle friends, Ringo Starr (who performed a very emotional 'Photograph', a song he wrote with Harrison) and Paul McCartney. McCartney performed an astounding and impassioned version of 'All Things Must Pass'.

The concert was filmed and directed by David Leland and was released on DVD on 10 October 2003. The album of the concert was released on 17 November 2003 by Warner Brothers and not Dark Horse. It is odd that it was not issued on Dark Horse since, at that time, Dark Horse was affiliated with Parlophone/EMI, and McCartney was still with the label at the time. However, Clapton was signed to Warner Brothers, which may explain why the album was released under that umbrella. The DVD *Concert For George* won a Grammy for Best Long Form Video in 2005.

With the success of *Brainwashed*, Olivia made the decision to bring Harrison's Dark Horse Records back and make available Harrison's albums that he had released on the label. With the success of *The Beatles Anthology 1* and the reissue of *Yellow Submarine*, The Beatles added many young fans,but if they were keen enough to explore each Beatle, a lot of Harrison's catalogue was simply not available. It is hard to believe that all of Harrison's albums released from 1976 to 1987 (as well as the two Traveling Wilburys albums) were no longer available to fans. The songs were still being played on the radio, but the albums were not in stores. Additionally, Harrison's solo catalogue was not available on iTunes, which by 2004 had become a major distribution method. But the idea of the albums being reissued was actually George's plan.

Author Alan Clayson wrote that by 2000, Harrison wanted his albums reissued. The reissue of *All Things Must Pass*, which he compiled, was superbly done and, justifiably well received by critics and fans. Harrison had planned to overhaul his catalogue, both the albums he made for Apple and his Dark Horse output. He also had plans to release material that was in his vaults. In February 2001, Harrison took part in an online discussion with fans. When asked about future reissues, he was very clear with his intentions: 'Well, hopefully during this year, I should at least get out a new album and all the other boxes of unreleased demos could possibly follow in eighteen months. I'm trying to get everything that has ever been done out there. It'll just take a little time'.

Harrison, during the same question and answer session, was also clear that he intended to re-release the other Dark Horse albums: 'Well along with my own catalogue of records, the other Dark Horse records will hopefully be finding a new home and coming out on CDs (remastered) sometime in the future', he responded to a question about the reissues.

Olivia and Dhani continued to work on reissuing Harrison's music. His five studio albums, as well as his double live album, *Live in Japan*, were remastered and, on 13 February 2004, were released separately and as part of a box set, *The Dark Horse Years, 1976–1992*, while Dark Horse continued its relationship with EMI/Parlophone. As Olivia Harrison stated in her beautifully written 'History of Dark Horse Records' essay included in the book that was part of the box set, 'The Dark Horse has come full circle now – back with EMI/Parlophone since 2002 – and the seven-headed horse still spins'. The compilation *Best of Dark Horse: 1976–1989* was not included in the set and was not reissued. That particular album has been out of print since 1994 and has not been re-released.

Each album was packaged beautifully, mirroring the original releases, with some additions. *Cloud Nine*, for example, contains commentary from Harrison. The entire box set was put together with extreme love and appreciation of Harrison's art. And it was great to have the albums back available on CD. Fans would have to wait until 2018 to purchase them on vinyl again, and there was no cassette version of the set released.

By the late 1990s, as albums were being re-released on CD, the record companies and artists felt they had to add songs to the CD as bonus tracks.

Not everyone was in favour of such bonus tracks. In fact, some critics had been outright against the whole notion. Caroline Sullivan, writing for *The Guardian*, wrote a rather amusing article: 'What's the Point of Bonus Tracks?'. She answers the question with, 'I've always found bonus tracks annoying because they are usually old songs that a band couldn't get rid of any other way'. She argues that the original release is the definitive version. Roger Daltrey of The Who has very strong opinions about adding bonus tracks to an album, especially 'demos' of songs. He was a guest on Alice Cooper's radio show and said, 'I don't get it. I mean, just 'cause the record company's lost control of the record industry, I just don't get all that crap, y'know? To me, it makes a perfect album imperfect. Putting demos on a finished record is an absolute joke'.

But the Harrisons felt that it was important to keep current with current marketing strategies. So, bonus tracks were added to each album. While these were welcomed (anything new by Harrison would be welcomed by fans), what is interesting is what was left off. Indeed, some of the decisions were downright confusing. Further more, other bonus tracks were available on the iTunes versions of each of the albums. This meant that if you wanted it all, you had to buy the download as well as the physical CD.

Somewhere in England was the most anticipated re-release by fans. Olivia and Dhani had restored the original artwork; it is easy to assume that the original version of the album, complete with the original four songs that were left off after Warner Brothers rejected it, would be the version fans found when they tore the cellophane off of the CD. Sadly, this was not the case. Although the original artwork (by Basil Pao) was restored, the decision was made to stay with the original *released* version. One of the four songs, 'Flying Hour', was added to the digital version while a demo of 'Save the World' was added to the CD. This is perhaps the one album that would have benefited from more bonus material. The four tracks could have been added to the CD, and the original album Harrison had created could have been released. It was an opportunity missed.

While the CDs sounded great, and the remastering job on each album was fantastic, there were three other omissions. Because *Best of Dark Horse: 1976–1989* was not included, the three 'new' songs Harrison had included on that album were now lost. 'Cheer Down' was in the box as a live track, but 'Poor Little Girl' and 'Cockamamie Business' were no longer available, not even on digital platforms. 'Sat Singing', one of the four songs removed from the original version of *Somewhere in England, was* also not included. These are huge omissions and could have been added to any CD, or there could have been a 'rarities CD' included in the box set capturing these and other stray songs. At the time of the writing, those songs continue to be missing in action, and if fans wish to hear them, one must find a copy of *Best of Dark Horse: 1976–1989*.

Also included in the box set, but initially not sold separately, was a DVD featuring a great deal of material. First and foremost, the DVD contained a short feature about Dark Horse Records, but all of Harrison's promo films he made for his Dark Horse Records releases were also there. Included in the set were 'Crackerbox Palace', 'This Song', 'Faster', both versions of 'Got My Mind Set on You', 'When We Was Fab' and 'This is Love'. Missing, however, was the promo film for 'True Love' and the videos for 'Blow Away' and 'All Those Years Ago'. These were very odd omissions, especially when clips of 'Blow Away' were used in the short 'Dark Horse Feature'. Therefore, once again, the set comes up short of being complete.

The DVD also contained live footage from the tour of Japan. 'Cheer Down', 'Devil's Radio', 'Cloud Nine' and 'Taxman' were all featured in very good quality, which leads the viewer to question what other footage and audio is sitting in the vault. Finally, three songs from *Shanghai Surprise* were featured: 'Shanghai Surprise', 'Someplace Else' and 'Hottest Gong in Town'. While these are excellent to watch and hear, there seems to be little reason why the songs could not have been featured as bonus tracks somewhere.

The set was extremely well put together and was well-received by critics and fans. James Griffiths, writing for *The Guardian*, wrote 'many of the actual songs ... are transcendentally lovely'. He added the lovely note that Harrison was 'The Under-Rated One, rather than the Quiet One...' Michael Endelman was less kind; in his review for *Entertainment Weekly*, he writes that the box set 'repackages some of his most dated and mediocre work – the sprightly *Cloud Nine* excepted'. John Metzger, writing for *The Music Box*, reviewed the DVD closely and, although he enjoyed parts of it, the DVD was far too short and 'it ultimately doesn't go far enough to really give Harrison his due'. Christopher Walsh, writing for *Billboard* magazine (and listed as a 'Vital Reissue') had much kinder words on the DVD and box set: 'Harrison's late 1970s/1980s work contains several overlooked or forgotten gems', he observes. 'Also in abundance is Harrison's outstanding guitar playing', noting how the influence of Indian music and his sense of melody helped him create his own 'unique style'. He also notes Harrison's 'spiritually inclined lyrics'. The box set did not chart, despite loosely coinciding with Harrison's birthday and his induction into the

Rock and Roll Hall of Fame. Tom Petty did the honours and inducted Harrison on 14 March 2004.

In 2009, a new album from the Dark Horse Records camp was announced. The label continued to be under the Umlaut umbrella and continued their association with Parlophone/EMI/Capitol records, allowing them access to Harrison's post-Beatles Apple solo recordings. On 14 April 2009, Harrison received his own 'star' on The Hollywood Walk of Fame. Olivia, Dhani, Paul McCartney, Eric Idle, Tom Petty, Tom Hanks and thousands of others were on hand to celebrate the event. Capitol/EMI also used the occasion to announce the release of a new George Harrison album: a 'best of' compilation scheduled to come out in June.

Dark Horse had partnered with Angel Records for the *In Celebration* box set released in 1996. For *Let it Roll: Songs by George Harrison*, Dark Horse and Apple (under the EMI/Capitol umbrella) combined forces, and came up with a very listenable collection, focusing on highlights and tried to give an overview of Harrison's solo output. The album was released worldwide on 16 June 2009 and did extremely well, despite not being released on vinyl or cassette.

The Best of George Harrison, released in 1976, was an album that Harrison disliked and had nothing to do with. The only solo compilation album Harrison ever had a hand in putting together was *Best of Dark Horse 1976 – 1989*. That new collection was put together by Olivia and she designed the beautiful packaging (with help from Drew Lorimer), which featured a stunning photo of Harrison taken from the Apple Archives. The set was remastered by Giles Martin, son of George, who had worked with The Beatles (and Harrisons) for the 2006 album *Love* and *The Beatles Rockband* game. The nineteen songs sounded fantastic, although collectors should note that a 20th song was added to the iTunes digital download album, a demo version of 'Isn't it a Pity'.

It did very well, and for the first time, there were no singles released off the album, either to radio or to record buyers. On 4 July 2009, the album peaked at number 24 on The *Billboard* Top 200 album charts. On the same day, it peaked at number nine on *Billboard*'s Top Rock Albums chart. In Canada, the album peaked at number eighteen on 4 July 2009, while in the UK, Harrison had his first Top Ten album since 1987's *Cloud Nine*, later awarded gold status in the UK.

In terms of reviews, the album received positively. Andrew Hultrans, writing for *Spin* Magazine, stated: 'The quiet Beatle arguably had a stronger, more consistent career than any of his bandmates' and 'forged a unique sound from quavering vocals, layered acoustic guitars and melodic slide playing'. He gave the album eight out of ten stars. While in *Uncut*, David Quantick gave the album a good review: '*Let it Roll* is a proper career retrospective ... and a toe in the water for anyone who, like me all those years ago (sorry), wonders just what George Harrison's music might sound like'. Daryl Easlea, writing for the BBC website, offered: 'George Harrison is the most deserving of all the Beatles for an anthology such as this', and further added, '*Let it Roll* is a celebration of one of the finest and most underrated soulful voices of his generation. And that's before we've even mentioned his guitar work ...' He added in his review that the two previous compilations were not sufficient as an overview of his career.

The album was not without controversy, however. For example, it included three songs from *The Concert For Bangladesh* album that were originally Beatle songs ('Here Comes the Sun', 'Something', 'While My Guitar Gently Weeps'). These are somewhat odd inclusions given Harrison's unhappiness with the use of Beatles songs on *The Best of George Harrison*. While these were solo versions performed live, the songs still date from The Beatles era. Secondly, as with *Best of Dark Horse: 1976–1989*, this was not a 'greatest hits', but rather a 'best of' or an overview. To that end, a number of hits are absent from the collection, such as 'Bangla Desh', 'You', 'Dark Horse', 'This Song', 'Ding Dong; Ding Dong' and 'Crackerbox Palace'. This meant that the only way for a fan to obtain the studio recording of 'Bangla Desh' was to purchase *The Best of George Harrison*, on which it was included.

In 2010, Dark Horse Records entered into yet another agreement, this time with Rhino Records, whose parent company is Warner Brothers. On 18 October 2010, the only joint Dark Horse/Rhino project was released. This box set coincided with Shankar's 90th birthday and was part of the many celebrations and honours that year. The project, released through Dark Horse Records and Rhino Records, was *Collaborations*: a set collecting all of Ravi Shankar's work with Dark Horse. This marked the first time that two entire non-George Harrison Dark Horse Records albums were re-released in their entirety. They were not available individually, but *Shankar Family & Friends* and *Ravi Shankar's Music Festival From India,* were remastered and reissued in the box set. Also included in the box set was the re-release of an album whose copyright was owned by The Harrison Estate, *Chants of India*. It also included a DVD featuring *Music Festival From India – Live at The Royal Albert Hall.*

Rhino Records was founded in 1978 and were originally set up as a reissue label. Originally specialised in novelty records, the label became recognised as one of the best reissue labels, taking great care in their reissues and showing a great deal of respect to the artist and the original work. By 1998, Rhino was purchased by Warner Brothers, and it became a Time Warner label. It retains a very good reputation for reissues.

Collaborations was no exception for Rhino or Dark Horse. This lavish, spectacular box set was near perfect. The original Dark Horse albums were painstakingly remastered and the sound was much enhanced. *Chants of India* had been released on CD, so there was minimal difference. However, to hear *Shankar Family & Friends* on compact disc made the album sound brand new. The same can be said for *Ravi Shankar's Music Festival From India*.

The packaging, designed by Olivia Harrison and Drew Lorimer, was well thought out and an example of how a box set could look. It set new standards for quality. As music fans will know, CDs are typically packaged in small sleeves (usually approximately five by five inches or 13 by 13 cm); for *Collaborations,* the CDs were packaged in 8 ½ by 8 ½ inches (21 ½ by 21 ½ cm) packaging. This allowed for a faithful and wonderful reproduction of the original artwork. As it was a limited edition, the box set also contained a certificate of authenticity. Each certificate was individually numbered.

The front picture of the box was taken by Clive Arrowsmith from his photo sessions for *Ravi Shankar's Music Festival From India* album. The photo captures the incredible relationship between Shankar and Harrison. On his website, Arrowsmith wrote, 'I was delighted when Olivia told me that she was putting together a box set of George and Ravi's music called *Collaborations*. She wanted to use the image of George and Ravi under the same scarf on the cover'.

Additional photos from the Harrisons and Shankars were collected for the beautiful book accompanying the CDs. This book, along with providing information on, and the history of, Harrison's relationship with Shankar, featured a fascinating and glowing introduction by Phillip Glass, an artist who had collaborated with Shankar on *Passages* in 1990.

The DVD contained the film of the first concert of Ravi Shankar's tour of the UK and Europe. The film was directed by Stuart Cooper, who had directed the movie *Little Malcolm and His Fight Against the Eunuchs*. This was a very important film for Harrison and Dark Horse and one could argue it is because of *Little Malcolm and His Fight Against the*

Eunuchs that Dark Horse exists. However, Cooper was given the task of filming the Royal Albert Hall performance on 23 September 1974. The film had not been well stored and, over time, the film and audio deteriorated and required a great deal of work in order for it to be ready for release, with some of the film missing. The audio was more complete and the DVD features a separate 'audio only' track, where one could hear a more complete concert.

Ravi Shankar's daughter, Anoushka Shanker, and Paul Hicks were tasked with the job of restoring the audio. Paul Hicks, son of Hollies member Tony Hicks, is a renowned music engineer and musician. He has worked with Paul McCartney, Ringo Starr, The Beatles, and Elliott Smith, and along with Dhani Harrison, he was also a member of the band thenewno2 (*Prisoner* fans will get that reference) With Dhani Harrison, he has also scored a number of television shows and films. Shankar and Hicks did an excellent job of restoring the music. On the DVD, there is a short documentary directed by David Kew of Anoushka Shankar and Hicks working in the studio, and they are visited by Ravi Shankar and Olivia Harrison. It is a very touching moment.

Although the concert had been shown on a few Public Broadcasting television stations in America, it is fantastic to have the entire film available on DVD. Even though, visually, it is not complete, the footage available makes for an astonishing experience. Writing for *Goldmine* Magazine, Gillian G. Gaar wrote, 'Both CD and DVD are mesmerising, the female vocals having an uncanny ability to imitate the sitar (or vice versa). The CD/DVD also features the most traditional Indian music of this set, as well as the most powerful performances'.

Elsewhere, the box set received generally positive reviews. Terry Staunton, writing in *Record Collector*, said that 'this box set is a strong testament to two friends' mutual respect and their desire to push musical boundaries'. Sophie Harris, writing for *Time Out: New York,* wrote a short but great (and humorous) review for the set, highlighting the influence the musicians have had on artists and the music world in general. She concluded the review with: 'Contained herein: awesome, spooky-sounding chanting, a live DVD, a glossy book and much more to rejoice about'.

On 6 November 2010, *Collaborations* entered the *Billboard* Top World Album chart at number three. This was also the peak position. It was kept from number one by two albums by the Irish band Celtic Thunder (number one was *Christmas*, while *It's Entertainment* had the number two position). It is interesting to note that almost half of the top fifteen records in the chart that week were Celtic albums. It seemed that in terms of the World Music chart, Irish/Celtic music was a dominant commercial force in this particular year. The fact that *Collaborations* cracked the Top Three is, therefore, even more impressive. Indeed, two of the three albums in this set had never made the charts prior to this re-release. In some ways, it was proof that Harrison and Dark Horse Records were ahead of their time. Perhaps the record-buying public were not ready for the albums in 1974 and 1976, but by 2010, the gates had been opened (with a great deal of help from Harrison and Shankar).

The music industry continued to change in the 2010s. One shocking piece of news was the end of EMI Records. In September 2012, it was announced that Universal Music would be taking over EMI for 1.2 billion pounds. EMI, which stood initially for Electric and Music Industries, was founded in 1931 and had become one of the largest record companies during the 1960s through to the 1990s. EMI was acquired by Citigroup (the third-largest banking institute in America) and by 2012, Citigroup broke the organisation up and sold its various departments to various music companies.

The collapse and sale of EMI were important to Dark Horse Records and the Harrison estate, as they had entered into a partnership with Parlophone/Capitol (both owned by EMI) and had released the critically acclaimed and successful *The Dark Horse Years: 1976 – 1989* box set on CD and the compilation *Let it Roll: Songs by George Harrison*. Now Dark Horse Records found itself with Universal.

In 2011, film director Martin Scorsese, released a documentary about Harrison, *George Harrison: Living in the Material World.* Made in cooperation with The Harrison family (Olivia was one of the producers of the film), the documentary provided an excellent overview of Harrison's career. Included were brief scenes of his 1974 tour with Ravi Shankar. The documentary debuted on HBO on 5 October 2011 and went on to win two Emmys (awards for American television shows/ movies) for Outstanding Directing for Nonfiction Programming and Outstanding Nonfiction Special. It was also nominated for four other Emmys – Outstanding Cinematography, Picture Editing, Sound Editing, and Sound Mixing. A book published by Abrams was also released in 2011, which was written by Olivia Harrison.

Finally, a soundtrack, of sorts, was also released, titled *Early Takes: Volume 1.* The album was available on vinyl, CD and as a digital download. However, The album was released on Universal Music (licensed from the George Harrison Estate). The CD features demos and early versions of ten songs, six of which were recorded for *All Things Must Pass* or during that era. Also included was Harrison's version of Bob Dylan's 'Mama, You've Been on My Mind', which, according to Giles Martin (who had compiled the album), was recorded in the 1980s, plus the demo for the song, 'Woman Don't You Cry For Me', and although it appears on the Dark Horse album, *Thirty Three & ⅓*, according to Martin, this is 'one of the earliest recordings on the album' Although the album was hugely successful, and Giles Martin noted in an interview that Harrison was a thorough archivist and there is a lot more material, in 2012, there were no concrete plans for a *Volume 2*. At the time of writing, a *Volume 2* has still not been announced.

Following the release of the *Early Takes: Volume 1,* the Dark Horse Records label made a return. On 24 February 2017, a mammoth box set was released by Universal Music titled *George Harrison – The Vinyl Collection*. This box set contained all of Harrison's solo studio albums (barring the compilation albums), as well as the double live *Live in Japan* album. This meant that all of his solo studio albums were collected in one place. The set includes *Wonderwall Music, Electronic Sound, All Things Must Pass, Living in the Material World, Dark Horse, Extra Texture (Read All About It), Thirty Three & ⅓, George Harrison, Somewhere in England, Gone Troppo, Cloud Nine, Live in Japan* and *Brainwashed*. The live collection, *The Concert For Bangla Desh,* was left out of the collection, as was an album of rarities and B-sides. Included in the box, however, were two 12" single picture discs, 'Got My Mind Set on You' and 'When We Was Fab'.

Ron Hart, writing for *The Observer,* noted in his very positive review of the box set that *George Harrison – The Vinyl Collection* provided '... the perfect opportunity to reconsider the work this quiet, spiritual, beautiful man delivered in increasingly sporadic doses...' Steve Matteo, writing for *Under The Radar,* noted the box set '... is housed in a beautiful box and each package is replicated exactly like the original album release, with the records themselves pressed on 180-gram heavyweight vinyl'. He gave the album an excellent review but did note that fans may be somewhat disappointed with the lack of rarities and bonus material.

On 10 August 2018, Dark Horse Records released *Ain't Love Enough: The Best of Attitudes.* This was a very significant release, confirming that Dark Horse Records were well and truly back. But this was a digital-only release, available for download through iTunes and other platforms, such as Amazon. The album was re-released on 24 January 2020 when Dark Horse Records entered into an agreement with BMG. Even though the album was only available as a digital release, it was an encouraging sign that some of the music from the label might be made available again.

This release was exciting news. It seemed that music recorded for Dark Horse Records, long unavailable, was resurfacing. Perhaps encouraged by the conversation Olivia Harrison had had with David Foster (as he noted in his book), this long overdue compilation was finally out.

However, it was not reviewed, nor did it chart. Promotion was kept to a minimum with a couple of radio interviews by band members, but overall, the release went largely unnoticed, other than by Beatles fans and fans of the individual members of Attitudes. This was a shame, but the *Good News* (pun intended) was that the album continues to be available on streaming platforms.

A New Decade, A New Start

On 22 January 2020, BMG announced on their website that Dark Horse Records had partnered with BMG and would be releasing new music. Their announcement went on to state that it is a new 'multi-faceted global partnership'. Further, it was stated that the label would be run by Dhani Harrison and his manager, David Zonshine. Of course, Harrison had experience running his own label H.O.T. (which stands for Henley-on-Thames), and he had done well in keeping it active for a number of years. While he did not sign other artists to the label, he was able to get his music to the public.

This was very big news, especially since the press release noted that Harrison's solo catalogue was set to be re-released; Dark Horse was set to reissue Harrison's Dark Horse Records and the other artists who had recorded for Dark Horse Records. Further, it was announced that there would be 'compilations, live albums and box sets featuring rare and unreleased recordings from the Dark Horse label – many of which will be made available digitally for the first time ever' A website (*www. darkhorse.com*) was launched. Dark Horse Records could also be found on social media platforms, such as Facebook, Twitter and Instagram.

The official press release from BMG read:

It is with great pleasure and excitement that I can finally announce a new chapter for Dark Horse Records in the music industry alongside our friends at BMG. The label, started by my father in 1974, has been a family business my whole life (and is, indeed, the reason that my parents met). From the Indian classical Ragas of Ravi Shankar to the rock 'n' roll of Attitudes, I look forward to reintroducing, to a new audience, all of those artists that my father loved so much. We will also be expanding the Dark Horse family with new artists and classic catalogues in the coming years to include a rich and varied roster of incredible musicians whom we love. Please watch this space! With love, Dhani Harrison.

The announcement also included the fact that Dark Horse Records would be joining with another label set up by the Harrison family, HarriSongs label. The HarriSongs label was an online platform that would allow for free streaming of the music. The label was launched on 18 April 2018 to commemorate Ravi Shankar's birthday (7 April

1920) and Ali Akbar Khan's birthday (14 April 1922). The only two releases on the label were *Chants of India* and a reissue of the 1972 Apple album *In Concert 1972*, also available as downloads. HarriSongs was established in partnership with Craft Records. Both albums, once under the HarriSongs label banner, were now copyrighted by the Estate of G.H., licensed to BMG. Umlaut and Dark Horse were not mentioned or noted.

However, by 2020, Dark Horse Records had found a home with BMG. In 2017, Dhani Harrison released his first solo album, *In///Parallel*, which was released on his H.O.T. (Henley-on-Thames) label through BMG. Although Harrison had released a great deal of material with his bands, thenewno2 (debuting in 2006 with an EP), Fistful of Mercy (2010) and his soundtrack work with Paul Hicks, *In///Parallel* was his first solo album, released in North America on 20 October 2017. It was not on Dark Horse Records.

BMG (Bertelsmann Music Group) Music, as it is known nowadays, established itself in 2008. Originally, it was part of Sony/BMG, but in 2008, the company sold its shares in Sony and went independent. BMG was started by Carl Bertelsmann in 1835 as a publishing house in Gütersloh, Germany, but by the 1950s, the company moved into music and formed the Ariola label. The label proved very successful and by 1985, Bertelsmann company acquired RCA and, with all the labels associated it, forming BMG Music. In 2003, BMG merged with Sony Music, forming Sony/BMG. By 2008, as an independent label, they launched a company built on 'fairness, service and transparency'. No doubt a model that the Harrison family would find attractive, and that George Harrison himself would approve of as a home for Dark Horse.

Dhani had been working with BMG since 2017. BMG had assisted him with his solo career, and obviously, Dhani Harrison felt that BMG could do the same with Dark Horse. They did promote the partnership, as articles appeared in the media, and at the same time, they gave the label high exposure, beginning on 25 January 2020 when BMG announced that BMG and Dark Horse would be co-hosting BMG's annual 'Wammys', a pre-Grammy's party. Dhani appeared (performing covers of Electric Light Orchestra's 'Wild West Hero' and Petty's 'You Don't Know How It Feels'). Other artists at the event included Jewel (who performed 'Here Comes the Sun' with Butch Walker and Lukas Nelson), Weird Al Yankovic (who performed 'Savoy Truffle' with Jimmy Vivino), Blur's Graham Coxon (performing 'Taxman'), Perry Farrell (performing 'Just

Like a Woman' with Etty Farrell and Danny Clinch) and Jakob Dylan (performing Petty's 'The Waiting').

On 24 January 2020, BMG announced that the initial releases on Dark Horse Records were being released through digital platforms only. In the list were *In Concert 1972, Chants of India* (both previously released through HarriSongs, but now under the Dark Horse label) and *Ain't Love Enough: Best of Attitudes*. These releases were available on streaming services and download platforms. However, four other titles were announced.

The first new release was a tribute to Tom Petty. 'For Real – For Tom', is a one-track single featuring Jakob Dylan, Dhani Harrison, Amos Lee, Lukas Nelson, Micah Nelson and Willie Nelson. 'For Real' was originally released on the 2019 compilation box set, *The Best of Everything* by Tom Petty and the Heartbreakers, having been recorded in 2000 by Petty and the Heartbreakers but was not released until 2019. It was released for charity, benefitting the homeless in Los Angeles, via Midnight Mission. The UK's *Far Out* Magazine gave the song a great review, referring to it as a 'wonderful tribute'.

Although the song/single received a great deal of written press, it did not chart. However, those who heard it seemed to like it and applauded the fact that it was a worthy cause. It was also nice to see a Harrison and a Dylan working together again, albeit their sons. It is an interesting and very positive Dark Horse Records debut for Dhani.

Dark Horse Records also signed a 'new' artist, Joe Strummer, to the label, the first artist since Keni Burke signed as a solo artist in 1977. The three albums by Joe Strummer & The Mescaleros – *Rock Art and the X-Ray Style, Global a Go-Go*, and *Streetcore* – were included in the four initial releases. Joe Strummer, of course, was a member of The Clash, a band with its roots firmly planted in the punk movement in the UK.

George Harrison was not a fan of punk, although he understood why it needed to exist. Harrison was quite critical of the movement. In talking with Mick Brown of *Rolling Stone* magazine, Harrison said, 'I don't think punk was inventing anything except negativity ... As far as musicianship goes, the punk bands were just rubbish – no finesse in the drumming, just a lot of noise and nothing'. Yet, at the same time, he understood where the noise and anger originated. '... I felt very sorry when the Sex Pistols were on television and one of them was saying, 'We're educated to go into the factories and work on assembly lines ...' and that's their future. It *is* awful, and it's especially awful that it should come out of

England because England is continually going through depression; it's a very negative country. But out of all that is born the punk thing, so it's understandable'.

Strummer, however, was a Beatles fan. The same man who wrote about phoney Beatlemania, also told Judy McGuire, 'I'd like to see somebody try and beat the Beatles. Many people have tried'.

Born John Graham Mellor on 21 August 1952, Strummer cut his teeth in music by first learning the ukulele. George Harrison would, no doubt, have loved that fact. After spending time in some local bands (Flaming Youth and The Vultures), Strummer formed The 101ers. While a member of The 101ers, he had the opportunity to perform a show opening for The Sex Pistols. The 101ers were not a punk band, but the energy of The Sex Pistols caught his attention, and when he was asked by manager Bernie Rhodes to join a band that was being formed with Mick Jones, he jumped at the opportunity. The new band became The Clash, and they made their debut on 4 July 1976 in Sheffield. In January of 1977, they released their debut album (*The Clash*, Epic/CBS) in the UK.

Five more albums would be recorded under The Clash banner, but by 1986, the band had run its course and Strummer officially went solo. He formed a new band, The Latino Rockabilly War, but after one studio album and a soundtrack, thet disbanded. In 1999, he formed The Mescaleros. Their first album, *Rock Art and the X-Ray Style,* was released on 18 October 1999 on the Hellcat label. The album received lukewarm reviews and did not chart.

This was followed by the more successful *Global a Go-Go*, released on 24 July 2001 on the Hellcat label. The album reached number 34 on *Billboard*'s 'Heatseeker' chart. Once again, the reviews were somewhat lukewarm, but it did mark a return to form of sorts for Strummer.

Strummer passed away quite suddenly on 29 December 2002 from an undiagnosed congenital heart defect. Like Harrison, his last solo album would be released posthumously. *Streetcore* was released on 21 October 2003, once again on the Hellcat Records label. The album was his most successful with The Mescaleros. It was his only album to make it on the *Billboard* Top 200 albums (peaking at 160 on 8 November 2003). One week later, it would make it to number eleven on *Billboard*'s Independent Chart.

The re-release on Dark Horse was initially only on digital platforms. To promote the catalogue coming to Dark Horse, an online/streaming event took place on Friday 21 August 2020. Advertised as being presented by

Gates of The West and Dark Horse Records, was called *A Song For Joe: Celebrating the Birthday of Joe Strummer*. Two years later, these albums would be released on vinyl and CD.

Gates of the West, while the name of a Clash song, is also a project founded by musician Jesse Malin and DJ Jeff Raspe. They bring together, on an annual basis, musicians to pay tribute to The Clash. In 2020, due to the COVID-19 pandemic, the show was put online and streamed. The shows typically benefit the Joe Strummer Foundation and Music & Memory. The 2020 show also benefitted 'Save Our Stages, which was being spearheaded by the National Independent Venue Association (NIVA) to preserve and protect the USA's independent live music venues and promoters'. As well as previously unreleased film footage of Strummer, the show also featured performances by Bruce Springsteen, Albert Hammond Jr., Dropkick Murphys, Hinds, Jesse Malin and many more. Dhani Harrison also appeared in the show, introducing Nicolai Fraiture (who performed 'Police and Thieves'). The livestream was a success and the show achieved its goal of raising money for a very important cause.

On 29 August 2020, Dark Horse Records released its first physical record since the George Harrison vinyl box set. The album *Chants of India* was pressed, for the first time, in a limited number on red vinyl. It was originally scheduled to be released on 18 April 2020 as part of Record Store Day, but due to the COVID-19 Pandemic, the date for Record Store Day was changed, and the album, in the limited number of 3000, sold out immediately when it eventually hit record stores.

Chants of India was released on vinyl as a double album, housed in a gatefold sleeve and was accompanied by a print of George Harrison and Ravi Shankar. It was a joint Dark Horse and HarriSongs release, but it was great to see the Dark Horse Records label once again spinning on a turntable.

Although *Shankar Family & Friends* was technically the second release from Dark Horse all those years ago in 1974, seeing *Chants of India* by Shankar, produced by George Harrison, playing on the record player, one could be forgiven for feeling as though one had been transported in time to 1974.

Since then, a Strummer compilation, *Assembly*, has been released by Dark Horse (in March 2021), which did very well on the charts and received very positive reviews. In August 2021, it was announced that Billy Idol had signed to Dark Horse Records with a debut EP released in 2021. Since then, Idol has released a Christmas album (*Happy Holidays*) as well as a second EP (*The Cage*). Dark Horse also re-released seventeen albums by the legendary Leon Russell (from 1984's *Hank Wilson Vol. 2* through to 2013's *Snapshot*) on digital platforms. In 2021, however, Leon Russell's 2001 album *Signature Songs* made its debut on vinyl (it had only been released on CD previously) on Dark Horse, with a CD released as well. Along with Russell's albums, Dark Horse signed a deal to re-release former Deep Purple member Jon Lord's solo albums.

In 2022, Dark Horse also released a compilation album of the original Dark Horse artists. The album *Dark Horse Records (The Best Of 1974 – 1977)* featured songs from all of the artists who had released music on the label through A&M. Once again, the album was released as a special release for Record Store Day. On the same day, they released a 12" single of Ravi Shankar's 'I Am Missing You'. As with most Record Store Day Releases, both of these were limited edition. But Dark Horse was not finished. In 2023, *Stairsteps 2nd Resurrection* and *Shankar Family & Friends* were re-released in limited quantities on coloured vinyl with accompanying CDs available.

In 2023, Dark Horse made two other announcements that created a great deal of excitement. First, Yusuf/Cat Stevens shared that he had signed with the label. In his interviews and press releases, Yusuf noted his kinship with George Harrison. 'While most of my generation was just into music, I was a bit like George, where music became the key to something much higher', he told Jonathon Cohen of *Spin* Magazine. The first single released by Yusuf/Cat Stevens was his acoustic version of 'Here Comes The Sun' in February 2023. This was followed by an album, *King Of A Land*, released in June. It charted at number 49 in the UK, making it the highest-charting non-George Harrison Dark Horse album.

The other big news in February 2023 (actually released on what would have been George Harrison's 80th birthday) was the announcement that his entire recorded catalogue was now owned by The Harrison family and all of it would be re-released on the Dark Horse label. Not only was his entire solo output going to be on Dark Horse, but the Harrison family also issued all of Harrison's music as a stream-only Dolby Atmos mix through Apple Music. Through Facebook, Dhani made the announcement and added, 'we will also be using this opportunity to make all the custom limited vinyl that we can get away with. Happy 80th Dad, we love you'.

Dark Horse Records seemed to be alive and kicking. Fans seemed to welcome the new Dark Horse phase but continued to wait for news of reissues of the classic albums. The albums were released, but as of 2023, only on digital platforms.

All of this news and these releases are very significant. For the first time, fans can legally download the albums they have read about over the years and ditch those dubious CDs.

The fact that Dark Horse released a compilation, *Dark Horse Records (The Best 1974 – 1977),* suggests that the label has a plan to reissue the albums physically in the future. The albums are full of great music that should be heard, while the Billy Idol, Joe Strummer and Leon Russell reissues are also indicative of a very active label.

Afterword

Dark Horse Records remains an interesting chapter in Harrison's life and career. He not only maintained a solo career but established a new record label that was not striving for international, huge successes, but rather a label that could sustain itself and introduce new music to the world. This also made it one that stood out in the music business, given its business model and desire to promote new and diverse music. But Harrison was also aware that his name would draw attention to the music being released on the label.

When Dark Horse Records debuted in September 1974 with Splinter's debut album *The Place I Love,* the main reason the album and the label received so much attention was because of the Beatles's involvement. Harrison made no secret of this; he was placed prominently in many of the print advertisements for the album. Harrison thought he would draw attention to music that he thought should be heard. They also had the talent to back up any attention they received. Splinter were a great band and it was understandable that Harrison would be a fan.

This model of nurturing a smaller number of artists, yet sustaining itself can be seen in subsequent labels such as Mute Records and Nonsuch. These are two examples of small, diverse labels that focus on the music rather than generating hits. The more successful artists provide the revenue needed for the rest to produce their music. For example, on Nonsuch, David Byrne's albums help fund the more experimental Laurie Anderson. This is what Harrison had hoped for Dark Horse 30 years before.

Harrison could have signed bigger, established artists to his label. However, he wanted to promote the artists and music that he enjoyed. The first three years of Dark Horse were exciting and very busy, with eight albums by six artists released between September 1974 and March 1976. Furthermore, unlike Apple, none of those albums were solo projects by George Harrison. Of those eight albums, Harrison was directly involved in half (i.e. he played on them or produced them) and he provided a great deal of support, encouragement and, yes, money to the other four.

Harrison never intended the label to be massive, wanting to sign artists who were friends (Shankar, Attitudes) and new, exciting artists who were original and had something positive to say. Harrison always enjoyed helping artists, as he demonstrated during the early days of Apple. Of all The Beatles, he was the most involved in signing artists, which he continued until Apple shut down. This helps us understand the reason for Dark Horse. He wanted to sign Splinter to Apple, but since there were legal issues, he formed Dark Horse instead.

Harrison also learnt from the issues at Apple Records, and he did not want to replicate the same problems that Apple suffered. Dark Horse offices were small (Dark Horse basically shared space with another A&M label, Ode Records) and when they moved to Warner Brothers, Dark Horse had small offices in LA and in London. Gone were the days of owning a building like 3 Savile Row. Harrison was also more involved with day-to-day operations than The Beatles had been with Apple. He chose singles, consulted with track selections of albums, helped with promotion and got bands on tours. But this was never about control, it was about care. Harrison wanted the best for the artists on his label. In many ways, he felt responsible for them.

Furthermore, Harrison tried to help the artists who recorded with Dark Horse as best he could. One could argue that aspects of promotion suffered and that mistakes were made, but Harrison did what he thought was best for the artists. He may not have produced every act or played on their albums, but he did provide support in other ways, if by no other means than by getting their music out into the world.

But the music business changed a great deal over time, as it always has and will. Harrison kept up with the times, but he also had a model of record promotion that became old-fashioned. By the late 1970s, simply sending a single to a radio station did not equate to a hit record and furthermore simply having a Beatle involved did not mean an instant hit. It may draw increased attention to a certain record, but it did not ensure a hit. And these things combined did not help with Harrison's morale. By 1979, all of the acts had been dropped by Dark Horse Records, and it almost forced Harrison focused on his own music career.

It is hard to blame him. When one looks at 1974 – 1975 and how much Harrison had accomplished, he had every right to be exhausted. By 1976, things had slowed down significantly, but when one considers that besides Dark Horse Records, he had written and recorded three solo albums, completed a tour, produced three other albums, and worked on numerous other records, it is clear. After *Thirty Three & 1/3*, he must have been exhausted. Moreover, his personal life was turbulent, not to mention the numerous court battles he fought regarding The Beatles' legal matters and legacy. It is completely understandable that he took a much-needed break in 1977. By 1978, he started recording and putting together *George Harrison*, but being on his own label, he had total control of release dates and albums. In theory, at least.

The circumstances surrounding *Somewhere in England*, in 1980 certainly did not help his morale or his perception of record companies. Having an album publicly rejected by your parent record company disturbed Harrison. 'Blood of a Clone', a song he wrote and recorded to replace the songs 'rejected' by Warner Brothers, is a clear attack on the record company and the music industry as a whole. Harrison was understandably disillusioned. In many ways, one can imagine that not only did he not want to deal with the music business, but had little interest in bringing new artists into such a corrupt system

Splinter's *Two Man Band* was the last non-George Harrison album released until *In Celebration*. Harrison, who was once again firmly established in the music business with his successful *Cloud Nine* album, not to mention The Traveling Wilburys, brought Dark Horse out of semi-retirement and partnered with Angel Records for the *In Celebration* box set (and *In Celebration Highlights*) to honour Ravi Shankar. The next year, Harrison helped Shankar with his beautiful *Chants of India* as a producer and helped him promote it. Both albums were very successful, critically and commercially. *Chants of India*, although released through Angel/EMI, might have been released on Dark Horse, as George Harrison held the copyrights. But he was smart enough to hold the copyright and license the album to record companies. The album, *Chants of India*, would eventually find a home at Dark Horse Records and be issued twice, once on CD (as part of the box set *Collaborations*) and once on vinyl.

Harrison had his own studio, his own label, his own cottage industry. He was truly independent. Many labels and artists claim to be independent, but by the 1990s, Harrison defined independence. And, in some respects, that was what he had always hoped for Dark Horse Records: an independent record company, self-sufficient, with his studio in England and, originally, the A&M studio in Los Angeles. But as Robert Burns once wrote, 'the best-laid plans o' mice an' men...' He ran into legal difficulties with A&M, Warner Brothers disappointed him and, in the end, all he had left was his own music.

Dark Horse Records, like Apple, was not a failure. It was a fantastic idea and, for a time, well executed. A lot of great music exists because of George Harrison and Dark Horse, which still deserves to be heard, played and enjoyed. It was an experiment and model that others have adapted and been very successful with, such as Sufjan Stevens' Asthmatic Kitty. He is an artist who has established his own independent label, which allows him to help out a great many other artists while being a mechanism to release his own music.

Although Dark Horse was a British label, it had its base in America. Harrison loved American music and grew up with it, from Bing Crosby as a child, to early rock 'n' roll, to RnB, to country rock, he loved American music. It is no wonder that all but three artists signed to Dark Horse were American. It was also clear that Harrison knew he had to establish the label and the artists in America, which is one of the reasons he spent so much time in Los Angeles during 1974 and 1975. However, in the 2020s, the label seems to be back home with the unusual release of music by Billy Idol and Joe Strummer. Much like the original version of label, one does not know what to expect from its current incarnation.

When Dark Horse Records debuted in 1974, artist-owned record companies were nothing new; A&M was a prime example. But what made Dark Horse different was that, despite the small size of the label, it was incredibly diverse. The first two releases could not be more different: an Indian ballet and a British folk album. Yet, fans of each could easily enjoy the other. Harrison signed a rhythm and blues band, a jazz/funk band, a rock band, and a British blues artist for Dark Horse's first two years. Had Harrison stayed with A&M, or Warner Brothers had been more invested, who knows who else Dark Horse would have signed. The fact that Dhani has re-released Joe Strummer's music makes total sense, considering Dark Horse's diverse history.

Dark Horse Records was not a vanity label set up exclusively for George Harrison's music. It was a record label and company that attempted – and succeeded – in being unique, that desired to make a difference. Harrison had a passion for helping artists and introduce them to the world. He felt there was room in the music business to accommodate many different styles and a label with diverse acts could not only exist but thrive. It was more of a philosophy than a business plan, and the world was a better place because of it.

Dark Horse Records Discography

Attitudes
Singles (US/UK/Australia)
Ain't Love Enough/The Whole World's Gone Crazy DH-10004/AMS 5504
09/12/75
Honey Don't Leave L.A./Lend A Hand DH-10008 31/05/76 (U.S. Only)
Sweet Summer Music/If We Want DH-10011/AMS 5508 23/07/76
Sweet Summer Music/Being Here With You DRC 8404 (US only)
13/06/77
Sweet Summer Music/Turning In Space DHS 6785 1977 (Australian only)
In A Stranger's Arms/Good News DRC 8452 (--/09/77) (U.S Only)

Albums (US/UK)
Attitudes SP- 22008/AMLH 22008 06/02/76
Good News DH – 3021/ K 56385 05/05/77
Ain't Love Enough: The Best of The Attitudes Digital/ Streamed/
Download Only 10/08/18

Keni Burke
Singles (US/UK)
Shuffle/From Me To You DRC 8474. 11/10/77 (US only)
Keep On Singing/Day DRC 8522 1978

Albums
Keni Burke DH 3022 16/08/77 (US Only)

Jakob Dylan, Dhani Harrison, Amos Lee, Lukas Nelson,
For Real Digital/Stream/Download

George Harrison
Singles
This Song/Learning How To Love You DRC 8294/K 16856 03/11/76
Crackerbox Palace/Learning How to Love You DRC 8313 24/01/77 (US
Only)

True Love/Pure Smokey K 16896 11/02/77 (UK only)

It's What You Value/Woman Don't You Cry For Me K 16967 31/05/77 (UK only)

Blow Away/Soft Hearted Hana DRC 8763 14/02/79 (US Only)

Blow Away/Soft Tough K 17327 14/02/79 (UK Only)

Love Comes To Everyone/Soft Hearted Hana K 17284 20/04/79 (UK Only)

Love Comes To Everyone/Soft Touch DRC 8763 11/05/79 (US Only)

Faster/Your Love Is Forever K 17423 30/07/79 (UK Only – also released as a picture disc)

All Those Years Ago/Writing's One The Wall DRC 49725/K17807 06/05/81

Teardrops/Save The World DRC 49785/K 17837 15/07/81

Wake Up My Love/Greece 7-29864/929864-7 27/10/82

I Really Love You/Circles 7-29744 07/02/83 (US Only)

Got My Mind Set On You/Lay His Head 7-28178/W8178 03/10/87 (Released as a 12-inch single)

When We Was Fab/Zig Zag 7-28131/W813103/01/88 (Also released as a 12-inch single)

This Is Love/Breath Away From Heaven 7-27913/W7913 12/05/88 (Also released as a 12-inch single)

Cheer Down/Poor Little Girl W2696 12/11/89 (UK Only – Also released as a 12-inch single)

Any Road/Marwa Blues 724355211774/R 6601 12/05/03

Albums

Dark Horse Records Presents A Personal Music Dialogue With George Harrison At 33 ¹/₃ PRO- 6491976 (US Only)

33 & ¹/₃ DH – 3005/ K 5631924/11/76

George Harrison DH – 3255/K 5656214/02/79

Somewhere In England DHK-3492/K 5687001/06/81

Gone Troppo 1-23734/ 923 734-127/10/82

Cloud Nine 1-25643/ WX-12302/11/87

Best Of Dark Horse – 1976 – 1989 1-25726 / WX-31217/10/89

Live In Japan 9 26964-2/7599-26964-1 13/07/92

Brainwashed 7243 5 41969 18/11/02

The Dark Horse Years 1976–1992 CDP 7243 5 97051 0 1/ GHBOX 1/7243 5 94232 0 323/02/04

Billy Idol
Eps
The Roadside DH0004 17/09/21
The Cage DH0008 11/11/22

Albums
Happy Holidays DH0005 04/11/21

Jiva
Singles
Something's Goin' On Inside L.A/Take My Love DH-10006 11/02/76 (US only)

Albums
Jiva SP-22003/AMLH 22002 06/10/75

Henry McCullough
Albums
Mind Your Own Business SP-22001 / AMLH 22001 25/09/74

Leon Russell
Albums
Signature Songs DH0011 17/03/23

Ravi Shankaar
Singles
I Am Missing You/Lust DH-10001/AMS 7133 06/11/74 (Released as a 12-inch single in 2022)

Albums
Shankar Family & Friends SP-22002/AMLH 22002 07/10/74
Ravi Shankar's Music Festival From India SP- 22007/AMLH 22007 06/02/76

Ravi Shankar/George Harrison
Albums
Collaborations R2-525469 19/10/10
Chants Of India DH001 29/08/20

Splinter
Singles
Costafine Town/Elly-May DH-10002/AMS 7135 07/11/74
Drink All Day/Haven't Got Time AMS 5501 07/02/75 (UK only)
China Light/Drink All Day AMS 55 02 21/02/75 (UK only)
China Light/Haven't Got Time DH-10003 07/03/75 (US only)
Which Way Will I Get Home/Green Bus Line AMS-5503 07/11/75 (UK only)
Which Way Will I Get Home/What Is It (If You Never Ever Tried Yourself) DH-10007 09/02/76 (US only)
Half Way There/What Is It (If You Never Ever Tried Yourself) AMS-5506 21/05/76 (UK only)
After Five Years/Half Way There DH-10010 16/07/76 (US only)
Round And Round/I'll Bend For You DRC 8439/K 17009 06/09/77
New York City (Who Am I)/Baby Love K 17116 --/02/78 (UK Only)
Motions Of Love/I Need Your Love DRC 8534 --/02/278 (US Only)

Albums
The Place I Love SP-22001/AMLH 2200120/09/74
Harder To Live SP-22006 (US)/ AMLH 22006 (UK)06/10/75
Two Man Band DH – 3073 (US)/K 56403 03/10/77

Stairsteps
Singles
From Us To You/Time DH-10005/AMS 5505 03/12/75
Pasado/Thrown' Stones Atcha AMS-5507 21/06/76 (UK only)
Tell Me Why/Salaam DH-10009 14/06/76 (US only)

Albums
Second Resurrection SP- 22004 (US)/AMLH 22005 (UK) 06/02/76

Joe Strummer
Singles
Junco Partner (Acoustic)/Junco Partner (Live) DH003 12/06/21

Albums
Assembly DH002 26/03/21
Live At Music Millennium DH0013 25/11/22

Joe Strummer & The Mescaleros
Albums
Joe Strummer 002: *The Mescalors Years* DH0009 16/09/22

Yusuf/Cat Stevens
Singles
Here Comes The Sun Digital/Stream/Download

Albums
King Of A Land 538868871 16/06/23

Various Artists
Dark Horse Radio Special Dark Horse Records (The Best Of 1974-1977) DH001225/11/22

Bibliography

Brennan, Tom http://badfinge.ipower.com/DarkHorseRecords/Jiva/ JivaLibrary.html

Brown, Peter; Gaines, Steven. *The Love You Make: An Insider's Story of The Beatles*. London: Macmillan Publishers, 1983.

Castleman, Harry and Podrazik, Walter J. *All Together Now: The First Complete Beatles Discography 1961–1975*, Ballantine Books (New York, NY, 1976; ISBN 0-345-25680-8)

Chaurasia, Hariprasad. Interview with Author, September 16, 2020.

Cicalo, Hank. Interview with Author September 2, 2020

Clapton, Eric. *Clapton: The Autobiography*. Broadway, 2007.

Clayson, Alan, *George Harrison*, Sanctuary, London, 2003

Cohen, Finn. 'The Day Prince's Guitar Wept The Loudest'. *New York Times,* April 28, 2004, retrieved November 16, 2020.

Coleman, Ray. 'Harrison Regains His Rubber Soul'. *Melody Maker*, November 27, 1976. p. 23

Coon, Caroline (1977). *1988: The New Wave Punk Rock Explosion*. Hawthorn, 1977

Davis, Andy (2010). *Encouraging Words* (CD booklet). Billy Preston. Apple Records.

DiLello, Richard. *The Longest Cocktail Party – An Insider's Diary of the Beatles, Their Million Dollar 'Apple' Empire and Its Wild Rise and Fall*. Playboy Press, 1972

Dogget, Peter. (2009) *You Never Give Me Your Money: The Beatles After The Break-up* HarperCollins, 2009.

Doyle, Tom. *Man On The Run: Paul McCartney in the 1970s*. Ballantine Books, 2014

Du Noyer, Paul. *The Illustrated Encyclopedia of Music*. Fulham, London: Flame Tree Publishing, 2003. p. 181.

Editors of *Rolling Stone*, The. *Harrison*, Rolling Stone Press/Simon & Schuster, 2002

Engelhardt, Kristofer. *Beatles Undercover.* Collector's Guide Publishing, 1998.

Engelhardt, Kristofer. *The Beatles Deeper Undercover*. Collector's Guide Publishing, 2010.

Geldof, Bob. *Is That It?* Pan MacMillan, 2005

Giddens, Gary. 'Dreaming A LIttle Dream With Bing Crosby: Nothing Is Dated On John Lennon's Jukebox'. *Town Topics*, May 3, 2017. Retrieved Oct. 1, 2020.

Gould, Jonathan. *Can't Buy Me Love: The Beatles, Britain and America*. London: Piatkus, 2008.

Granados, Stefan. *Those Were the Days: An Unofficial History Of The*

Beatles' Apple Organization: An Unofficial History of the 'Beatles' Apple Organization 1967–2001. Cherry Red Books, 2002.

Green, Derek. Interview with Author. July 21, 2019.

Hall, Ron. *The Chum Chart Book. 1957 – 1986 A Complete Listing Of Every Charted Record.* Stardust Productions, 2007.

HariSongs. www.harisongs.com.

Harrison, George. George Harrison Dark Horse Radio Special. Dark Horse Records. November 1974.

Harrison, George. Dark Horse Records Presents A Personal Music Dialogue With George Harrison At 33⅓. Dark Horse Records/Ganga PRO 649 1976

Harrison, George. *I Me Mine. The Extended Edition.* Genesis Publications, 2017.

Harrison, Olivia and Holorn, Mark. *Living In The Material World: George Harrison.* Harry N. Abrams, 2011.

Harry, Bill. *The Paul McCartney Encyclopedia*, Virgin Books, 2002.

Harry, Bill *The George Harrison Encyclopedia*, Virgin Books, 2003.

Heatley, Michael. Liner Notes, *Henry McCullough Band Live At Rockpalast* CD, Repertoire. 2014

Chris Hunt (ed.), *NME Originals: Beatles – The Solo Years 1970–1980.* IPC Ignite!, 2005, p. 22.

Huntley, Eliot J., *Mystical One: George Harrison – After the Break-up of the Beatles* (Guernica Editions, 2006.

Lanning, Michael. (Music and Art Interviews, 12 Mar 2013)

Lanning, Michael. Facebook Performance. July 15, 2020.

Lavezzoli, Peter. *The Dawn of Indian Music in the West*, Continuum, 2006.

Leng, Simon. *While My Guitar Gently Weeps: The Music of George Harrison*, Hal Leonard, 2006.

Lewisohn, Mark (1988). The Beatles's Recording Sessions (1st Ed.), Harmony Books, 1988.

Leenheer, Franck, and Dickmann. *The International Dark Horse & Ring O'Records Discography. Updated and Extended Edition.* Self Published, 2004.

Lewisohn, Mark (1992). *The Complete Beatles Chronicle:The Definitive Day-By-Day Guide To the Beatles' Entire Career* (2010 ed.). Chicago Review Press, 2010 ed.

Lorimer, Dre and Harrison, Olivia. Collaborations Box Set Book. Dark Horse Records/Rhino Records, 2010.

Madinger, Chip & Easter, Mark. 'Eight Arms To Hold You: The Solo Beatles Compendium. 44 1 Productions Inc; 1st edition (October 1, 2000)

Margouleff, Robert. Interview with Author September 9, 2020.

Materialworldfoundation.com

Mojo Staff, (2015) 'Jeff Lynne: 'Bob Dylan Wanted To Call Us Roy & The Boys". *Mojo* magazine. 4 November 2015, retrieved 2 November 2020.

O'Dell, Chris; with Ketcham, Katherine. *Miss O'Dell: My Hard Days and Long Nights with The Beatles, The Stones, Bob Dylan, Eric Clapton, and the Women They Loved*, New York, NY: Touchstone, 2009.

Ostin, Mo (2007). 'The History of The Traveling Wilburys: Introduction'. *The Traveling Wilburys Collection* (CD Booklet). Wilbury Recordings.

Purvis, Robert. Quoted in Tom Brennan's SPlinter Library (http://badfinge.ipower.com/Splinter/AnotherChance.html). Retrieved November 26, 2020.

Pythons, The. *Autobiography of The Python*. Thomas Dunne Books/St Martin's Press, 2003. ISBN 0-312-31144-3.

Reed, Jack. Interview with Author November 4, 2018.

Rodriguez, Robert. *Fab Four FAQ 2.0: The Beatles' Solo Years, 1970 – 1980*. Backbeat Books, 2010.

Romanowski, Patricia; George-Warren, Holly; Pareles, Jon, *The New Rolling Stone Encyclopedia of Rock & Roll*. New York: Fireside/Rolling Stone Press, 1995.

Schaffner, Nicholas. *The Beatles Forever*. Cameron House, 1977.

Scott, Tom. Interview with Author September 5, 2020.

Sellers, Robert. *Always Look on the Bright Side of Life: The Inside Story of HandMade Films*. Hushion House, 2004.

Shapiro, Mark. *Behind Sad Eyes*. St. Martin's Press, 2002.

Shankar, Ravi (Edited by Harrison, George). *Raga Mala: The Autobiography*. Welcome Rain Publishers, 1999.

Shankar, Ravi. *Ravi Shankar:In Celebration* CD Box Set Liner notes. CDCD 7243 5 55577 2 8

Shankar, Ravi. Chants Of India CD Liner notes CDQ 7243 8 55948 2 3

Sharp, Ken. *Starting Over: The Making of John Lennon and Yoko Ono's Double Fantasy* MTV Books, 2010.

Slawek, Stephen (2001). 'Shankar, Ravi'. In Sadie, Stanley (ed.). *The New Grove Dictionary of Music and Musicians*. 23 (2nd ed.). London: Macmillan Publishers.

Soocher, Stan. *Baby You're a Rich Man: Suing the Beatles for Fun and Profit*, University Press of New England, 2015.

Spedding, Chris. Interview with author

Spizer, Bruce. *The Beatles Solo on Apple Records*, 498 Productions , 2005

Strauss, James. Interview with Author.

Tayler, Alvin. Interview with Author.

Taylor, McComas. *Seven Days of Nectar: Contemporary Oral Performance of the Bhāgavatapurāṇa*. Oxford: Oxford University Press, 2016. p. 187.

Wallgren, Mark. *The Beatles On Record*. A Fireside Book, 1982.

Womack, Kenneth. *The Beatles Encyclopedia: Everything Fab Four*, ABC-

CLIO (Santa Barbara, CA, 2014; ISBN 978-0-313-39171-2).

Wright, Gary (2014). Dream Weaver: A Memoir; Music, Meditation, and My Friendship with George Harrison. Jeremy P. Tarcher/Penguin, New York ISBN 978-0-399-16523-8

Zane, Warren. Liner notes for *Let It Roll: Songs By George Harrison*. Universal Music, 2009

Derek Taylor: For Your Radioactive Children

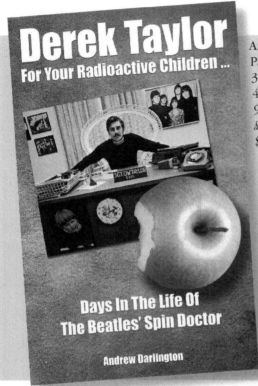

Andrew Darlington
Paperback
336 pages
47 colour photographs
978-1-78951-038-5
£20.00
$29.95

Days In The life Of The Beatles' Spin Doctor

Derek Taylor lived a charmed life. It started on Saturday, 7 May 1932, in the Liverpool 17 suburb of Toxteth Park South, and it saw him become a writer best known as the press agent for the Beatles. He became the band's friend and intimate across thirty years. Indeed, there are no shortage of claimants to the 'honorary' or 'fifth Beatle' status, but Derek's claim is more valid than most. Indeed, his urbane charm, his easy intelligence and the value of his contribution to the Beatles' collective story are beyond dispute. He put spin on stories decades before the term 'spin doctor' was concocted, with his droll, idiosyncratic way of speaking.

It all began in 1964, when he co-wrote A Cellarful Of Noise, the best-selling autobiography of Brian Epstein. Soon after, he became Epstein's personal assistant and The Beatles' press agent. In 1965 he moved to Los Angeles, where he started his own public relations company working for bands like Paul Revere And The Raiders, The Byrds and The Beach Boys, and also co-created the historic Monterey Pop Festival in 1967. Brian Wilson called him a 'PR whiz' and 'a colourful, slick-talking Brit'. Later, he returned to England to work for the Beatles again as the press officer for the newly created Apple Corps.

This is the definitive biography of a man that was at the heart of the music world of the 1960s and 1970s. It is essential reading for anyone with an interest in the Beatles of course, but also to anyone yearning for a deep dive into the colourful world of a man who helped define an era.

George Harrison in the 1970s
Decades

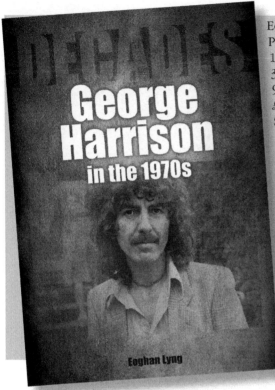

Eoghan Lyng
Paperback
128 pages
37 colour photographs
978-1-78951-174-0
£15.99
$22.95

A crucial decade in the career of this ex-Beatle.

Depending on who you asked, George Harrison was many different things to different people. There was his songcraft, which won over the affections of producer savant Phil Spector; there was his musicianship, that captured the hearts of blues geniuses Eric Clapton and Delaney Bramlett; and then there was his penchant for comedy, which made him an obvious shoo-in for Rutland Weekend Television and Saturday Night Live.

But behind these traits stood a fragile man, aching for enlightenment and peace in an industry that strove to rid him of any of it. Keenly aware of this conflict, Harrison was brave enough to commit it to tape on the wistful Dark Horse, a confessional album written against the backdrop of a regrettable American tour. But Harrison was always ready to brave the conflict, and it served him better to ride it out than to return to The Beatles for an easy paycheque. He was known as 'The Quiet Beatle', although this title did him a disservice, considering his intellectual focus and thoughtful nature. Instead, he was arguably 'The Chameleonic Beatle', a moniker that only serves to understand this deeply complex guitar player better. And in a deeply complicated decade, Harrison's artistry flourished.

Also available from Sonicbond

Badfinger - *on track*
every album, every song

Robert Day-Webb
Paperback
128 pages
45 colour photographs
978-1-78951-176-4
£15.99
$22.95

**Every album released
by this Welsh band
who signed to Apple
and were much loved
by The Beatles.**

Generally regarded as one of the most tragic tales in the history of rock music, the story of Badfinger makes for an impressively sombre Hollywood-style film script. A Welsh and Liverpudlian hybrid, the band were signed to Apple Records, became protégés of The Beatles and produced four global hit singles. Two of its members also co-wrote the now perennial pop standard 'Without You', covered most notably by Harry Nilsson. Yet Badfinger found themselves plagued by ruinous misfortune and through a combination of unscrupulous business management, record label neglect and just plain bad luck, the dream soon lay in tatters with the

band's story ultimately culminating in the suicides of two of its members, Pete Ham and Tom Evans.

This book helps redress the band's legacy and refocuses some much-needed attention on the brilliance of their music. It casts a keen critical eye over their entire musical output – albums and singles – recorded and released during their lifetime. This detailed and definitive guide not only examines and assesses the recordings but also provides valuable historical context for each album and while not ignoring the financial and legal issues that blighted the band, this book ultimately focuses on Badfinger's considerable musical legacy.

1967: A Year in Psychedelic Rock

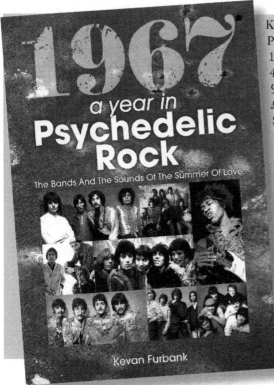

Kevan Furbank
Paperback
160 pages
41 colour photographs
978-1-78951-155-9
£14.99
$21.95

**The bands and
sounds of the
Summer Of Love.**

It was the year the Sixties really started swinging - the Summer of Love, when the Rolling Stones said 'We Love You' and The Beatles pointed out that 'All You Necd Is Love'. At the centre of the year's tumultuous social and cultural change was the mind-expanding music called psychedelic rock, a multi-coloured mixture of amazing sounds, when imagination and experimentation ran riot and the old musical boundaries were torn down in a haze of hallucinogenic abandon.

Kevan Furbank looks at the roots of psychedelic rock and examines the contributions made by some of the biggest bands of the year, including The Beatles, The Doors, Jimi Hendrix, the Rolling Stones, Love, Pink Floyd and The Beach Boys.

He examines the hits and misses, the successes and failures, the bands that were born to be psychedelic and those that had psychedelia thrust upon them – sometimes with disastrous results. And he shows how the genre planted the seeds for other forms of popular music to take root and flourish. If you love music and want to know why 1967 was such a watershed year, then you will want this book. It is eye-popping, mind-opening and horizon-expanding – and a splendid time is guaranteed for all.

On Track series

Allman Brothers Band – Andrew Wild 978-1-78952-252-5
Tori Amos – Lisa Torem 978-1-78952-142-9
Aphex Twin – Beau Waddell 978-1-78952-267-9
Asia – Peter Braidis 978-1-78952-099-6
Badfinger – Robert Day-Webb 978-1-878952-176-4
Barclay James Harvest – Keith and Monica Domone 978-1-78952-067-5
Beck – Arthur Lizie 978-1-78952-258-7
The Beatles – Andrew Wild 978-1-78952-009-5
The Beatles Solo 1969-1980 – Andrew Wild 978-1-78952-030-9
Blue Oyster Cult – Jacob Holm-Lupo 978-1-78952-007-1
Blur – Matt Bishop 978-178952-164-1
Marc Bolan and T.Rex – Peter Gallagher 978-1-78952-124-5
Kate Bush – Bill Thomas 978-1-78952-097-2
Camel – Hamish Kuzminski 978-1-78952-040-8
Captain Beefheart – Opher Goodwin 978-1-78952-235-8
Caravan – Andy Boot 978-1-78952-127-6
Cardiacs – Eric Benac 978-1-78952-131-3
Nick Cave and The Bad Seeds – Dominic Sanderson 978-1-78952-240-2
Eric Clapton Solo – Andrew Wild 978-1-78952-141-2
The Clash – Nick Assirati 978-1-78952-077-4
Elvis Costello and The Attractions – Georg Purvis 978-1-78952-129-0
Crosby, Stills and Nash – Andrew Wild 978-1-78952-039-2
Creedence Clearwater Revival – Tony Thompson 978-178952-237-2
The Damned – Morgan Brown 978-1-78952-136-8
Deep Purple and Rainbow 1968-79 – Steve Pilkington 978-1-78952-002-6
Dire Straits – Andrew Wild 978-1-78952-044-6
The Doors – Tony Thompson 978-1-78952-137-5
Dream Theater – Jordan Blum 978-1-78952-050-7
Eagles – John Van der Kiste 978-1-78952-260-0
Earth, Wind and Fire – Bud Wilkins 978-1-78952-272-3
Electric Light Orchestra – Barry Delve 978-1-78952-152-8
Emerson Lake and Palmer – Mike Goode 978-1-78952-000-2
Fairport Convention – Kevan Furbank 978-1-78952-051-4
Peter Gabriel – Graeme Scarfe 978-1-78952-138-2
Genesis – Stuart MacFarlane 978-1-78952-005-7
Gentle Giant – Gary Steel 978-1-78952-058-3
Gong – Kevan Furbank 978-1-78952-082-8
Green Day – William E. Spevack 978-1-78952-261-7
Hall and Oates – Ian Abrahams 978-1-78952-167-2
Hawkwind – Duncan Harris 978-1-78952-052-1
Peter Hammill – Richard Rees Jones 978-1-78952-163-4
Roy Harper – Opher Goodwin 978-1-78952-130-6

Jimi Hendrix – Emma Stott 978-1-78952-175-7
The Hollies – Andrew Darlington 978-1-78952-159-7
Horslips – Richard James 978-1-78952-263-1
The Human League and The Sheffield Scene –
Andrew Darlington 978-1-78952-186-3
The Incredible String Band – Tim Moon 978-1-78952-107-8
Iron Maiden – Steve Pilkington 978-1-78952-061-3
Joe Jackson – Richard James 978-1-78952-189-4
Jefferson Airplane – Richard Butterworth 978-1-78952-143-6
Jethro Tull – Jordan Blum 978-1-78952-016-3
Elton John in the 1970s – Peter Kearns 978-1-78952-034-7
Billy Joel – Lisa Torem 978-1-78952-183-2
Judas Priest – John Tucker 978-1-78952-018-7
Kansas – Kevin Cummings 978-1-78952-057-6
The Kinks – Martin Hutchinson 978-1-78952-172-6
Korn – Matt Karpe 978-1-78952-153-5
Led Zeppelin – Steve Pilkington 978-1-78952-151-1
Level 42 – Matt Philips 978-1-78952-102-3
Little Feat – Georg Purvis - 978-1-78952-168-9
Aimee Mann – Jez Rowden 978-1-78952-036-1
Joni Mitchell – Peter Kearns 978-1-78952-081-1
The Moody Blues – Geoffrey Feakes 978-1-78952-042-2
Motorhead – Duncan Harris 978-1-78952-173-3
Nektar – Scott Meze – 978-1-78952-257-0
New Order – Dennis Remmer – 978-1-78952-249-5
Nightwish – Simon McMurdo – 978-1-78952-270-9
Laura Nyro – Philip Ward 978-1-78952-182-5
Mike Oldfield – Ryan Yard 978-1-78952-060-6
Opeth – Jordan Blum 978-1-78-952-166-5
Pearl Jam – Ben L. Connor 978-1-78952-188-7
Tom Petty – Richard James 978-1-78952-128-3
Pink Floyd – Richard Butterworth 978-1-78952-242-6
The Police – Pete Braidis 978 1-78952-158-0
Porcupine Tree – Nick Holmes 978-1-78952-144-3
Queen – Andrew Wild 978-1-78952-003-3
Radiohead – William Allen 978-1-78952-149-8
Rancid – Paul Matts 989-1-78952-187-0
Renaissance – David Detmer 978-1-78952-062-0
REO Speedwagon – Jim Romag 978-1-78952-262-4
The Rolling Stones 1963-80 – Steve Pilkington 978-1-78952-017-0
The Smiths and Morrissey – Tommy Gunnarsson 978-1-78952-140-5
Spirit – Rev. Keith A. Gordon – 978-1-78952- 248-8
Stackridge – Alan Draper 978-1-78952-232-7

Status Quo the Frantic Four Years – Richard James 978-1-78952-160-3
Steely Dan – Jez Rowden 978-1-78952-043-9
Steve Hackett – Geoffrey Feakes 978-1-78952-098-9
Tears For Fears – Paul Clark - 978-178952-238-9
Thin Lizzy – Graeme Stroud 978-1-78952-064-4
Tool – Matt Karpe 978-1-78952-234-1
Toto – Jacob Holm-Lupo 978-1-78952-019-4
U2 – Eoghan Lyng 978-1-78952-078-1
UFO – Richard James 978-1-78952-073-6
Van Der Graaf Generator – Dan Coffey 978-1-78952-031-6
Van Halen – Morgan Brown – 9781-78952-256-3
The Who – Geoffrey Feakes 978-1-78952-076-7
Roy Wood and the Move – James R Turner 978-1-78952-008-8
Yes – Stephen Lambe 978-1-78952-001-9
Frank Zappa 1966 to 1979 – Eric Benac 978-1-78952-033-0
Warren Zevon – Peter Gallagher 978-1-78952-170-2
10CC – Peter Kearns 978-1-78952-054-5

Decades Series
The Bee Gees in the 1960s – Andrew Mon Hughes et al 978-1-78952-148-1
The Bee Gees in the 1970s – Andrew Mon Hughes et al 978-1-78952-179-5
Black Sabbath in the 1970s – Chris Sutton 978-1-78952-171-9
Britpop – Peter Richard Adams and Matt Pooler 978-1-78952-169-6
Phil Collins in the 1980s – Andrew Wild 978-1-78952-185-6
Alice Cooper in the 1970s – Chris Sutton 978-1-78952-104-7
Alice Cooper in the 1980s – Chris Sutton 978-1-78952-259-4
Curved Air in the 1970s – Laura Shenton 978-1-78952-069-9
Donovan in the 1960s – Jeff Fitzgerald 978-1-78952-233-4
Bob Dylan in the 1980s – Don Klees 978-1-78952-157-3
Brian Eno in the 1970s – Gary Parsons 978-1-78952-239-6
Faith No More in the 1990s – Matt Karpe 978-1-78952-250-1
Fleetwood Mac in the 1970s – Andrew Wild 978-1-78952-105-4
Fleetwood Mac in the 1980s – Don Klees 978-178952-254-9
Focus in the 1970s – Stephen Lambe 978-1-78952-079-8
Free and Bad Company in the 1970s – John Van der Kiste 978-1-78952-178-8
Genesis in the 1970s – Bill Thomas 978178952-146-7
George Harrison in the 1970s – Eoghan Lyng 978-1-78952-174-0
Kiss in the 1970s – Peter Gallagher 978-1-78952-246-4
Manfred Mann's Earth Band in the 1970s – John Van der Kiste 978178952-243-3
Marillion in the 1980s – Nathaniel Webb 978-1-78952-065-1
Van Morrison in the 1970s – Peter Childs - 978-1-78952-241-9
Mott the Hoople and Ian Hunter in the 1970s –
John Van der Kiste 978-1-78-952-162-7

Pink Floyd In The 1970s – Georg Purvis 978-1-78952-072-9
Suzi Quatro in the 1970s – Darren Johnson 978-1-78952-236-5
Queen in the 1970s – James Griffiths 978-1-78952-265-5
Roxy Music in the 1970s – Dave Thompson 978-1-78952-180-1
Slade in the 1970s – Darren Johnson 978-1-78952-268-6
Status Quo in the 1980s – Greg Harper 978-1-78952-244-0
Tangerine Dream in the 1970s – Stephen Palmer 978-1-78952-161-0
The Sweet in the 1970s – Darren Johnson 978-1-78952-139-9
Uriah Heep in the 1970s – Steve Pilkington 978-1-78952-103-0
Van der Graaf Generator in the 1970s – Steve Pilkington 978-1-78952-245-7
Rick Wakeman in the 1970s – Geoffrey Feakes 978-1-78952-264-8
Yes in the 1980s – Stephen Lambe with David Watkinson 978-1-78952-125-2

On Screen series
Carry On... – Stephen Lambe 978-1-78952-004-0
David Cronenberg – Patrick Chapman 978-1-78952-071-2
Doctor Who: The David Tennant Years – Jamie Hailstone 978-1-78952-066-8
James Bond – Andrew Wild 978-1-78952-010-1
Monty Python – Steve Pilkington 978-1-78952-047-7
Seinfeld Seasons 1 to 5 – Stephen Lambe 978-1-78952-012-5

Other Books
1967: A Year In Psychedelic Rock 978-1-78952-155-9
1970: A Year In Rock – John Van der Kiste 978-1-78952-147-4
1973: The Golden Year of Progressive Rock 978-1-78952-165-8
Babysitting A Band On The Rocks – G.D. Praetorius 978-1-78952-106-1
Eric Clapton Sessions – Andrew Wild 978-1-78952-177-1
Derek Taylor: For Your Radioactive Children –
Andrew Darlington 978-1-78952-038-5
The Golden Road: The Recording History of The Grateful Dead – John Kilbride 978-1-78952-156-6
Iggy and The Stooges On Stage 1967-1974 – Per Nilsen 978-1-78952-101-6
Jon Anderson and the Warriors – the road to Yes –
David Watkinson 978-1-78952-059-0
Magic: The David Paton Story – David Paton 978-1-78952-266-2
Misty: The Music of Johnny Mathis – Jakob Baekgaard 978-1-78952-247-1
Nu Metal: A Definitive Guide – Matt Karpe 978-1-78952-063-7
Tommy Bolin: In and Out of Deep Purple – Laura Shenton 978-1-78952-070-5
Maximum Darkness – Deke Leonard 978-1-78952-048-4
The Twang Dynasty – Deke Leonard 978-1-78952-049-1

and many more to come!

Would you like to write for Sonicbond Publishing?

At Sonicbond Publishing we are always on the look-out for authors, particularly for our two main series:

On Track. Mixing fact with in depth analysis, the On Track series examines the work of a particular musical artist or group. All genres are considered from easy listening and jazz to 60s soul to 90s pop, via rock and metal.

On Screen. This series looks at the world of film and television. Subjects considered include directors, actors and writers, as well as entire television and film series. As with the On Track series, we balance fact with analysis.

While professional writing experience would, of course, be an advantage the most important qualification is to have real enthusiasm and knowledge of your subject. First-time authors are welcomed, but the ability to write well in English is essential.

Sonicbond Publishing has distribution throughout Europe and North America, and all books are also published in E-book form. Authors will be paid a royalty based on sales of their book.

Further details are available from www.sonicbondpublishing.co.uk. To contact us, complete the contact form there or email info@sonicbondpublishing.co.uk